Insuring Cyberinsecurity

Insuring Cyberinsecurity

*Insurance Companies
as Symbolic Regulators*

Shauhin A. Talesh

UNIVERSITY OF CALIFORNIA PRESS

University of California Press
Oakland, California

Suggested citation: Talesh, S. A. *Insuring Cyberinsecurity:
Insurance Companies as Symbolic Regulators*. Oakland:
University of California Press, 2025. DOI: https://doi.org
/10.1525/luminos.243

Library of Congress Cataloging-in-Publication Data

Names: Talesh, Shauhin A. author
Title: Insuring cyberinsecurity : insurance companies
    as symbolic regulators / Shauhin A. Talesh.
Description: Oakland, California : University of
    California Press, [2025] | Includes bibliographical
    references and index.
Identifiers: LCCN 2025001905 (print) | LCCN 2025001906
    (ebook) | ISBN 9780520422575 cloth |
    ISBN 9780520401501 paperback | ISBN 9780520401518
    ebook
Subjects: LCSH: Cyber insurance—United States |
    Computer security—Risk management—United States |
    Insurance companies—United States
Classification: LCC HG9978.3 .T35 2025 (print) |
    LCC HG9978.3 (ebook) | DDC 368.8/10973—
    dc23/eng/20250501

LC record available at https://lccn.loc.gov/2025001905
LC ebook record available at https://lccn.loc.gov
/2025001906

GPSR Authorized Representative: Easy Access System
Europe, Mustamäe tee 50, 10621 Tallinn, Estonia,
gpsr.requests@easproject.com

34 33 32 31 30 29 28 27 26 25
10 9 8 7 6 5 4 3 2 1

To my wife, Jasmine—thank you for your help and support through this journey. To Cyrus and Leila—thank you for your energy and spirit; you inspire me to be my best. To my father, Khosrow (Tom), and my mother, Shaheen, for all the love and sacrifice that you made to help me succeed—you are my heroes. To my brother, Rameen—I am still looking up to you.

CONTENTS

Acknowledgments

ix

PART I. THE INTERPLAY BETWEEN INSURANCE
INSTITUTIONS, LAW, AND CYBERSECURITY

1. Introduction

3

2. A New Institutional Theory of Insurance

27

PART II. INSURANCE COMPANIES AS REGULATORS

3. The Influence of Technology and Big Data
on Cyber Insurance

59

4. The Effects and Implications of the Technologization
of Insurance

83

5. Cyber Insurance Risk Management: Ineffective,
Symbolic Regulatory Interventions
109

6. How Cyber Insurers and Managed Security
Companies Influence the Meaning of Privacy Law
and Cybersecurity Compliance
132

PART III. POLICY REFORMS
AND PATHWAYS FORWARD

7. What Can Be Done? Policy Reforms and Pathways
Forward for Cyber Insurers and Governments
159

8. Symbolic Regulation and Insurer Influence
on Private Organizations and Public Law
198

Notes 225

Bibliography 233

Index 251

ACKNOWLEDGMENTS

The law and society community is my intellectual home and has provided me pathways for focusing on law, inequality, and social change. I have benefited from the work and guidance of many scholars over the years, but I am especially grateful to Lauren Edelman and Tom Baker. Lauren's mentorship and guidance as I became a law and organizations scholar was invaluable. My work has gone in directions different than hers did, but some of my theoretical framework derives from the generative and foundational work that she did for almost thirty years on law and organizations. Similarly, Tom Baker's guidance way back in law school (and after) provided me a fundamental anchoring in insurance law, policy, and theory. More important, Tom was part of a small community of scholars studying insurance from a law and society perspective. In many respects, this book is (I hope) an illustration of what is possible when one combines these subfields into theoretically informed empirical research and pushes these concepts into understudied areas.

This book is an outgrowth of work that I undertook in the past decade on the role between insurance, regulation, organizations, and cybersecurity. Articles that I published earlier helped me cultivate the larger ideas concerning how insurance companies influence the content and meaning of privacy law and cybersecurity compliance. These articles include "Uncle Sam RE: Improving Cyber Hygiene and Increasing Confidence in the Cyber Insurance Ecosystem via Government Backstopping" (authored with Bryan Cunningham), *University of Connecticut Insurance Law Journal* 28 (2021–22): 1–84; (with Bryan Cunningham) "The Technologization of Insurance: An Empirical Analysis of Big Data and Artificial Intelligence's Impact on Cybersecurity and Privacy," *Utah Law Review* 5 (2021): 967–1027; "Planet of the Insurers: How Insurers Shape and Influence Law and Impact Access to Justice," in *Research Handbook on Modern Legal Realism*, edited by S. Talesh, E. Mertz, and H. Klug (Cheltenham, UK: Edward Elgar, 2021); and "Data Breach, Privacy, and Cyber Insurance: How Insurance Companies Act as 'Compliance Managers' for Businesses," *Law and Social Inquiry* 43 (2018): 417–40.

I also benefited from workshopping portions of articles, chapters, and ultimately the book as they were in early formative stages at various conferences and academic institutions, including Information Society Project's faculty workshop, Yale Law School (2025); University of Connecticut School of Law faculty workshop, sponsored by the Insurance Law Center (2023); Initiative for Inclusive Civil Justice conference, University of California, Irvine (UCI), School of Law (2023); UCI's conference Exploring a Potential Federal Insurance Response to Catastrophic Cyber Risk, (2023); Hemispheric Insurance Conference in Latin America, Panel on Cybersecurity, Inter-American Federation of Insurance Companies, Rio de Janeiro, Brazil (2023); Insurance Institute, FGV (Fundação Getúlio Vargas)

Direito Rio School of Law, Brazil (2023); the Committee on Insurance and Pension Regulation, Insurance Institute, FGV Direito Rio School of Law (2023); British Insurance Law Association (2023); Arizona State University (ASU) College of Law, 9th Annual Governance of Emerging Technologies and Science Conference, sponsored by ASU College of Law and the Beus Center for Law and Society (2022); Power and Accountability in Tech Workshop, University of California, Los Angeles, School of Law (2021); Center for the Study of Law and Society, Faculty Workshop Series, University of California (UC), Berkeley, School of Law (2021); Privacy Law Scholars Conference, hosted by Georgetown Law School (2021); A Cyber Cyber Insurance Conference, University of Minnesota Law School and University of Connecticut Insurance Law Center Joint Conference (2021); Socio-technical Cybersecurity Research Interest Group, University of Maryland, School of Information Sciences (2021); Cyber Insurance and Cyber Resilience: A Workshop for Researchers and Practitioners, University of Pennsylvania Law School (2019); Baldy Center Law and Social Policy Distinguished Speaker, University of Buffalo School of Law, Faculty Workshop (2018); UCI Cybersecurity Policy and Research Institute Workshop (2018); Association of American Law Schools Annual Conference (2018, 2025); Institut d'études politiques de Paris (Sciences Po), Laboratoire Interdisciplinaire d'Evaluation des Politiques Publiques (LIEPP), Faculty Workshop, Paris, France (2017); Society for the Advancement of Socio-economics (2017); American Bar Foundation (2017); UC Berkeley School of Law, Center for the Study of Law and Society (2017); University of Minnesota Faculty Workshop (October 2016); University of California, Hastings, Faculty Workshop (2016); Society for the Advancement of Socio-Economics, UC Berkeley (2016); Clifford Symposium on Tort Law and Social Policy, DePaul University Law School (2016); Drexel University Law School

Faculty Workshop (2016). Thank you to all the faculty and students who attended and engaged with my scholarship at these conferences and workshops.

I also benefited enormously from my time spent as a visiting scholar in Sciences-Po, Laboratory for Interdisciplinary Evaluation of Public Policies, FGV Direito Rio School of Law, and UC Berkeley. In these settings I often wrote and revised portions of the manuscript and benefited from conversations with scholars.

The research for and the writing of this book was a long journey, and I owe thanks and gratitude to many people. I offer thanks to Bryan Cunningham, who collaborated with me on portions of the larger project. Bryan's expertise in cybersecurity and privacy law helped shape (and, in many cases, reshape) my perspectives on the project. I cannot thank him enough for his thoughtful collaboration on articles that we coauthored. I also thank my three research assistants, Stephanie Lee, Amruta Trivedi, and Hedyeh Tirgardoon, for invaluable research and assistance on the project, including coding, statistical analyses, references, and legal research, all with precision and accuracy.

Maura Roessner, executive editor at the University of California Press, has been outstanding to work with. I appreciate her advice and counsel as the project developed. I also thank Sam Warren, editorial assistant, and all the staff at the University of California Press, as well as the two anonymous reviewers who provided excellent feedback.

Finally, I am grateful for the support of a number of organizations that helped fund and support the project, including the Herman P. and Sophia Taubman Foundation, the UC Irvine Cybersecurity Policy and Research Institute, a UC Irvine School of Law Research Grant, and UC Irvine Beall Applied Innovation.

PART I

The Interplay between Insurance Institutions, Law, and Cybersecurity

CHAPTER ONE

Introduction

> Perhaps no modern commercial enterprise directly
> affects so many persons in all walks of life as does the
> insurance business. Insurance touches the home,
> the family, and the occupation or the business of almost
> every person in the United States.
>
> Justice Hugo Black

Cyber risks—loss exposure associated with the use of electronic equipment, computers, information technology, and virtual reality—are among the biggest threats facing businesses and consumers. Malware, ransomware, phishing scams, viruses, tracking software, robocalls, and solicitation lead to identity theft and compromised personal, financial, and health information. Cyber risks threaten societies, governments, businesses, and individuals across the world. From the NotPetya malware that spread across computer systems in 2017, to the Colonial Pipeline Ransomware Attack in 2021 that led to the largest attack on an oil pipeline infrastructure in the United States, to Russia's continual cyberattacks on Ukrainian electricity and transportation services, cybersecurity threats know no boundaries. Systemic, catastrophic risks are also a major concern, as governments increasingly engage in cyberwarfare as a tactical response to political conflicts and wars. Moreover, the increasing digitization of society opens more possible attack vectors for cybercriminals. In 2021, more than 4,100 publicly disclosed breaches occurred and exposed more than 22 billion records (*Security* Magazine 2022). When cybercriminals are not engaging in cyberattack errors, cybersecurity providers can unwittingly cause systemic failure, as demonstrated by the failure of CrowdStrike in July 2024. In that case, a software update from a single cybersecurity company (CrowdStrike) was the root cause of problems with computers and technology systems across the world, underscoring the fragility of the global economy and its dependence on computer systems and periodic system updates. Cyber risks are also expensive. The global cost of cybercrime is expected to rise in the next five years from $8.44 trillion to $23.84 trillion by 2027 (Statistica 2023). In addition to financial and public relations damage, data breach events threaten an organization's survival.

Organizations also face compliance hurdles as they navigate between various, sometimes overlapping, federal and state laws and regulations concerning the collection and use of personal data. The proliferation of security breaches in the past ten years has resulted in an expansion of privacy laws, regulations, and industry guidelines. No single, comprehensive federal law regulates the collection and use of personal data in the United States. Instead, the United States has a patchwork of federal and state laws that sometimes overlap. The major federal laws that regulate privacy in different ways include, but are not limited to, the Federal Trade Commission Act, the Financial Services Modernization Act, the Health Insurance Portability and Accountability Act, the Fair Credit Reporting Act, and the Electronic Communications Privacy Act. Many laws at the state level regulate the collection and use of personal data.[1]

The United States is not alone in dealing with cybersecurity challenges as countries across the world try to regulate rights and responsibilities among organizations and their citizenry. In 2018, the European Union (EU) passed the General Data Protection Regulation (GDPR) to enhance EU citizens' control over the personal data that companies can legally hold. In the US context, the increased flow of data across state boundaries, coupled with the enactment of additional data protection–related statutes, creates significant challenges for organizations operating on a national level to comply with the state and federal legal requirements.

Despite legal, reputational, financial, and survival threats, prevailing research suggests that private organizations are not significantly changing their behavior. Although many organizations do have formal policies in place, the majority of organizations do not believe they are sufficiently prepared for a data breach; have not devoted adequate money, training, or resources to protect consumers' electronic and paper-based information from data breaches; and fail to perform adequate risk assessments (*Business Wire* 2015; Ponemon Institute 2015, 2016). The US Cybersecurity and Infrastructure Security Agency (CISA) found in January 2021 that "despite the use of security tools . . . organizations typically had weak cyber hygiene practices that allowed threat actors to conduct successful attacks" (CISA 2021).[2] Focusing on recent attacks against cloud services, the CISA report concluded that the victims were not employing even some of the most basic cybersecurity protective techniques, such as enforcing multi-factor authentication and training employees against phishing attacks. A 2018 study found woeful adoption by surveyed users across most key aspects of good cyber hygiene, including password usage, response to phishing scams, sharing sensitive personal information in emails and even over social media, and the use of antivirus scans (Cain, Edwards, and Still 2018). The United

States Cyber Solarium Commission, a blue ribbon panel created in 2020 by Congress and the President in the wake of the NotPetya attacks to explore how the United States can defend against significant cyberattacks and what policies and legislation are needed, concluded that "The United States now operates in a cyber landscape that requires a level of data security, resilience, and trustworthiness that neither the U.S. government nor the private sector alone is currently equipped to provide. Moreover, shortfalls in agility, technical expertise, and unity of effort, both within the U.S. government and between the public and private sectors, are growing" (US CSC 2020).

A *privacy paradox* exists among organizations, much as it does among individuals (Acquisti, Brandimarte, and Loewenstein 2020; Gerber, Gerber, and Volkamer 2018). That is, a disconnect exists between an organization's desired level of privacy protection and its privacy protection behaviors. Yet cybersecurity is an issue virtually every business must address to advance its digital transformation.

Because of business underpreparation and undercompliance and the fragmented, inconsistent, and weak legal regulatory oversight, insurance companies have stepped in during the past decade and begun offering cyber insurance. Cyber insurance is designed to provide both first-party loss and third-party liability coverage for data breach events, privacy violations, and cyberattacks. Although the types of available policies vary, insurers offering cyber insurance provide some risk shifting for the costs associated with having to respond, investigate, defend, and mitigate against the consequences surrounding cyberattacks.

Cyber insurance is one of the fastest-growing lines of insurance. Whereas no cyber coverage existed twenty-five years ago, the cyber insurance market is growing rapidly with 45 percent of organizations purchasing some form of cyber coverage in 2022 (US GAO 2023). The United States cyber market increased by 50% from 2016 to 2019, when it reached $3.1 billion in written premiums (US GAO 2021). The insurance industry estimates that 150 insurance groups are now writing $6.5 billion in direct written premiums (NAIC Staff 2022). In addition to offering risk transfer and indemnification, cyber insurers also offer policyholders a series of risk management services aimed at preventing, detecting, and responding to cybersecurity incidences. In this respect, insurers have responded to the fragmented legal framework and organizational underpreparation by attempting to function as regulators. This development is consistent with a long history of insurers acting as gatekeepers to services and products and attempting to regulate the behavior of insureds. Although cybersecurity is a growing global concern that virtually every business must address and although cyber insurance is expanding across the world, we know less about what role cyber insurers as de facto regulators have played and whether it is working well. How do insurers manage uncertainty about underwriting risks where little actuarial data exist? Do insurance as a form of regulation and insurance companies as de facto regulators work?

Insuring Cyberinsecurity: Insurance Companies as Symbolic Regulators explains how cyber insurers manage cybersecurity and privacy law compliance among organizations and why it has not been more successful in curtailing cybersecurity breaches. In doing so, I offer a complete explication of my *new institutional theory of insurance* to explain how insurance institutions as legal intermediaries shape and influence the content and meaning of law and compliance among organizations that purchase insurance. In response to vague and fragmented privacy laws and a lack of strong government oversight, insurers, as intermediaries, offer cyber insurance and a series of risk management services to organizations interested in buying this insurance. These risk management services exude legitimacy to the public and to buyers of cyber insurance but fall short of improving the cyber hygiene of organizations, rendering such interventions largely symbolic. Cyber insurers, in partnership with managed-security companies, have flooded the market with high-level technical tools that they claim mitigate risk and have institutionalized a norm that policyholders need these tools to avoid cybersecurity incidences. Over time, federal and state regulatory agencies and industry-based rating agencies defer to cyber insurer practices regarding cybersecurity policy without evidence that such interventions improve the cybersecurity of organizations. A new institutional theory of insurance not only helps to explain the limitations of insurance companies as regulators and how insurers manage uncertainty, but also provides a comprehensive theoretical statement of the interplay between insurance, organizations, and law.

Using a variety of empirical methods, including interviews with and participant observation among insurance industry actors, content analysis of insurance industry documents, and quantitative analysis of big data, I find that emerging technologies and big data have transformed the delivery of insurance in the cyber context. Unlike most traditional areas of insurance, cyber insurers lack significant amounts of loss history and actuarial data to rely on when making risk assessments. Because cyber insurance is new, uncertain, and constantly evolving, cyber insurers covet data from data providers. Cyber insurers are turning to big data, AI, and predictive analytics to assist in the underwriting and risk and claims management processes and, as a result, redefining the business of insurance.

Despite the theoretical promise that cyber insurers significantly enhance their insureds' cybersecurity, the promise remains just that: theoretical. The reasons for this failure include (1) a "soft" insurance market in which insurers hotly compete for market share;[3] (2) the resulting reluctance on the part of cyber insurers either to reward good cyber citizens with lower premiums or to punish those insureds unwilling or unable to improve their cybersecurity posture—whether through denial of coverage or higher premiums; (3) the unreliability of the big data and information security provider security scans that insurers and brokers heavily rely on; and (4) the frequent use of emerging technologies to improve policy sales and increase profit margins rather than to incentivize good cyber citizenship. Although mainstream cyber insurers are turning to big data and technology as mechanisms for managing uncertainty in the cyber market, such models are not fully integrated into the underwriting and risk management processes. Moreover, cyber insurers evaluate and treat prospective buyers of cyber insurance differently based on the size of the company, creating unequal, tiered levels of treatment in terms of quality and depth of analysis and care. This book thus offers a theoretically informed explanation of how insurance as regulation in this context has not succeeded. I also offer a series of recommendations that insurance companies and the government should consider in seeking to improve the cyber hygiene of society.

UNDER WHAT CONDITIONS CAN INSURERS EFFECTIVELY REGULATE BUSINESSES?

Consistent with the global turn away from command-and-control regulation and toward more public-private partnerships and self-regulation, insurance scholars are increasingly discussing the role of private insurance as a form of regulation of individuals and organizations. Through insurance policy terms, exclusions, conditions, and pricing, insurance companies can also establish norms of conduct. Insurance serves a gatekeeping function in society in that it is a prerequisite for other activities. Many insurance law scholars argue that insurance covering product liability, workers' compensation, automobiles, homeownership, environmental liability, and tax liability regulate individuals and businesses in ways that are more constructive than government regulation.

Omri Ben-Shahar and Kyle Logue (2012) have argued that insurers, with their superior access to information and commercial sophistication, use a set of techniques to improve the safety and conduct of their policyholders and are better regulators than regulatory, legislative, or judicial institutions. Other scholars have explored the relationship between insurance loss prevention and policyholder moral hazard across a variety of domains, including medical malpractice (Baker 2005b), legal malpractice (G. Cohen 1997; Davis 1996), the motion picture industry (Hubbart 1996), corporate directors and officers (Baker and Griffith 2010), firearms (Baker and Farrish 2005), personal injury (Sugarman 1989), policing practices (Rappaport 2017), food safety (Lytton 2022); kidnapping for ransom (Baker and Shortland 2022a, 2022b), burglaries and home safety (O'Malley 1991), college fraternities (Simon 1994), vessels and marine insurance (Heimer 1985), and the limits of regulation by insurance (Talesh 2015a, 2018; Abraham and Schwarcz 2022; Baker and Shortland 2022b). As insightful as this work and that of others who discuss insurance as a form of regulation is, studies in this area focus primarily on insurance policy language, actuarial techniques, underwriting, and claims practices as generating a form of regulatory oversight. Most (though not all) work in this area has been theoretical and has approached the topic through a law and economics analysis. Rarely is there a strong empirical focus on the regulatory role that insurance companies play. Most important, little empirical research has been designed to uncover the processes and mechanisms through which insurers engage in risk regulation. How do insurers as risk regulators work in action? Under what conditions does insurance as a form of regulation work?

Cyber insurance is an ideal area in which to explore these questions, because the federal government continuously turns to cyber insurers as potential agents of change and reform concerning cybersecurity and privacy law. Regarding cybersecurity policy, the United States government has continuously leaned on private organizations to take the lead in addressing noncritical infrastructure threats. The National Strategy to Secure Cyberspace in February 2003 emphasized that the private sector was "best equipped and structured" to address cyber threats (US DHS 2003, ix). This report noted that the insurance industry has been successful in other areas that impact "the economy or the health, welfare or safety of the public" (24). Josephine Wolff (2022), in her analysis of the history of cyber insurance, observes that "regulators returned, repeatedly, to the idea that the security of civilian data and networks was, primarily, an area for companies to tackle with their superior technical expertise and greater resources" (Wolff 2022, 15).

In 2012, the US Department of Homeland Security (DHS) National Protection and Programs Directorate convened working sessions and roundtables with the insurance industry to discuss ways to make public and private institutions more cybersecure. While acknowledging that the cyber insurance market is nascent as compared to other lines of insurance, the DHS report concluded that cyber insurance is vital: "A robust cybersecurity insurance market could help reduce the number of successful cyberattacks by: (1) promoting the adoption of preventative measures in return for more coverage; and (2) encouraging the implementation of best practices by basing premiums on an insured's level of self-protection" (US DHS 2017a). Moreover, the report devoted extensive attention to improving risk management within organizations and suggested that cyber insurers have an active role to play (US DHS 2017a; see also NPPD 2014). As recently as March 2020, the US Cyberspace Solarium Commission stressed the need to use cyber insurance to promote cybersecurity and suggested insurers can incentivize organizational cybersecurity (US CSC 2020).

Aside from critical infrastructure sectors such as energy and transportation, calls for public-private partnerships to deal with cybersecurity and privacy issues have been vaguely defined. Federal and state governments remain unwilling to mandate security best practices or announce standards or expectations for businesses to avoid liability for cybersecurity incidences. State privacy laws focus more on an organization's responsibilities to notify consumers in the event of a breach. These factors set the stage for the insurance industry to offer cyber insurance and attempt to play a regulatory intermediary role in fostering improved cyber hygiene among organizations.

Insuring Cyberinsecurity draws from and builds on existing studies of the impact of cyber insurance. Trey Herr (2021) identified cyber insurers as taking on a private governance role in cybersecurity by their standard-setting and enforcement practices. He suggests that insurer interventions as a quasi-regulator are the product of "private advance," the idea that organizations as regulators have some financial incentive in setting and enforcing standards and that their approach satisfies those seeking to be regulated. Herr prognosticates that cyber insurers as market actors can help bring to light the best practices that organizations should employ to improve the overall cyber hygiene of society:

> Cyber insurance is a rapidly expanding market whose ability to recognize trends across customers and identify best practices could serve not only to enforce, but also to eventually recognize new best practices. . . . The prospect for insurers to act as arbiters of best practice would be an evolution from the current status quo but holds potential to greatly improve the evolution and promulgation of standards in cybersecurity. . . . This governance, which works to break down information asymmetries in the private sector and helps to enforce security standards, could well serve as [a] model for policymakers. (Herr 2021, 111)

Others offer a more pessimistic prognostication. Daniel Woods and Tyler Moore (2020) suggest insurers may face many challenges in governing the cybersecurity practices of organizations. Romanosky and colleagues analyzed cyber insurance policies and concluded that premium discounts as an incentive for client behavior were rarely deployed by insurers (Romanosky et al. 2019). Another study found that cyber insurance premiums fell in absolute terms from 2009 to 2019, suggesting that a soft market and a prioritization of issuing insurance did not nudge cybersecurity upgrades on the part of insurers (Woods, Moore, and Simpson 2019). Most recently, Baker and Shortland conducted twenty-five interviews with insurers familiar with kidnapping, ransomware, and cyber insurance and concluded that kidnap and ransom insurers in Europe focus on containing criminal extortion, while liability insurers in the United States focus on reducing liability rather than reducing crime (Baker and Shortland 2022b; see also Mott et al. 2023; Talesh 2015a). These articles all address various aspects of cyber insurance, but none undertakes qualitative empirical research exploring how cyber insurers actually attempt to regulate cybersecurity behavior or responses by organizations.[4]

Josephine Wolff, in *Cyberinsurance Policy* (2022), offers a careful and comprehensive analysis of the historical origins of the cyber insurance market and its evolution over the past twenty years. In doing so, Wolff maps the growth of the cyber insurance market and how that growth has challenged earlier notions of the quantification, management, and assessment of risk. Relying largely on analysis of lawsuits, cyber insurance policies, government records, and media coverage, Wolff explores the development of the cyber insurance market by examining regulatory changes, legal battles in courtrooms, and shifts in public policy. Wolff spends considerable time charting how cyber evolved into a siloed line of insurance. Wolff shows that, unlike CGL (commercial general liability), property, auto, flood, and fire insurance, cyber insurance does not cover a single, coherent type of threat or set of damages. Wolff's book provides an excellent and well-documented history of the interrelated story of cybersecurity and cyber insurance.

In many respects, Wolff's *Cyberinsurance Policy* and this book work in tandem and provide a compelling account of cyber insurance and cybersecurity. As opposed to historical context, *Insuring Cyberinsecurity* focuses more on what is currently happening on the ground. Unlike Wolff's top-down account of how courts and regulatory pressures shape insurance, *Insuring Cyberinsecurity* picks up the story in near-real time in a finer-grained manner with a variety of empirical methods that show how cyber insurance acts as a form of regulation and the conditions in which insurance can act as a positive or negative form of regulation. Indeed, *Insuring Cyberinsecurity* turns the tables a bit by showing how insurance company interventions and actions ultimately shape and influence legislation and regulation, often relying on insurer information that is incomplete and unreliable. This contribution is especially important because of the US government's lack of stringent oversight over organizations' privacy responsibilities and cybersecurity compliance and because this lax oversight creates space for insurers to step in and offer insurance as a form of quasi-regulation. Moreover, this book provides insights concerning the conditions in which insurance companies act as substantive or symbolic regulators.

The new institutional theory of insurance framework is novel in that it places less emphasis on law and economic cost-benefit analysis than on framing insurance as regulation within the growing sociology of organizations literature that examines how norms, values, and institutionalized policies and practices shape compliance behavior. My institutional theory of insurance draws from new institutional organizational sociology studies of how organizations respond to legal regulations. Lauren Edelman's *Working Law: Courts, Corporations and Symbolic Civil Rights* (2016) posits "legal endogeneity theory" to explain how employers shape the content and meaning of civil rights laws designed to regulate them, including influencing how judges resolve antidiscrimination claims. As legal endogeneity makes clear, employers respond to ambiguous laws by creating, adopting, and institutionalizing policies and procedures, but they interpret and implement these law-like structures through a managerial lens that waters down strong legal protections and affords the employers considerable discretion. Eventually, courts defer to the presence of these structures as evidence of antidiscrimination efforts by employers without interrogating whether these structures work.

Legal endogeneity serves as a jumping-off point for my new institutional theory of insurance. Whereas Edelman focuses on organizations' influence of judicial decisions, *Insuring Cyberinsecurity* highlights how cyber insurer responses influence legislation, regulation, and private standard setting. Whereas Edelman focuses on how managerial values shape the way law is implemented by employers, *Insuring Cyberinsecurity* highlights how risk and managerial values complement each other and ultimately how, in the cyber context, emerging technologies are a mechanism through which organizations mobilize managerial and risk responses. In doing so, the book extends the "governing through risk" framework developed by Tom Baker and Jonathan Simon (2005) and shows not just how managerial values shape compliance, but also how risk management services and risk-based logics institutionalized in the insurance industry shape what organizations are told privacy laws mean and how they should respond to a data breach event. Finally, whereas Edelman highlights how employment policies and procedures are often symbolic gestures of compliance, I illuminate how insurers, as legal intermediaries, act as *symbolic regulators*.

In addition to advancing new institutional theory and law and society in new directions, *Insuring Cyberinsecurity* provides novel insights into the larger debates on public-private partnerships and co-regulation and on the role of legal intermediaries. Given that organizations continue to look to insurers as potential intermediaries, this book provides a closer analysis of the ways insurers facilitate or hinder cybersecurity among organizations and of their effort to comply with privacy laws. In doing so, this book speaks directly to larger conversations concerning the increased involvement, delegation, and deference to nonstate actors (Levi-Faur 2005).

Moreover, *Insuring Cyberinsecurity* also contributes to the burgeoning literature and public policy debates on privacy law, science, and technology. Although scholars are exploring the ways that code, technology, and information regulate society

(Boyle 1996, 2003; Chander and Sunder 2004; Chon 2006; Lessig 1999; Reidenberg 1998; Benkler 2006; Frischmann 2012; J. Cohen 2019), existing research—across many economic sectors and aspects of society—primarily focuses on the theoretical and normative challenges of big data and emerging technologies (Swedloff 2020). While theoretical and normative frameworks are helpful, much current scholarship lacks information on how these tools operate and what is actually happening on the ground.[5] This is due not to a lack of interest but rather to the secrecy and lack of disclosure on the part of data providers, data harvesters, and corporations that collect and use these data and operate these technologies (J. Cohen 2019).[6] Moreover, although the insurance industry has been moving toward "insurtech" models of underwriting and delivery of insurance for the past decade, there has not been a fine-grained analysis of how technology shapes the delivery of insurance. By specifying the mechanisms through which cyber insurers manage and regulate cybersecurity compliance among organizations (risk-management services, emerging technologies, and big data), this book serves as a template for scholars on how to empirically examine the role technology plays in other industries as well. Most important, I offer a comprehensive theory of the interplay of law, insurance, and organizations and explain how insurers manage uncertainty, describe the conditions under which insurers as regulators will likely fail, and reveal why privacy laws and cybersecurity policy makers are limited in their capacity to mobilize insurers as agents of regulation and social change.

MOBILIZING EMPIRICAL EVIDENCE

Insuring Cyberinsecurity relies on a variety of empirical data that I collected from 2016 to 2022, sometimes with collaborators (Talesh

2018; Talesh and Cunningham 2021; Cunningham and Talesh 2021–22). These data come from interviews with various members of the cyber insurance field; participant observation at cyber insurance conferences; an analysis of big data obtained from a cyber insurance data provider; and content analysis of insurance applications, insurance policies, webinars, websites intended for cybersecurity professionals, and professional literature on cyber risks. In addition to my own empirical analyses, described below, I draw on relevant legal and social science scholarship to develop a broad theoretical model of the relationship between law, insurance companies, and the organizations that purchase insurance. I also explore the process through which law and compliance is influenced and transformed by insurance institutions as legal intermediaries.

Interviews with Members of the Cyber Insurance Field

I conducted seventy semistructured in-depth interviews with members of the insurance field, including insurance underwriters, brokers, risk managers, actuaries, forensics experts, lawyers, data brokers, information security providers who actively partner with insurers, data scientists, and engineers who develop big data databases. A series of subquestions aimed at exploring how cyber insurers act as quasi-regulators guided my inquiry: (1) How does the insurance industry shape the way organizations respond to data theft breaches and the accompanying privacy laws? (2) How does the insurance industry characterize the objectives of privacy laws? (3) How does the insurance industry characterize the problem of cybersecurity? And (4) How do formal considerations of risk impact the way the insurance field responds to cyber security threats? I also asked all interviewees about the role that predictive analytics, big data, and emerging technologies play in the underwriting, pricing, and purchasing of cyber insurance; whether and how cyber insurer risk management services influence insureds' cybersecurity; and what best practices had been developed to improve cyber insurance and cybersecurity in society.

All in-depth interviews were confidential, lasted sixty to ninety minutes, and were digitally recorded and transcribed with the consent of the interviewees. To encourage candor, I agreed not to identify any interviewee. I used qualitative coding software, ATLAS.ti, to code the interview data. This allowed an additional layer of transparency, systematization, and formality to the coding process.

Participant Observation
at Cyber Insurance Conferences

Over a period of five years, I attended eight national conferences where the entire cyber insurance industry comes together to discuss all aspects of the field. Cyber insurance conferences are the place where most actors involved in drafting, marketing, buying, and selling cyber insurance engage one another. These conferences allowed me to explore how the insurance industry thinks about data breaches and privacy laws, discusses the most important issues, and advises one another on best practices.

Quantitative Analysis of a Big Data Provider

Because cyber insurance is an emerging field, most brokers lack historical and actuarial data with which to assess cyber risk and price insurance. Insurance underwriters and brokers,

therefore, rely on expensive, commercial third-party databases developed by providers that compile information on cyber
incidents and losses. Today, cyber insurers rely on three or four
major data providers.

Despite the difficulty of accessing big data sources, I purchased access to one of the major databases that insurance companies and brokers use. The database contains more than 90,000
records from publicly available sources about cyber events and
presents information about different types of cyber risks.[7] The
data are organized into peer groups by company, industry type,
and revenue amount. In addition to recording the parent company, its size and type, and the industry of each cyber event, the
database also includes information about the number of records
affected in each event, the types of loss suffered, how the breach
occurred, and the types of cyber risk posed.

Users seeking to sell or buy insurance may run simulations to
understand the estimated impact a cyber breach may have on a
company of a particular industry, size, and number of records
possessed. Brokers use such data to recommend policy limits for
prospective buyers of insurance by running simulations on similarly situated buyers.

In order to understand how underwriters, brokers, and buyers
use the information presented in the database, I ran three hundred simulations across various industry sectors, including agri-
culture, forestry, manufacturing, finance, insurance, and health
care. These industries reflect a broad cross-section of companies
that frequently experience cybersecurity breaches. I focused on
observing patterns and inconsistencies in visual information
presented in the database and assessing its utility for buyers
of insurance in determining whether and how much coverage
is appropriate, with a recognition of how such information is

presented in the database. Most important, I attempted to identify whether the database is used as a tool to encourage buyers to purchase higher limits of coverage (and, therefore, pay more premiums). These data allowed me to explore the processes through which predictive analytics, big data, and emerging technologies transform the delivery of insurance, and the implications and effects of such practices for broader concerns such as consumer privacy and algorithmic justice in society.

Content Analysis of Cyber Professional Literature and Risk Management Services

To evaluate how cyber insurers engage in a regulatory intervention with the pre- and postbreach services that they market aggressively to prospective buyers of insurance, I reviewed over thirty different risk management services offered by insurers and third-party vendors. These data revealed the ways the insurance industry acts as a compliance manager and de facto regulator well beyond the traditional services that the insurance industry offers. I also reviewed industry reports and executive summaries by risk management consultants who conduct research on the kinds of cyber liability insurance coverage offered by insurers.

Webinars

I observed, transcribed, and coded cyber insurance webinars administered by risk management consultants and brokers, insurance industry and cyber security experts, and attorneys. These webinars simultaneously market cyber insurance and educate webinar participants about what cyber insurance is and how it is used and the various pre- and postbreach risk management services provided to organizations that purchase cyber insurance. Similar to conferences, cyber insurance webinars allowed me to explore how various organizational actors discuss the interplay between insurance, data theft, and privacy laws.

Content Analysis of Cyber Insurance Policies

Cyber insurers' focus on law and compliance can be evaluated in part by examining how they construct their insurance policies and what level of scrutiny and attention is paid to holding their insureds accountable to the prevalent privacy laws and cybersecurity standards. The extent to which cyber insurers care about whether their insureds comply with privacy laws may be reflected in their insurance policies. To evaluate whether insurance policy language explicitly references law to promote or prioritize proactive cybersecurity behavior by insureds, I analyzed twenty-six cyber insurance policies and evaluated whether insurance policies reference various specific laws such as HIPAA, HITECH, GDPR, Graham Leach Bliley, PCI, or other, related regulations and standards. If the insurance policy did make references to specific laws, I evaluated whether the policies interpret or define requirements, articulate specific requirements for compliance, or offer incentives or impose penalties for noncompliance.

Content Analysis of Cyber Insurance Applications

To explore how insurance industry officials evaluate and account for a prospective insured's security measures in the underwriting process, I obtained and analyzed sixty cyber insurance application forms that insurance companies ask prospective insureds to fill out. I evaluated the similarities and differences across policies and to what degree insurance applications meaningfully solicit information concerning the loss control and cybersecurity protections that a policyholder maintains.

In sum, this mixed-method approach provides multiple vantage points from which to explore how cyber insurers manage an uncertain environment and function as quasi-regulators.

ORGANIZATION OF THE BOOK

The book is organized into three parts. Part 1, "The Interplay between Insurance Institutions, Law, and Cybersecurity," provides the context for the empirical study and the theoretical and legal background. Chapter 2 explains my new institutional theory of insurance and develops the theoretical framework. I introduce my model of how insurance companies serve as intermediaries in shaping the meaning of law and compliance among organizations. Because this chapter links my institutional theory of insurance to existing theories of organizations, it is more abstract and involves somewhat more jargon than the remaining chapters. It also situates the framework within larger debates over insurance as a form of regulation and the role of public-private regulatory frameworks in society.

Part 2, "Insurance Companies as Regulators," draws from my empirical research to explore how insurers, as legal intermediaries, influence the way organizations understand and address cybersecurity compliance and privacy law more broadly. Chapter 3 highlights how technology and data have transformed the delivery of insurance in the cyber context. Unlike most traditional areas of insurance, cyber insurers lack significant amounts of loss history and actuarial data to rely on when making risk assessments. Cyber insurers covet data from data providers because cyber insurance is new and uncertain and because cyber attackers continue to evolve their methods and strategies. Cyber insurers are turning to big data, AI, and predictive analytics to assist in the underwriting and risk and claims management processes and, as a result, are redefining the delivery of insurance. Emerging technologies are mobilized as tools for managing uncertain cyber and legal risks and regulating policyholders in a manner that not only is efficient but also allows insurers managerial discretion.

Chapter 4 discusses the effects and implications of the "technologization of insurance." Although reliance on technology and data is increasingly transforming the way insurers advertise, underwrite, and price insurance, the actual impact on insurer behavior seems to have remained minimal and largely symbolic. I find that insurtech interventions and innovations have been, to date, largely ineffective in enhancing organizations' cybersecurity and assisting insurers in managing uncertainty in the market. I highlight a variety of ways that insurers largely act as "symbolic regulators," or play a gatekeeping and oversight role concerning privacy law and cybersecurity compliance, while they ultimately mask informal practices that deviate from regulatory and legal goals.

Chapter 5 focuses on cyber insurer risk management and loss prevention services touted as symbols of an effective regulatory response by insurers. Insurers attempt to play a de facto regulator role by offering a series of pre- and postbreach risk management services to purchasers of cyber insurance that, they argue, prevent, detect, and respond to cybersecurity breaches. This chapter reveals that although risk management services are a mechanism through which insurers attempt to regulate and nudge organizational behavior, the impact of these services is largely symbolic because organizations fail to use the prebreach services. I explore the reasons for this disuse. I also reveal that although organizations have used insurer-provided postbreach services, because those services are used *after* the cyber breach occurs, they are not helpful in preventing breaches.

Chapter 6 brings together chapters 3–5 in two important ways. First, I show how cyber insurers and affiliated entities interpret and construct what privacy laws and cybersecurity compliance mean for organizations. Second, I explore how these insurer constructions of what privacy laws mean influence the manner in which legislatures, regulatory agencies, and private rating agencies understand privacy laws and cybersecurity compliance. Despite the ineffectiveness of cyber insurers as regulators, legislatures and regulatory agencies continue to defer to cyber insurance as a legitimate form of regulation in the cybersecurity and privacy law context without evidence that such interventions improve the cybersecurity of organizations.

Part 3, "Policy Reforms and Pathways Forward," attempts to recenter the debate and offer a way forward for insurers and governments interested in improving the cyber hygiene of organizations and, more broadly, society. Chapter 7 offers a series of recommendations for how insurers and the government can improve cybersecurity in society and foster greater algorithmic justice. Despite the problems identified with cyber insurers as regulators in prior chapters, this chapter suggests cyber insurers could play a meaningful role in improving their insureds' cybersecurity posture and, eventually, society. In particular, I put forward a prioritized and interconnected set of proposals to strengthen the cyber insurance field and incentivize needed improvements in our overall cyber hygiene, including creation of a federally funded financial backstop. I also offer suggestions on how to address catastrophic cyberattacks that could also pose existential threats to the cyber insurance ecosystem.

Chapter 8, the conclusion, explores the policy implications of insurance companies as regulators, not just in the cyber context but in other areas as well. This chapter also explores the potential for the new institutional theory of insurance to better explain how insurers in the twenty-first century manage risk and act as intermediaries between organizations that purchase insurance and the set of rules and laws that organizations must comply with. The chapter also discusses the theoretical significance of the new institutional theory of insurance for the study of law and organizations, law and regulation, legal intermediaries, and law and social change. Insurance companies do not just pool and spread risk, they increasingly shape and influence the meaning of law and compliance for organizations that purchase insurance. I draw on other examples of how insurers shape the content and meaning of law and compliance among the National Association of Insurance Commissioners, property and casualty insurance, and employment practice liability insurance. This chapter thus not only reveals the conditions in which insurers can work more effectively as regulators but also evaluates the role of emerging technologies and big data as mechanisms for managing uncertain risk as insurers increasingly turn to these tools.

CHAPTER TWO

A New Institutional Theory of Insurance

Insurance law scholars often analyze the forms and functions of insurance and discuss the various ways insurance institutions (i.e., companies, brokers, and agents) impact society. As traditionally conceived, insurance is a voluntary contractual agreement that transfers a risk of loss to a party whose business is selling such contracts. However, insurance scholars also examine how insurance functions in society as regulation (Baker 2002; Ben-Shahar and Logue 2012), as governance (Heimer 1985; Ericson, Doyle, and Barry 2003), as a public utility (Abraham 2013), and as a product (Abraham 2013). In addition to serving as a basis for knowledge production and capital accumulation and allocation, insurance increases and decreases social stratification in society. Insurance regulates many aspects of our lives. Insurance companies establish underwriting criteria and standards and charge premiums. These mechanisms allow insurance companies to act as gatekeepers controlling who can or cannot obtain insurance. Liability insurance in particular acts as a form of tort regulation and, in doing so, finances the civil litigation system

(Baker 2005a). Private insurance policies for life, health, and property often take the form of private legislation or regulation through exclusions and conditions.

Within these frameworks, scholars often draw from law and economics principles to understand insurance company and insured behavior.[1] Analyses of insurance law assume that law is top-down and exogenous to the insurance institutions that draft, market, and sell insurance. In other words, law is treated as formed and defined outside insurance institutions by courts, legislatures, and administrative agencies, and the role of the insurance industry is limited to reacting to law by either complying or not complying with it, often due to the industry's rational, strategic considerations. By exploring how and why insurance impacts society, and why insurance companies wield considerable influence in society, insurance law scholars lay an excellent foundation for thinking about insurance and insurance institutions. While existing approaches are helpful, there is not an insurance theory anchored in organizational behavior, culture, and decision making that explains how insurance companies respond to law and shape the compliance behavior of organizations that purchase insurance.

This book suggests that the relationship between legal regulation and insurance institutions is more bottom-up than we think. The interaction between insurance companies and legal regulation is best illustrated not by examining the forms or functions of insurance or the insurance industry's broad impact on society, but rather through a processual model in which insurance companies, often as legal intermediaries, influence not just private law but public law. Drawing on new institutional organizational sociology studies, this chapter, therefore, offers an institutional theory that explains insurance industry behavior and, in particular, *how* insurance companies respond to laws in ways that end up influencing the meaning of law and compliance for organizations that purchase insurance, not just in insurance companies' own legal environment but also among public legal institutions. Moreover, I theorize how insurance companies act as legal intermediaries by positioning themselves as de facto regulators of organizations and regulating the compliance behavior of organizations. In doing so, I offer an alternative theoretical framework for understanding the relationship between legal regulation, organizations, and insurance companies that issue insurance to organizations. Whereas most accounts attempt to specify the conditions under which organizations comply or do not comply with law, my institutional theory of insurance focuses on the *processes* through which organizations construct the meaning of cybersecurity and privacy law compliance. Figure 1 provides a visual of the processual model of how insurance companies as intermediaries influence the meaning of privacy law and cybersecurity compliance.

I start by identifying the conditions that make it more likely that insurance companies and other organizations will shape how compliance is understood among organizations; I pay special attention to a regulatory environment that encourages co-regulation and public-private partnerships, to the ambiguity of legal regulations, and to complexity of laws and new subject areas. The interaction of these three elements creates greater space for nontraditional actors to emerge and influence law and makes insurer intermediation more likely. Indeed, a wide variety of legal and nonlegal actors among and within organizations that come into contact with law have increasing discretion in their legal environments.

I suggest that legal intermediaries shape law and compliance for organizations, with varying degrees of success, in two primary ways: (1) law is filtered through nonlegal logics emanating from various organizational fields; (2) law is professionalized

Figure 1. The processual model through which insurance companies, as intermediaries, influence the way organizations go about responding to privacy laws and cybersecurity compliance issues. Risk and managerial values that dominate the insurance field shape the way insurance companies, acting as intermediaries, assist organizations responding to cybersecurity threats as they market insurance policies and accompanying risk management services. Emerging technologies, big data, and information security shape how cyber insurance providers market themselves as assisting organizations in preventing, detecting, and responding to cyber risks. Despite limited success, public legal institutions defer to cyber insurance's potential as a quasi-regulator.

by nonlegal actors, that is, it is increasingly filtered through and by professionals with varying degrees of connection to law. By "nonlegal actors," I mean actors who are *not* working or inscribed in the legal field as professionals such as lawyers, judges, or legislators. Insurance companies, brokers, information security analysts, and risk managers are some of the nonlegal actors that play critical roles in and among organizations attempting to become cybersecure. To show the expansive arc of legal intermediaries, I argue that professionalization and the filtering of nonlegal logics work together to facilitate and inhibit cybersecurity compliance among organizations.

In response to this legal environment, organizations often "legalize" themselves with written policies and procedures to construe the law's meaning. In this case, insurance companies as intermediaries offer insurance and partner with managed security companies. In addition to insurance, they offer pre- and postbreach services aimed at curbing cybersecurity incidents for the organizations purchasing cyber insurance. These insurance and managed-security companies working together have filled in this space and constructed what compliance means on the ground.

As organizations develop policies and procedures, managerial and risk values shape the way insurers offer risk management and give loss-control advice and guidance to organizations. Unlike prior new institutional studies that focus on how managerial and risk logics shape the way organizations understand law, cyber insurers are turning to big data, information security, and high-end technology tools to manage uncertainty in the cyber market. Thus, in the cybersecurity context, technology and big data are mechanisms through which managerial and risk responses are constructed by organizations.

These quasi-regulatory responses are decoupled and not fully integrated into the underwriting and risk management processes. As a result, they do not make organizations more cybersecure or compliant with privacy laws. In fact, insurance-as-regulation responses are often primarily focused on avoiding litigation and regulatory fines rather than making organizations more cybersecure (Talesh 2015a, 2018; Baker and Shortland 2022b). Thus, insurance company regulatory interventions tend to be seen as symbolic and ineffective. As insurers institutionalize a way of operating through conferences, professional literature, and training programs, insurer quasi-regulatory responses come to be seen as legitimate. Ultimately, private industry and federal and state lawmakers and regulators end up deferring to the insurance industry as a viable tool for assisting organizations in complying with privacy laws and protecting themselves against cybersecurity threats. This deference bubbles up not only into private standards but also public laws, standards, and regulations at the federal and state levels and ultimately allows insurers tremendous space to influence and shape cybersecurity policy in society. In sum, insurance companies and affiliated entities are acting as symbolic regulators and influencing what privacy law and cybersecurity compliance means on the ground in ways that ultimately do not make organizations more likely to be cybersecure.

Thus, my new institutional theory of insurance should be viewed as an extension and refinement of Edelman's legal endogeneity theory. While normative, instrumental, political, and cultural processes through which law produces social change and influences compliance behavior remain important (Edelman 2016; Dobbin 2009; Stryker, Docka-Filipek, and Wald 2012), this new institutional theory of insurance approach helps explain the underlying mechanisms that drive those different processes in the cybersecurity context. In particular, political, cultural, and institutional theories about how law is influenced are often *derived from and influenced by* the increasing professionalization of law by nonlegal actors and how these nonlegal actors encounter and filter what law means through nonlegal logics. By highlighting the conditions that lead to greater legal intermediation and the processes and mechanisms through which intermediaries can facilitate and inhibit compliance and ultimately social change, I set forth a framework for scholars to use in future studies of intermediaries, insurance or otherwise. In this respect, my framework provides the backstory for what shapes organizations and civil society actors' political, cultural, and instrumental choices for how best to respond to various laws.

The remainder of this chapter lays out in a fine-grained way the stages of my institutional theory of insurance and explains the process through which insurance companies act as intermediaries and influence organizational compliance.

STAGE ONE: THE REGULATORY AND LEGAL ENVIRONMENT CONDUCIVE TO INSURANCE INSTITUTIONS INFLUENCING LAW AND COMPLIANCE

What conditions lead intermediaries to be increasingly involved in not just the implementation of legal rules but law's construction and meaning? I view this question as essential to understanding how and when different kinds of legal intermediaries operating in different institutional and social environments influence organizational compliance behavior and facilitate or inhibit social change. Focusing less on public legal institutions than on the rising role of intermediaries is crucial because the location of lawmaking has shifted. In particular, the regulatory environment has gradually moved from a government to governance model that places a greater role on legal and nonlegal actors tasked with interpreting, implementing, and constructing law.

From Government to Governance and Increasing Co-regulation

Insurance companies have greater opportunities to shape the regulatory behavior of organizations they issue policies to because regulation has changed. For much of the twentieth century, scholars across a variety of disciplines studied law as a top-down process, a system of rules coming from the command of government or, more precisely, public legal institutions. Traditional instruments of lawmaking by public legal institutions such as legislatures, courts, and administrative agencies include formal rules and stipulations, adversarial methods, enforceable means of dispute resolution, and command-and-control regulatory mechanisms.

Interest groups, as intermediaries, directly participate in governmental processes such as those undertaken by legislatures and administrative agencies. In particular, interest groups form advocacy coalitions that lobby, negotiate for favorable laws, build (or set) an agenda in their strategic favor, or exert direct influence on government decision makers through campaign contributions. While instrumental, structural, and public choice approaches are all different, they each analyze interest groups as rational, strategic intermediaries seeking direct influence over governmental institutions. Businesses also attempt to "capture" regulatory institutions such that regulation is "acquired by the industry" and designed and operated primarily for its benefit (Stigler 1971, 3; see also Posner 1974 and Becker 1983). At all times, public law is produced by government. In this view law is exogenous to organizations even as it is open to organizational influence.

More recently, business and civil society actors' relationship with regulatory institutions has undergone a dramatic shift due to the transformation of the regulatory state over the past forty years. In particular, the location of governmental decisions has shifted away from traditional public governmental institutions. The top-down, command-and-control regulation of the 1960s and 1970s spawned heightened capture and interest group pluralist behavior. In response to political change at the executive and congressional levels of government, the 1980s and 1990s saw a shift toward free market capitalism, privatization, and devolution of power to the private sector in the United States and Europe (Talesh 2021).

Despite popular belief that regulation was abandoned when neoliberalism was adopted around the Western world beginning in the 1980s, empirical evidence suggests that privatization, deregulation, and the nurturing of markets under neoliberal governments expanded and extended regulation across the world (Vogel 1996; Levi-Faur 2005; Braithwaite 2008). Thus, the alleged deregulation and move toward free markets led to a slow re-regulation of free markets in softer, less stringent forms aimed at perfecting market performance (Majone 1997; Levi-Faur 2005). In this new era of public-private partnerships between corporations, state actors, civil society groups, nongovernmental actors have taken a more active role in governing themselves and trying to maintain the public good (Majone 1997; Braithwaite 2002; Lobel 2004; Freeman 1997, 2000; Ansell and Gash 2008). Regulation is still an important component of governance, but governance schemes go beyond mere regulation in that they are consensus oriented, deliberative, and aim to allow private industry more direct involvement and control in implementing public policies (Braithwaite 1982; Kagan, Gunningham, and Thornton 2003; Lobel 2004; Freeman and Minnow 2009).

New instruments and techniques of regulation, including negotiated rulemaking and management-based regulation follow the logic of governance (Coglianese 1997; Coglianese and Nash 2001; Gunningham 1995; Gunningham and Sinclair 1999, 2009; Ayres and Braithwaite 1992). State, business, and civil society actors act as "rule intermediaries" that affect, control, or monitor relations between rulemakers and ruletakers (Abbott, Levi-Faur, and Snidal 2017; Levi-Faur and Starobin 2014; Locke 2013). This framework suggests that rulemakers create law for ruletakers and the rule intermediaries largely monitor, verify, test, audit, and certify legal rules (Levi-Faur and Starobin 2014; Abbott, Levi-Faur, and Snidal 2017).

Scholarship in this vein has produced far more empirical research on the rise and character of governance than on its translation into practice (Schneiberg and Bartley 2008). Moreover, political scientists who have studied regulatory governance and rule intermediaries still position rulemaking as within the domain of public legal institutions as the rulemakers. Whereas previous studies of intermediaries have examined how intermediaries monitor, verify, or certify legal rules (Abbott, Levi-Faur, and Snidal 2017), few have examined closely the processes and mechanisms through which intermediaries shape the meaning of law and compliance itself and, in doing so, facilitate and inhibit social change. Because the regulatory state has shifted from command-and-control government to governance, there is far more room for stakeholders such as insurance companies to intervene and actively shape and influence the compliance behavior of organizations that it issues policies to.

The Ambiguity of Legal Regulations

The changing structure of the regulatory state from government to governance is coupled with the fact that laws regulating society and businesses, in particular, are often ambiguous as to how to comply with them and increasingly complex and technical. Vague and ambiguous legal provisions create greater opportunities for rule intermediaries to shape the rules. Research in the new institutionalist tradition has shown that legislation is often unclear and judicial rulings interpreting ambiguous statutes often provide little guidance on how to translate and implement legal standards into everyday organizational practice (Edelman and Talesh 2011). For example, Title VII of the Civil Rights Act of 1964 codified strong protections against employment discrimination but failed to specify the meaning of "discrimination" (Edelman 1990, 1992). In particular, statutes often constrain procedures more than substantive outcomes and focus on issues such as shifting burdens of proof or the availability of various kinds of relief (Edelman et al. 1992; Edelman and Talesh, 2011).[2] Powerful laws are also often accompanied with weak or declining enforcement mechanisms (Edelman, Abraham, and Erlanger 1992). I am not suggesting that all laws are ambiguous and incapable of providing appropriate guidance to civil society actors. For example, administrative agencies often provide guidelines and regulations that help clarify the meaning of legal rules. Nonetheless, intermediaries often have considerable room in which to interpret and construct legal rules due to the lack of clarity.

The Complexity of Legal Rules

Not only are many laws and regulations ambiguous with respect to how to comply with them, but they are also more complex than ever before. An increasing number of scholars across the world have examined the complexity of legal rules and its impact on judges and juries (Kades 1997; Müller-Graff and Mestad 2014). Laws such as the Health Insurance Portability and Accountability Act (HIPAA), the Foreign Corrupt Practices Act, bankruptcy laws, the United States Tax Code, the Wage and Hour Laws in France, the Registration, Evaluation, Authorization and

Restriction of Chemicals (REACH) in Europe, and many other environmental laws across the world are dense, technical, complex, and indeterminate and require specialized sets of knowledge. Privacy laws in the United States have largely consisted of notification statutes that require a series of specific responses and must be complied with to avoid regulatory fines. There has never been a time when law was considered completely simple.

However, the growth of new industries, markets, and technologies in areas such as intellectual property, financial services, the internet, and transnational legal settings has prompted formal and informal legal institutions to define the scope of permissible and impermissible behavior. The rising complexity of legal rules requires greater specialization in the legal profession but also greater involvement and coordination with specific industries and the organizations that these laws impact. Cybersecurity and data breach events often involve sophisticated techniques of corrupting, destroying, or stealing information stored on computers. In turn, forensics experts and other managed and information security companies are often brought in because of their specialized sets of knowledge, and they are often charged with identifying the cause of the data breach and restoring a company's network. A society concerned about various risks has emerged and created the need to manage, regulate, and govern these risks through various laws and legal rules that are increasingly complex, sophisticated, or technical.

Three Conditions That Call for Insurer Intermediation

These three conditions—the move from government to governance, the ambiguity in legal rules, and the complexity of legal rules—have created conditions and an environment where insurance companies are more prone to act as intermediaries regarding how organizations go about complying with privacy laws and dealing with cybersecurity threats. There is no federal privacy law. There is no federal cybersecurity law. Many federal laws such as HIPAA, the HITECH (Health Information Technology for Economic and Clinical Health) Act, and the Graham-Leach-Bliley Act touch on privacy law principles but are not the key components or focus of such laws. These laws sometimes contain a maze of technical requirements. With few exceptions, most states have focused largely on notification statutes and some general parameters regarding cybersecurity but have not provided the kind of mandate or guidance on how organizations should go about complying with privacy laws and maintaining a cybersecure environment. To the extent that laws push for organizations to develop "reasonable security measures," these laws are not defined and vague. Moreover, the technical nature of how to address cybersecurity and data breach events when stored information is corrupted, destroyed, or stolen from computers makes even well-meaning organizations hesitant or tentative about how to comply. Technical security requirements concerning how to avoid attack by cybercriminals at times leaves organizations feeling overwhelmed and requiring knowledge they do not possess internally or cannot access easily. As the Cyber Solarium Commission's 2020 report noted and continual surveys of organizations underscore, organizations are undercompliant with and underprepared to meet laws (Cunningham and Talesh 2021–22). Under these conditions, organizations such as insurance companies and other civil society actors have tremendous discretion and opportunity to shape the meaning of legal rules. These are not necessary conditions but are certainly sufficient conditions that help us understand why rule intermediation by nonlegal actors is more prevalent than ever before across the world. Thus, insurance companies have entered this marketplace offering not just first-party and third-party insurance but risk management services that they claim prevent, detect, and reduce cyber risk.

STAGE TWO: THE LEGALIZATION OF ORGANIZATIONS WITH INSURANCE COMPANIES AS INTERMEDIARIES

In situations where laws regulating organizations are ambiguous or complex, organizations do not resist or avoid law but instead respond by creating written rules, procedures, and structures to fill in the law's meaning. For example, Edelman (2016) shows how organizations responded to Title VII by creating new offices and developing written policies, rules, and procedures to achieve legal legitimacy while simultaneously curbing the law's impact on managerial power and unfettered discretion over employment decisions. In a sample of 346 organizations, only 30 had created antidiscrimination guidelines by 1969, 118 instituted guidelines in the 1970s, and 75 additional organizations created guidelines in the 1980s (Edelman 1990, 1992). There was also a noticeable increase in other forms of legalization in the 1970s, including a proliferation of special offices devoted solely to civil rights issues and special procedures for processing discrimination complaints. Initially, early adopters created these structures, but eventually they spread among other similarly situated organizations. Similarly, in the consumer protection context, Talesh shows that automobile manufacturers that faced strong consumer warranty laws first developed internal grievance structures and then eventually ceded them to external third-party organizations that contracted with manufacturers to administer these grievances (Talesh 2009,

2012, 2014). Thus, powerful consumer rights to resolve disputes in court were routed into alternative dispute resolution forums where fewer rights and less relief exists.

These legalization processes in organizations bear mixed results. On one hand, civil rights offices, grievance procedures, and other antidiscrimination rules serve as visible indicators of attention to law and give the appearance of legitimacy. On the other hand, these structures often allow compliance in form but do not require or lead to substantive change in the workplace for employees or consumer protection for consumers. As more and more organizations put such structures into practice and they become the taken-for-granted norm, these structures come to be seen as "rational" forms of compliance though they have become largely symbolic.

STAGE THREE: PROFESSIONALIZATION OF LAW BY NONLEGAL ACTORS AND THE RISE OF MANAGERIAL LOGICS

As new institutional organizational sociology studies reveal, law becomes managerialized as values such as rationality, efficiency, and management discretion operating within an organizational field influence the way organizations understand law, legality, and compliance (Edelman, Fuller, and Mara-Drita 2001). The professionalization of legal services by legal and nonlegal actors is coupled with the filtering of law through various organizational logics operating in particular fields or industries.

In addition to focusing on institutionalized logics, prior new institutional research shows that the professions are key carriers of ideas among and across organizational fields. In particular, we have seen a professionalization of legal services by nonlegal actors that operate and interact with law in tangible ways. In particular, human resource officials, personnel managers, management consultants, risk management consultants, insurance officials, and in-house lawyers communicate ideas about law as they move among organizations and participate in conferences, workshops, training sessions, and professional networking meetings and publish professional personnel literature (Jacoby 1985; Baron, Dobbin, and Jennings 1986; Abzug and Mezias 1993; Edelman, Erlanger, and Lande 1993; Edelman, Fuller, and Mara-Drita 2001; Edelman et al. 2011; Talesh 2015a). Professional associations, conferences, and other forums offer opportunities for the diffusion of new solutions to perceived managerial problems such as the threat of employment lawsuits or consumer complaints (Edelman, Abraham, and Erlanger 1992; Bisom-Rapp 1996, 1999; Talesh 2015a).

In particular, organizations struggle to find rational modes of response to legal ambiguity and devise strategies to preserve managerial discretion and authority while maximizing the appearance of compliance with legal principles. When legal ideals conflict with business goals and agendas, compliance officers often interpret law and compliance in ways that tilt toward business values. Compliance is interpreted so as to incorporate managerial values, logics, and ways of understanding the world derived from organizational fields. As this process takes place, law becomes managerialized, or infused with managerial values and interests, which in turn leads to symbolic structures or structures less likely to further social justice goals. Existing empirical research reveals that when organizations attempt to comply with laws, managerial conceptions of law transform sexual harassment claims, for example, into personality conflicts and interpersonal disputes and reframe, deflect, or discourage complaints rather than offering informal resolution (Edelman, Erlanger, and Lande 1993; Marshall 2005; Edelman 2016).

STAGE FOUR: PROFESSIONALIZATION OF LAW BY NONLEGAL ACTORS AND THE ROLE OF RISK LOGICS

Intermediaries are driven not just by managerial logics. Empirical studies demonstrate that institutional logics coexist and coevolve over time (Dunn and Jones 2010), while often one institutionalized or dominant logic is replaced or abandoned for a new dominant logic (Stryker 1994, 2000; Haveman and Rao 1997; Thornton and Ocasio 1999; Thornton, 2002; Lounsbury 2002; Rao, Monin, and Durand 2003). Moreover, field actors often mobilize multiple logics within organizational fields (McPherson and Sauder 2013; Talesh 2015c). Recent work in this area focuses on how organizational field logics influence the legal field, that is, "the environment within which legal institutions and legal actors and in which conceptions of legality and compliance evolve" (Edelman 2007, 58). The tensions between the logics of organizational and legal fields—one anchored in efficiency and rationality, the other in rights and justice (and more recently informality in the form of alternative dispute resolution)—come into play when organizational and legal actors and institutions interact (Edelman 2007; Stryker 1994, 2000; Pélisse 2011; Talesh 2012).

More recently, scholars have started to broaden the framework beyond managerialization and explore how other, nonmanagerial logics influence the way organizations understand the meaning of law and, in particular, the role of intermediaries who are not legal professionals (Pélisse 2014, 2016). Consumer, risk, science, and prison logics emanating from various organizational fields can influence organizations' understanding of law (Stryker, Docka-Filipek, and Wald 2012; Verma 2015; Talesh 2012, 2014, 2015a, 2015b). Managerial logics can contest or complement these other logics (Talesh 2015a). In particular, another series of studies have looked at how risk logics and risk management principles operating within a field can mediate the meaning of law and compliance. Different professions are anchored in different logics, and these logics shape the prism through which law is interpreted, implemented, and even constructed.

Risk logics and, in particular, risk reduction and risk management principles shape the way professional safety officers interpret and implement a variety of environmental, health, and safety rules (Silbey 2017). Professional safety officers in many industries have to ensure compliance with various international laws, industry guidelines, and government agency mandates aimed at protecting the environment and worker health and safety. Safety officers in scientific laboratories in France and the United States use their extensive training and technical skills and knowledge concerning safety, chemical products, and health risks to interpret and implement many legal regulations surrounding health and safety in work settings (Talesh and Pélisse 2019). They use surveillance technology and build and maintain databases to manage hazards (Silbey and Agrawal 2011) and develop "relational regulation practices" in science laboratories (Huising and Silbey 2011). Safety officers also use the authority of legal rules to manage risks, influence safe practices, and develop safe working conditions (Pélisse 2017; Borelle and Pélisse 2017).

The insurance industry, as an active intermediary for organizations, uses the logic of risk to shape the way organizations that purchase certain lines of insurance understand law. Specifically, the insurance field (companies, agents, brokers, and risk management consultants), through employment practice liability insurance (EPLI) and the accompanying risk management services that the insurance field offers, construct the threat of employment law and influence the nature of civil rights compliance (Talesh 2015a). Insurers began offering EPLI in response to perceived threats of employment discrimination lawsuits. Unlike other insurance policies, EPLI policies provide defense and indemnification coverage to employers for claims of discrimination and other employment-related allegations made by employees, former employees, and potential employees. Insurers increasingly offer, and employers increasingly purchase, this insurance. Insurers encourage employers to avert such risk, and act as a regulatory intermediary, because employers have an incentive to avoid discrimination. But, in playing this intermediary role, insurers help organizations avoid litigation rather than fostering fair governance, due process, and equality in the workplace.

Drawing from participant observation and interviews at EPLI conferences across the country, as well as content analysis of EPLI policies, loss-prevention manuals, EPLI industry guidelines, and webinars, this book shows how insurance companies and institutions use a risk-based logic and institutionalize a way of thinking centered on risk management and reduction. Faced with an uncertain and unpredictable legal risk of discrimination violations on the part of organizations, insurance institutions elevate the risk and threat in the legal environment and offer risk management services that, they argue, will reduce the risk for employers that purchase EPLI. Insurers use policy language to build discretion into legal rules and often reframe the rules and principles around a nonlegal risk logic that focuses on avoiding risk and making discrimination claims more defensible (Talesh 2015a, 2015b).

By framing employers' legal environment in these terms, the insurance industry creates a space in which to encourage employers to engage in managerialized responses and develop formalized policies and procedures by using the various risk management services offered by insurers. Thus, in this instance, risk and managerial values complement each other and allow insurers as rule intermediaries greater influence over compliance issues concerning employers (Talesh 2015a, 2015b).

Insurer risk management services can have positive and negative impacts on social change. On one hand, insurer risk management may reflect some best practices and lead to improved employment policies and procedures and greater equality in the workplace. On the other hand, they may also make it easier for employers to become lethargic concerning compliance, as by developing policies and procedures without actively participating in their creation. In particular, insurance company guidance on these issues largely focuses more on how to avoid litigation than on how to maintain a discrimination-free work environment. As with managers and human resource officials in the employment context (Edelman 2016), here the insurance field filters law through a nonlegal risk logic in ways that make it harder for law to achieve social change.

Insurer intermediation, however, is not a foregone conclusion. Sometimes intermediaries are well positioned to engage in social change but choose not to. For example, Baker and Griffith (2010) show how insurance companies offering directors and officers (D&O) insurance to a corporation have opportunities to engage in loss and risk prevention and discourage wrongful or even illegal behavior, but fail to take action. Concerns about corporate malfeasance by corporate directors and officers at the expense of shareholders and broader corporate social responsibility remain present in the increasingly global economy. Empirical studies of the relationship between D&O insurance and corporate actors reveal that such insurance significantly weakens the deterrent effect of shareholder litigation and thus undermines such private lawsuits brought to enforce securities laws as forms of regulation

(Baker and Griffith 2010). Despite having financial incentives to do so, D&O insurers neither monitor nor provide loss prevention programs to the corporations they insure. In particular, D&O insurers do not condition the sale of insurance on adopting loss prevention policies. Brokers and risk managers note that loss prevention advice is not highly valued or binding on public corporations (Baker and Griffith, 2010). Thus, intermediaries in this instance have opportunities to improve the legal and ethical conduct of corporate directors and effectuate positive social change, but do not.

Cyber insurance is an ideal location in which to explore insurer intermediation and quasi-regulatory interventions, because organizations are admittedly underprepared for data breach events and do not comply fully with privacy laws. Moreover, cybersecurity risks are a major concern for businesses, consumers, and governments. Tapping into fear of cyber threats, in the past twenty years the insurance field has stepped in and offered first-party loss and third-party liability coverage for data breach events, privacy violations, and cyberattacks. Emphasizing the need for organizations to prevent, detect, and respond to risks, cyber insurers also provide a set of risk management services that actively shape how an organization's various departments tasked with preventing and addressing data breaches respond to such an event; among these departments are in-house counsel, information technology, compliance, and public relations. In the cyber context, managerial and risk logics complement each other as cyber insurers attempt to advise clients and manage uncertain risk.

STAGE FIVE: PROFESSIONALIZATION OF LAW BY
NONLEGAL ACTORS AND THE ROLE OF TECHNOLOGY

As noted, risk, managerial, prison, and consumer logics or ways of thinking are pathways through which intermediaries filter the law's meaning. But this list is not exhaustive. I suggest that technology is a key pathway through which managerial and risk values influence how organizations go about complying with law. Artificial intelligence (AI), predictive analytics, and big data are taking over society (J. Cohen 2019). Governments, businesses, banks, advertisers, schools, health care, finance, and policing institutions all over the world are turning to emerging technologies and predictive analytics. The shift from an industrial economy focused on money, labor, and property as commodities to an economy focused on information is reconstructing labor, money, and property as "datafied inputs to new algorithmic modes of profit extraction" (J. Cohen 2019, 25). Data providers, harvesters, and refineries are paving the way for the "Fourth Industrial Revolution," one that extracts information from the available pool of consumers so that it may be reliably identified, analyzed, and used for profit (Schwab 2017). Julie Cohen (2019) describes the process of information capitalism as involving data cultivation, harvesting, refining, and ultimately marketing and selling this information to interested parties.

Proponents of big data and emerging technology argue that these processes provide businesses with insights and perspectives on their customers, increase the efficiency of their operations, offer competitive advantages, and improve the use of existing products and services (Brookman 2015; Thomas and McSharry 2015). Opponents argue that corporate use and exploitation of consumer information threaten privacy and data security (Crawford and Schultz 2014). Moreover, state and private sector producers of surveillance technologies cultivate a global economic and social environment where very little is private. It remains an open question whether the technological and big data revolution is transformative, disruptive, or harmful. The pivot toward technology in society, however, appears irreversible.

Drawing on legal, political, and economic theories, scholars offer theoretical and normative arguments for and against big data, technology, and algorithmic governance in various contexts. We have less empirical scholarship on how these tools operate and impact society. In addition, prevailing research on big data and technology focuses on the impact on individuals and ignores the impact data have on businesses operating across multiple sectors. The lack of disclosure by data providers, data harvesters, and corporations that collect and use these data and operate these technologies make accessing information a challenge. "The most noteworthy attribute of the personal data economy," Julie Cohen (2019) notes, "has been its secrecy, which frustrates the most basic efforts to understand how the internet search, social networking, and consumer finance industries sort and categorize individual consumers" (62). Frank Pasquale (2015) has highlighted how data processing practices of platform firms and data providers revolve around secrecy. Efforts by government and consumer advocacy organizations to access this information have failed (Cohen 2019). There has been little empirical analysis of precisely *how* big data and technology influence important aspects of society. What are the processes and mechanisms through which big data and emerging technology influence society? This book explores how big data, artificial intelligence, technology, and security operate on the ground in specific settings. My empirical research reveals how technology and big data operate as mechanisms through which risk and managerial constructions of law and compliance influence organizational compliance. Moreover, I show how insurers lean into and rely on emerging technologies and big data as they attempt to nudge organizations' cybersecurity hygiene.

Cybersecurity and cyber insurance in particular are ideal locations to explore the current way organizations understand compliance. Technology and data have transformed the delivery of insurance in the cyber context because, unlike most traditional insurers, cyber insurers lack significant amounts of loss history and actuarial data to rely on when making risk assessments (Herr 2021). These challenges are coupled with the evolving attacks by cybercriminals and lead cyber insurers to covet data from providers.

This analysis supports a fundamental argument to new institutional theories of law and organizations: big data, AI, and emerging technologies are not all the same, organizations and, more important, organizational fields shape the way these tools operate. In this case, the insurance field plays a big role in how big data, emerging technologies, and AI are developed and mobilized. The empirical research presented in the following chapters reveal that emerging technologies are not neutral but are configured and constructed in subtle ways by individuals and organizations that develop these technologies.[3] Thus, the issue is not whether data and technology are good or bad, or effective or ineffective, but rather under what conditions these technologies lead to socially desirable or undesirable outcomes. My insights come from within the corporate world and reveal how this "technologization of insurance" is mobilized and leads to nonneutral outcomes that further the insurance industry but do not necessarily make businesses or individuals (or society) more cybersecure. Thus, insurer risk management responses render insurance companies symbolic regulators that exude the traditional signals that regulators possess but provide limited effective interventions that change organizational behavior—in this case, cybersecurity practices and hygiene.

STAGE SIX: PUBLIC LEGAL INSTITUTIONS' DEFERENCE TO ORGANIZATIONAL RESPONSES TO LAW

The infusion of technological, managerial, and risk logics into how organizations go about complying with laws is not limited to organizations but also eventually influences the content and meaning of judicial decisions, legislation, and regulation. New institutionalists have shown how law becomes endogenous as legal rules derived from court cases come to be determined by organizations—the very group that such laws are designed to regulate. Similar to employers, employees, compliance professionals, and lawyers, judges over time end up equating the symbolic structures that organizations create in response to civil rights law, for example, with the protection of civil rights in organizations (Edelman 2016). Judges in employment cases increasingly defer to the presence of organizational structures as evidence of nondiscriminatory treatment without evaluating whether these structures do anything substantively to curb discrimination and without examining the evidence suggesting that these structures fail to protect employees' legal rights.

Industrial organizational psychologists, as nonlegal intermediaries, helped lay the foundation for the disparate impact theory of discrimination under Title VII, a theory ultimately adopted by courts (Stryker, Docka-Filipek, and Wald 2012; Stryker 2011). Industrial organizational psychologist's research pertaining to performance-related worker characteristics, performance evaluations of employees, and human resource management helped influence judicial thinking on disparate impact. Similarly, insurers have influenced public legal institutions through insurance. The institutionalized practice and increasing legitimacy of EPLI ultimately lead public legal institutions to defer to EPLI considerably. In addition to courts expanding coverage afforded to those insured under EPLI, federal, state, and municipal governments have adopted the logics of EPLI insurers and have encouraged and, in some instances, required public organizations and government institutions to purchase EPLI (Talesh 2015b).

In the realm of consumer protection legislation and regulation, a similar deference has been shown to organizational practices. In response to powerful but ambiguous consumer protection laws and regulations, automobile manufacturers were able to reroute the protection of significant consumer rights from courts to alternative disputing forums that they created where consumers had far fewer rights and where managerial values shaped the manner in which these processes operated. Ultimately, the legislature deferred to these structures and adopted use of these disputing forums into law and required consumers to use them (Talesh 2012). As a result, intermediaries have inhibited law's ability to achieve social change in the employment and consumer contexts. In the cybersecurity context, this book highlights a similar deference to insurer-sponsored risk management interventions by legislators and private standard rating agencies.

INSURANCE COMPANIES AS SYMBOLIC REGULATORS

The processual model that I articulate in this chapter explains how private organizations (in this case, insurance companies) become symbolic regulators. To summarize, my new institutional theory of insurance contains six stages:

Stage 1   The regulatory and legal environment that leads
               to insurance institutions influencing law and
               compliance

Stage 2   The legalization of organizations with insurance
               companies as intermediaries

Stage 3   Professionalization of law by nonlegal actors
               through managerial logics

Stage 4   Professionalization of law by nonlegal actors
               through risk logics

Stage 5   Professionalization of law by nonlegal actors
               through technology

Stage 6   Deference to organizational responses to law
               by public legal institutions

Stage 1 suggests that organizations operate in a regulatory
and legal environment where privacy laws are ambiguous and
cybersecurity compliance is complex. The move away from
command-and-control regulation invites public-private partnerships and stakeholder involvement amidst a self-regulatory or at
best co-regulatory framework. Stage 2 reveals that in response
to this legal and regulatory environment, organizations legalize
themselves, that is, they create cybersecurity policies and
procedures or look to insurers for assistance in developing a
cybersecurity response and in complying with privacy laws
through insurers' policies and accompanying risk management
services. As organizations legalize themselves, a "technologization of insurance" occurs: insurers as intermediaries offer a
series of pre- and postbreach services and tools that they claim
help organizations prevent, detect, and reduce risk in the event
of a data breach. Here, stages 3 and 4 work in tandem. Although
insurers filter what privacy law and cybersecurity compliance

means for organizations through a managerial and risk lens (consistent with the logics that dominate the insurance field), insurers use information security and high-end technology tools to manage uncertainty in the cyber market, and organizations use these tools to mobilize and implement managerial and risk responses. In stage 5 this technologization of insurance permeates the cyber insurance field and thereby shapes how organizations deal with cybersecurity challenges. As the following chapters show, this diffusion and mobilization of risk management services and cyber insurance initiatives within organizations, though institutionalized and normalized within and among organizations, is largely symbolic. This ineffectiveness results in insurance companies acting largely as symbolic regulators in light of the soft, government oversight in the privacy law arena. In stage 6, things come full circle. Ultimately, private standard rating agencies and public legal institutions defer to insurer quasi-regulatory responses: they accept use of information security and technology tools as evidence of compliance without evaluating whether such responses work. Thus, this new institutional theory of insurance helps us understand how insurance companies influence the manner in which organizations comply with privacy legal rules or cybersecurity mandates and shape the content and meaning of laws designed to regulate organizations. It also reveals how insurers as intermediaries manage uncertainty, act as de facto regulators, and become symbolic regulators.

Having already addressed in chapter 1 how the legal and regulatory environment with respect to privacy law and cybersecurity compliance is ambiguous and complex and operates in a co-regulatory environment with little involvement by state and federal governments, the following chapters use empirical research to focus on stages 2–6 and explain how insurance companies as intermediaries engage in de facto regulation in ways that do not strengthen organizational cyber hygiene, and also show how insurers influence what law and compliance means to organizations attempting to address evolving privacy and cybersecurity challenges.

PART II

Insurance Companies as Regulators

The Influence of Technology and Big Data on Cyber Insurance

This chapter highlights how technology and big data have transformed the delivery of insurance in the cyber context. I use the term *technologization of insurance* to refer to the process whereby technology influences and shapes the practice and delivery of insurance (underwriting and risk and claims management). A self-regulatory or at best co-regulatory environment where privacy laws are ambiguous and organizations are underprepared for data breach events creates an environment that invites stakeholder involvement and interventions by insurance companies acting as intermediaries. In this environment organizations try to legalize themselves by creating a series of policies and procedures to address cybersecurity and privacy law compliance. In contrast to prior cases evaluating the way organizations legalize themselves (Edelman 2016; Talesh 2009), in this instance, technology is a mechanism through which insurance companies construct managerial and risk responses concerning cybersecurity and compliance.

I begin by briefly exploring the slow influence of technology on insurance and then turn to how technology shapes the delivery of cyber insurance. I then reveal how cyber insurance applications as currently constructed do not properly allow insurers to evaluate and price risk faced by prospective buyers of insurance. I find that brokers and insurers, two key actors in delivering cyber insurance, are managing the uncertainty of evaluating cyber risk by using big data and other emerging technologies at every stage of the insurance cycle. Insurance brokers and underwriters rely on technology to assess the risk of the prospective insured. Technology, predictive analytics, and security surveillance supplant the traditional insurance application and interview process. Brokers and insurers also use big data to compile information about past losses and breaches of similar companies to develop benchmarks, predict the risk to which companies seeking insurance are exposed, and set appropriate premiums.

THE BLENDING OF INSURANCE AND TECHNOLOGY FIELDS

In the insurance field, the innovative use of technology, big data, cloud infrastructure, peer-to-peer, usage-based, and on-demand insurance is commonly referred to as *insurtech*. Insurtech is marketed as improving the experience of insureds because it can collect and analyze data in ways that provide better services to the insured. Although the use of data is not new to the insurance industry, technological advances have made data more easily accessed and usable for enhancing or replacing traditional functions in the insurance industry such as back-office systems, risk assessment, underwriting, fraud detection, and claims processing. In theory, this affects how insurance is distributed and reduces costs for both the insurer and the insured.

Insurtech activity is significantly increasing across the insurance industry, having attracted $16.5 billion in investments over the past decade (NAIC 2020). Some insurers use on-demand insurance platforms that allow customers to enroll or disenroll whenever they want—they do not have to commit to an annual policy as required by traditional insurance companies. Insurtech approaches also include insurance apps that allow consumers to purchase coverage through their smartphones and use AI to analyze trends and improve risk modeling. While many of these technologies were pioneered by technology startups, some established insurance companies are incorporating these innovative technologies into their business practices.

In addition, big data has been increasingly incorporated into the practice of insurance. Data are fundamental to insurance. Although the industry was slow to adopt insurtech innovations, throughout the 2000s, insurers expanded their use of big data analytics and started using data from social networks and other third-party sources rather than obtaining information solely by asking insureds directly (Elliot 2017). For example, in the property and casualty insurance industry, policies were historically priced based on fewer than twenty variables and were fine-tuned with a standard list of questions. Now, insurers use additional data from new and nontraditional sources, with more than one thousand variables and granular rating classes (Hagan 2018). In fact, digital broker Acxiom said in 2018 it had intelligence on 700 million individuals (Acxiom Corporation 2018), which could—among other things—reveal "3,000 propensities for nearly every US consumer" (Acxiom Corporation 2014).

Although insurers have always analyzed information in order to make underwriting decisions, big data has transformed how data scientists analyze information. Real-time data are now seen as more trustworthy than static parameters such as insurance applications. In contrast with understanding movements and regularities in the aggregate, predictive analytics focus on the individual. Big data leads data scientists to look "at each individual in their irreducible differences, rather than discarding them, and assessing their risk as if each individual were their own class" (Barry and Carpentier 2020, 6).

Consequently, big data is integrated into the marketing, underwriting, claims handling, and risk management of an insurers' operations. Insurtech companies and large insurers across health, life, property, and casualty insurance aggressively pursue ways to incorporate big data into their operations. In fact, the insurance industry financially invests heavily in big data technologies, including over $4 billion in 2024 (Parashchak 2024). A 2017 study (Brothers et al.) revealed that 51 percent of insurers surveyed use big data analytics for claims modeling in efforts to reduce claims, and 42 percent use analytics for actuarial model testing and underwriting. These numbers are increasing rapidly as technology advances and insurers realize the benefits of its use.

Emerging technologies and big data, therefore, are especially attractive tools for cyber insurance. Cyber insurers and brokers face the difficult task of assessing risk in the absence of the sort of reliable actuarial data that has been developed for other lines of insurance. Whereas automobile, property, and commercial general liability insurance can rely on decades of predictive data to assess and evaluate risk, the relative lack of information makes cyber insurance risk evaluation far less dependable. In addition to the lack of data, cyberattackers constantly modify their tactics as adaptive adversaries.

Insurers attempting to evaluate and price risk use the insurance application to gather information on the prospective buyer of insurance and decide whether to issue insurance. The application process provides an opportunity for the insurer to learn more about the prospective buyer and gather information. One key problem with cyber insurance underwriting is the relative lack of expertise of those who fill out applications on behalf of potential insureds. As a result, many in the insurance industry regard applications alone to be an incomplete and unreliable tool for evaluating the risk profile of a prospective policyholder. As one insurance coverage lawyer noted, "In my view, it's that insurers are still trying to figure out how to evaluate the risk. They're not quite sure how to really monetize what the granting of any particular coverage is" (insurance coverage lawyer, interview 27, August 14, 2019). In addition to uncertainty related to the lack of claims history, insurers rely on technology also because the insurance applications do not reliably capture the applicant's cybersecurity posture, as one provider explained:

> The applications aren't necessarily getting the entire job done. And there's a few different issues there. One is you're not necessarily going to get a fully filled out application. . . . [Also, w]ho's filling out this application? So, if someone from cybersecurity within a company is filling it out, you're going to get very different answers than if the CFO's filling it out. . . . And so the quality of the data that you're

capturing is still pretty uncertain. [Y]ou don't necessarily get an opportunity to ask those follow-up questions for various reasons. (information security provider, interview 36, March 16, 2020)

Another problem identified by the people that I interviewed is that insurance applications are not thoroughly inquiring into the cybersecurity health of the organization. My own analysis confirms this problem. To examine how insurers use the application questionnaire to manage uncertainty in the underwriting process and probe the cybersecurity health of the organization, I coded sixty cyber insurance applications from the market from 2011 to 2019 that insurers required prospective buyers of cyber insurance to complete in order. More specifically, examining these insurance applications allowed me (1) to explore the variation between and among cyber insurance applications; (2) to understand what type of information insurance providers find salient and relevant enough to collect from companies seeking insurance; and (3) to assess, together with information collected from interviews with brokers, the relative importance these applications have in decisions made by brokers and insurance companies in setting premiums and deductibles for the companies seeking insurance. I focused the coding on six categories: (1) data storage and privacy risk; (2) security practices; (3) use and monitoring of third-party service providers; (4) compliance with laws, regulations, and industry standards; (5) current coverages and history of losses; and (6) use of the Internet of Things.[1]

My findings reveal that although there was variation among insurers, with some offering more detailed applications than others, most insurance applications do not probe deeply enough into the cybersecurity posture and history of the organizations to make a meaningful evaluation of the cyber health of the organization. Two-thirds of the insurance applications evaluated do not make probing inquiries into the security practices or ask questions that would allow a reviewing body to follow up or verify. For example, although over three-fourths of the sixty applications that I analyzed ask if applicants collect or store personally identifiable information and ask for the number of records collected, few applications were concerned about the specific types of data collected.

Similarly, most applications asked whether the applicant had a privacy and security policy for data classification, governance, storage, and transmission of private information. However, only two applications asked for proof of such privacy practices. Indeed, only one insurance policy provided space for the company to provide additional comments on its privacy practices and data storage. Risk managers that I spoke with repeatedly expressed frustration with the inability to tailor responses to a company's particular profile.

Most insurers inquired about whether organizations encrypt files but did so in a cursory way. For example, 50 percent of the applications probed whether the organization used encryption over public networks, when data were stored on mobile devices, or when they were stored on company assets such as databases, backups, and proprietary file share systems. Notably, while most applications asked about the existence of plans for responding to cyber incidents, less than 30 percent (17 applications) asked about the amount of time the company's system would need in order to reboot and resume operations in the event of a breach or outage. Thus, these types of inquiries were incomplete at best and not tailored to sufficiently evaluate the cyber hygiene of the applicant.

Questions about whether applicants complied with federal and state standards, laws, or regulations also varied across the applications. Table 1 highlights the number of insurance applications that inquired about specific laws. Of note, inquiries concerning legal compliance rarely probed deeply into the documented procedures or due diligence that the organization undertook to

TABLE 1

Compliance with standards, laws, and regulations

Legal standard	Number (and percentage of total) of applications that specifically asked about compliance (n = 60)
ISO Standards for Information Security Controls[a]	6 (10%)
Sarbanes-Oxley Act[b]	7 (12.72%)
Payment Card Industry Data Security Standard (PCI-DSS)	38 (63%)
Health Insurance Portability and Accountability Act (HIPAA)[b]	23 (41.82%)
Health Information Technology for Economic and Clinical Health (HITECH) Act[b]	13 (23.63%)
Gramm-Leach-Bliley Act[b]	15 (27.27%)
Statement on Standards for Attestation Engagements (SSAE 16 or SSAE 18)	2 (3.3%)
Federal Information Security Modernization Act of 2002[b]	4 (7.27%)
National Institute of Standards of Technology (NIST) standards	5 (8.3%)
Compliance with any state regulation or law	6 (10.91%)
Applications that asked about compliance with at least one of the above	41 (68.3%)

[a]ISO/IEC 27002:2013 was the most current standard at the time of this study.
[b]The sample size for this standard was 55 because compliance with this law does not apply to international applications.

comply with laws. Only 6 applications asked about compliance with specific state laws.

Surprisingly, insurers also engaged in little inquiry over whether an applicant currently had different lines of insurance coverage. Less than one-quarter (14 applications) asked if the applicant had ever been declined for cyber insurance or if a prior policy had ever been canceled. Only 1 in 6 applications (10 applications) even asked about whether the company currently had some form of cyber liability or cyber breach coverage. No application that I reviewed asked questions about the use of Internet of Things (IoT) devices or software or whether the company used such devices despite the fact that many interviewees said this was essential given the rising interconnectedness of devices.

To be clear, there was variation in cyber insurance applications. The most thorough applications all asked whether a company collected private or personally identifiable information, had encryption practices, possessed an incident response plan, backed up data regularly, used detection software, and used secure processes to allow remote access to its networks. However, in general, insurance applications are not effective tools for evaluating or managing uncertain cyber risk. The inquiries into the cyber hygiene of prospective buyers of insurance are not probing enough in scope and types of questions. Relatedly, the cyber insurance applications do not necessarily elicit the types of information needed for insurers to subsequently know how to recommend changes and regulate the insurer.

MANAGING UNCERTAINTY WITH TECHNOLOGY AND SECURITY TOOLS

Because cyber insurers lack significant amounts of loss history and actuarial data to rely on when making risk assessments, because cyber risks and attacks from cybercriminals are constantly changing, and because insurance applications are an imprecise tool for evaluating and pricing cyber risk, cyber insurers covet data from providers (see also Herr 2021). Cyber insurers are turning to big data, AI, and predictive analytics to assist them in the underwriting and risk and claims management processes and, as a result, are redefining the delivery of insurance.

Insurers' decision whether to issue a policy to a particular insured and whether and how to underwrite the risk largely hinges on the use of big data, technology, and AI. "I've been surprised," one attorney told me, "at the level of sort of big data and predictive analytics that it seems like insurers are using, brokers are using. There are third-party companies [data providers] that market this information. And that seems like it's playing a big role and an increasing role in part because there's not a lot of good data on cyber" (cyber insurance attorney, interview 15, June 26, 2019). Information security and forensic companies and big data providers have penetrated the cyber market using technology. Although there are a handful of big data providers that harness and aggregate loss data, the insurance field is crowded with information security and cyber forensics companies eager to assist insurers with underwriting and risk and claims management. Some large insurance companies rely on their own big data and have hired security and forensics engineers to develop their own information security tools. However, the majority of insurers are contracting with a variety of information security providers and big data suppliers rather than developing these skills in-house.

Facing similar challenges, insurance brokers have resorted to a variety of big data, predictive analytics, and security tools to help assist clients in seeking cyber insurance and managing uncertainty in the cyber market. First, a brief word about what insurance brokers do. Insurance brokers represent interested buyers of insurance and generate business by connecting their clients with insurance companies offering coverage. Insurance brokers do not work for insurance companies and cannot bind them by entering into insurance contracts on their behalf. Rather, brokers direct clients to insurance agents, or directly to insurance companies, with whom the clients can then enter into insurance contracts. Brokers do have a financial stake in the transaction, in the form of commissions earned on policies that they place.

Insurance brokers face significant barriers to servicing their clients interested in purchasing cyber insurance. Similar to cyber insurers, insurance brokers are desperate for reliable data: "I think . . . cyber brokers and agents will take anything that they can get because, for a long time, we haven't had very much" (wholesale broker, interview 22, July 26, 2019). Insurance brokers are often stuck with insurance application forms that are confusing, not detailed, and too static. They also do not have access to insurance company information or enough of their own data across multiple industries. In response, brokers have turned to analytical tools such as big data, predictive analytics, and security and surveillance tools to assist clients seeking cyber insurance. These "analytical brokers" attempt to use data to their advantage.

Some of the large brokerage firms use a team of actuaries who develop models based on real claims data that draw from examples and instances of claims that the brokers have handled. These are put into a quantified cyber model that relies on the organizations' revenue, records, and other variables to evaluate the likelihood of a data breach. Then, the brokers try to build "the ideal insurance program to provide the greatest return on investment based on all these data points and information that we have" (broker, interview 3, June 17, 2019).

To make up for the lack of actuarial data, brokers combine their own data with those they purchase from big data brokers to articulate a more persuasive case to the prospective buyer: "And so we are very mindful of that. We do use third parties such as Advisen or Net Diligence for benchmarking data, but we also keep track of and are very mindful of trying to use our own data to our advantage. So, when we're pitching a client, we can say, 'We have 35 or 40 other retail or health care organization clients that we work with that kind of have a similar profile from a revenue standpoint, record standpoint, control standpoint'" (broker, interview 3). In addition to relying on big data, analytical brokers, particularly when dealing with large organizations, use security and surveillance tools to analyze the risk profile of a consumer. The larger, "high touch" brokers contract with security organizations to scan the network of a prospective insured to evaluate its vulnerabilities. The scan is used in conjunction with the broker's evaluation of the insurance application, use of big data, and meeting with risk managers or officers of the company interested in purchasing insurance. Brokers dealing with smaller or medium-sized businesses rely more heavily on these scans and the big data models discussed earlier (in lieu of probing insurance applications and meetings with the company managers). Many brokers graft the information security firms' risk ratings and risk factors into their own model and market it to the public as their own. "If you look at insurance brokers, for example, . . . what they do is they use our analytics and then they take their expertise, provide consulting services, and really use it as a tool in theirs" (information security provider, interview 42, December 23, 2020).

In sum, big data, predictive analytics, quantifiable models, and security and surveillance tools dominate the work brokers do with businesses interested in buying cyber insurance. At times, these technological tools deemphasize or supplant the insurance application and interview stages. Insurance brokers manage the uncertainty of cyber risk by relying on third-party data brokers and security firms because the brokers are not experts in cybersecurity or in the technical components of an organization's cyber hygiene. It appears they use these tools to evaluate the risk profile of the prospective insurance buyer and to better gauge the amount of insurance policy limits that brokers recommend be purchased. Although loss control measures and security are evaluated, little attention is paid to improving data security, though brokers sometimes offer additional services that can help the cybersecurity profile of the prospective buyer.

DATA AGGREGATED ON CLAIMS AND EVENTS THAT HAVE ALREADY OCCURRED

I now explore more precisely how big data, AI, and emerging technologies are changing the business of cyber insurance. Insurers and brokers use data primarily in three different ways. Data brokers collect information on thousands of claims and losses from public records and nonpublic information from brokers and insurers and then sell the aggregated information back to insurers and brokers attempting to understand the extent of the cyber insurance market and types of breaches that may reasonably be expected. As one underwriter noted, "[Big data providers] are kind of aggregating claims data and then, you know, providing trends of, you know, like law firms are more likely to get hit than manufacturing firms by a cyberattack. And when they do [get breached], the average cost of a claim is X. . . . [They are] aggregating stuff that has already happened" (interview 35, February 28, 2020). Insurance brokers and companies also buy big data from data brokers in order to develop pricing and underwriting models.[2]

Through collecting and analyzing information on cyber breaches, including amounts and types of information lost, big data allows insurers to explore the scope of cyber events in a way not previously possible. For specific peer groups selected, the database that I analyzed provides details about prior cyber events experienced by similar companies, including the dates of prior breaches, amounts of records lost, types of breach, and actual or estimated costs that victim companies incurred as a result of the breaches. This allows insurance underwriters and brokers to understand the frequency of breaches in that peer group, and what types of data have historically been affected—and through what type of breach. They can then compare all that with information about the company seeking insurance.

While not necessarily predictive of risk, such historical information can lend reliability to decisions to insure and to the price points for various cyber insurance options. One executive of a large insurer noted that most large insurers purchase big data but rely primarily on those data acquired about their own insureds, whereas smaller insurers often rely more heavily on purchased big data to enhance their models: "[It's] more helpful for companies that don't have as substantial a book of business, if I'm being honest" (underwriter, interview 35).[3]

Insurance brokers whom I interviewed routinely noted that these aggregated databases allow brokers to provide to their customer companies "detailed analysis of where some of their peers may be purchasing, what type of limits are being put up, and then how much [is reasonable to pay] based on client claims data from our carriers" (wholesale broker and underwriter, interview 23, July 29, 2019). These data also have the potential to persuade a prospective insurance buyer to purchase specific amounts of coverage and limits based on what similarly sized organizations in the same industry have bought.

Brokers routinely present findings derived from big data analytics directly to clients to help these prospective buyers understand why the broker is recommending coverage within particular parameters: "When we are pitching a client, we can say, 'We have thirty-five or forty other retail or health care organization clients that we work with that kind of have a similar profile from a revenue standpoint, record standpoint, control standpoint'" (broker, interview 3). Big data providers are supplying insurers and insurance brokers with aggregate data about breaches that have already happened to similarly situated organizations. Thus, big data from these entities fuels the expansive use of technology, analytics, and AI in the cyber insurance field. Big data providers were not hesitant to recognize the importance of their data for the cyber insurance field:

> INTERVIEWER: [I]s it fair to say [that providing the data], the underbelly of the insurance lifecycle here for cyber, is based in part on [the information that your company] has compiled?
>
> DATA BROKER: Yes, I think that's fair to say. (data aggregator and big data provider, interview 33, part 1, December 6, 2019)

Moreover, AI and other emerging technologies rely on big data to generate outputs.

DRIVING SALES WITH AGGREGATE RISK ANALYSIS

Relying partially on big data, a growing number of information security companies are focused on modeling aggregate or systemic risk based on an insurer's portfolio:[4]

> [It] is more geared to aggregation, and what they're doing and doing pretty well is to say, "Okay, if this kind of scenario happened, you might have a portfolio of 30,000 customers, and 5,000 of those 30,000 are all using the same cloud provider," and maybe we [the insurer]

don't know that, but maybe [the information security company] can help us understand that.

[T]hen we say, "Aha. Are we comfortable with that kind of potential aggregation?" Because if those 5,000 customers maybe don't each [have a data breach] event, but they're reliant on the same vendor and that vendor has an event that could cause a ripple effect on our [insurance] portfolio. So, they help model out both kinds of those scenarios and what that looks like across a portfolio of business. (underwriter, interview 35)

Information security companies evaluate the insurer's client population and then use analytics and modeling to evaluate aggregate risk. These security companies use technology, security, and insurance experts to understand aggregate risks: "In-house we have people like me who are actuaries, underwriters, brokers. And then we have the . . . cybersecurity experts, intelligence experts, [and] economists. And so, we have all these professionals sitting under the same roof who have been trying to speak the same language and solve this problem together. We've got the experts there" (information security provider, interview 36).

To convince buyers to purchase insurance and avoid worst-case scenario exposures, insurers use these tools to translate data and analytics into risk avoidance and cost containment:

I think that the common language is dollars and probabilities. And that's what the boardroom can respond to. If I'm the technical IT guy and I come to you and say we have two million botnets on our network and five hundred high-severity vulnerabilities, and you are a board member, you're going to look at me and say, "I have no clue what that means."

But if you come to me and you say, "Sir, we believe that there's a 1 percent chance that we have any of these events occur in the next twelve months. And the worst-case scenario is a billion-dollar loss."

That's a much different conversation. That's the way that you can corral resources and start to actually manage the risk and manage the exposure and not have kind of these blind-siding type events. (insurer and information security provider, interview 32, October 4, 2019)

Technology and big data tools, therefore, are driving the insurance sales process by translating aggregate risk into a language that buyers of insurance understand: potential profit and loss. In this respect, managerial values of efficiency and cost containment are operationalized around technology when discussing cyber insurance with prospective insureds. Insurance brokers whom I interviewed indicated that organizations purchase additional insurance based on the extent to which the insurance that many major companies had proved insufficient when they experienced a major breach: "I think it was Anthem, Target, and Home Depot. They all had $100 million limits on cyber, and they all experienced losses between $200 million and $300 million. The reason they all had $100 million of cyber insurance is because they all looked at each other and said 'Oh, they have 100, so we should have 100.' But that doesn't give you the proper benchmarking exercise. That doesn't take you through the proper benchmarking exercises as to what Target needs" (insurance underwriter, interview 1, June 17, 2019). Clearly, in an uncertain market, organizations look to one another (even if the comparison is not entirely reliable) for guidance on evaluating and understanding cyber risk, and insurers play an influential role by modeling aggregate risk.

CYBERSECURITY HEALTH EVALUATIONS AND SCANS

Other information security providers are contracting with insurers to evaluate the cyber hygiene and vulnerability of prospective insureds. These companies are less focused on the aggregate, systemic risk to an insurer's large portfolio of clients than on individual companies looking to buy insurance. The security providers give each specific potential insured a score or rating that helps underwriters determine its risk level and whether to issue insurance to the company: "[Cyence, BitSight, and Security Scorecard are] more looking specifically [whether] this particular company, ABC Inc., has a vulnerability because they have a poor patching cadence. And we know they have poor patching cadence because they're still running software that's facing the internet that hasn't been patched. So they're telling you more specifically about an individual account" (underwriter, interview 35).

Using security and technology tools, these companies conduct endpoint vulnerability assessments and rate the company based on information gathered from its IP address, domain name, and other publicly accessible information, as well as on information about the company posted on the dark web.[5] One information security provider referred to these companies as an "intelligence service for the underwriters. . . . A lot of times the clients have no idea" (forensic security consultant, interview 16, July 15, 2019). A big data provider whom I interviewed noted that their company's data are often used to validate information produced from the security provider's scoring systems: "Companies that do scoring based on various attributes of a company's cybersecurity profile—they use our data to demonstrate the veracity of their scoring systems" (data aggregator and big-data provider, interview 33, part 1). One information security provider has the ability to go "inside" the company's firewall to evaluate its cybersecurity.[6] This information security provider explained:

> [W]e have exclusive rights to [the data from] . . . one of the largest security companies in the world. We're the only ones that have it, and that's going to give us data that's from inside the firewall. So

we're not just doing network scans and looking from the outside in. We can also look from the inside out. Now, [the security provider we work with] has to anonymize and aggregate this, so we get it on what we call microsegment level. So it's groups of companies that have the same kind of profile. [It] looks at region, revenue band, and industry.

We still believe that's still very helpful. And the insurance industry is very comfortable looking at risks on a homogeneous risk basis. . . . We also work with . . . up to ten or twelve companies that we're contracted with to grab other data. And a lot of that is outside the firewall—so, network scanning of different kinds. (information security provider, interview 36)

In addition to assisting with pricing, insurers believe the scores increase their efficiency and accuracy in pricing and setting the specific terms they offer in cyber insurance policies, rendering answers in the insurance application less important:

If somebody has a good cybersecurity hygiene, I can rely on third-party data to help me, which makes it more convenient for the customer because they don't have to fill out a lengthy application. I don't have to worry about, does the person filling that application out even understand the question I asked them? Are they just checking "yes" because they feel like a "no" would result in a bad outcome? So it's easier it's more accurate, it's more granular, and I can then set my pricing more accurately to reflect that individual risk. (underwriter, interview 35)

Insurers engaging large organizations often use the security score to open a deeper conversation with their clients about cybersecurity.

Insurance brokers working with large organizations also contract with security organizations to scan networks of prospective insureds to evaluate their vulnerabilities. The security organization issues a score that can be used to help the insurance broker counsel the prospective insured on their cyber hygiene and the likelihood of coverage. "We do partner with some firms from an outsider's perspective that . . . scan . . . their network from the perimeter to see where there may or may not be some vulnerabilities," a broker and former underwriter told me. "But the score is very helpful for just having a dialogue with the client" (interview 10, June 25, 2019).

Some insurance brokers graft the information security firm's rating and risk factors onto their own model for marketing purposes: "If you look at insurance brokers, . . . for example, . . . [w]hat they do is they use our analytics, and then they take their expertise, provide consulting services, and really use it as a tool in theirs" (insurer and information security provider, interview 32). Virtually all insurance industry actors that I spoke with indicated that insurance companies need big data, AI, and other technologies that the information security companies provide in order to stay viable: "Underwriters are now recognizing [that they] . . . need to have one or more of those tools in the shops to be able to continue to be competitive in the marketplace" (data aggregator and big data provider, interview 33, part 1).

ARTIFICIAL INTELLIGENCE AND INSURANCE COMPANY EFFICIENCY

The technologization of insurance involves not just big data, predictive analytics, and advanced security and forensic tools. My interviews reveal that AI is playing an increasing role as well. Information security providers use AI to assist insurers in building predictive models and, in this way, enhance efficiency in the underwriting process. One of the leading information security providers highlighted the connection between big data, AI, and the insurance underwriting process:

And so what we did is we started collecting all that data, as well as looking at things like dark web data, and building out machine-learning algorithms and natural language–processing algorithms to actually sort through all this stuff at scale. And so now, instead of only having your population of companies that you've either underwritten and actually written the policy or have come and shopped with you, you can now compare people to the universe and use that to really try to fine-tune your strategy.

So underwriters can get company-specific information—sets of risk factors, [from] technical things like vulnerabilities to behavioral things like employee sentiment, for example. And then we'll build out frequency and severity models and provide analytics on all this stuff so that underwriters could understand, if I write a particular layer of coverage, based on [these] models, what are the dollars and probabilities associated to losses? (insurer and information security provider, interview 32)

This interviewee's explanation highlights the technologization of insurance. It reveals the interconnection between big data, AI, and the predictive analytics that mobilize such data and, more important, the manner in which insurers operationalize such data in the delivery of insurance. Insurance companies are short-circuiting the traditional underwriting process and are able to "plug in" information from a prospective buyer of insurance and receive a report geared toward assisting the insurer with pricing the risk. The same interviewee referred to "Other people that are taking those risk assessments that we do on an individual company basis and using them kind of more loosely in their guidelines, using it to dictate [underwriting] authority. . . . There's people that are working it into their underwriting guidelines" (interview 32). Other insurance officials suggest that insurers and information security providers engage more in machine learning and natural-language processing than in predictive analytics. One data aggregator noted that insurers and information security providers are "using machine learning and, to a lesser degree, natural-language processing to be able to rate, quote, and bind nearly instantaneously for small businesses" (data aggregator and big data provider, interview 33, part 2, December 6, 2019). One insurer and information security provider noted the various ways insurers are using machine learning and AI:

> That's where these more sophisticated machine-learning techniques come in. And carriers are using them all over. And then they're building models using those techniques to identify jumper claims— [to] try to know more quickly if a claim is going to be a bad one and how you should jump on it. This movement is definitely happening. There's companies that are out there that are checking policy language using artificial intelligence. They can automatically parse through a portfolio of hundreds of thousands of policies and come back with a structured data set of it that could tell you information about your aggregate exposures or help you parse through the document more easily in that one time. (interview 32)

One of the major managed-security providers that partners with insurers describes the fusion of AI with insurance at the underwriting, reinsurance, and regulatory levels:

> And so actuaries will use that to influence their own models. They'll use it as another reference point, like a counter view to their own view of risk. And then from there, it's used both internally when carriers are looking at their own books, as well as when Lloyds Syndicates reports to Lloyds. . . .
>
> So, they'll use it to manage aggregate exposures and pricing internally, as well as use it to report out to regulators. Reinsurance brokers, for example, also use our software and our models to model these exposures. And then use that to service their clients as well as approach the market with portfolios of cyber risks to go buy reinsurance for. (interview 32)

In terms of actual use, most in the insurance field agreed that AI is in its infancy and developmental stage. However, there is a clear desire to expand and integrate AI into the practice of cyber insurance. As one underwriter and former insurance broker observed: "What we hope to do is build a big data lake and use artificial intelligence to start finding some correlations that maybe others haven't found yet. That's the dream. It's a long way from being realized. I think in terms of the data aggregators that are out there, there's not one that's going to provide all the data that you would hope to have" (interview 13, June 26, 2019).

The information security companies and forensics analysts are also trying to find the best way to utilize AI: "You have to sort through tons and tons of data. And so, yes, we would use things like AI—where we're building out our AI. And we just got a patent on a threat correlation engine, and there's some real machine learning and intelligence in there—and a lot more than just putting a bunch of *if* statements in your software code" (forensic and information security expert, interview 14, June 26, 2019). Although AI is still in the experimental phase with insurers who deal with cyber risk, clearly, it is an area of future development and growth.

In sum, the traditional underwriting process for most noncyber lines of insurance, anchored by the insurance application, client consultation, and actuarial loss history built over decades, is being supplanted by a process that relies largely on information security companies that partner with insurers and use big data, AI, and other predictive analytics (or insurers are bringing these tools in house). Brokers and insurance companies manage the uncertainty of cyber risk by also using these tools to evaluate the risk profile of the prospective insurance buyer and to better gauge the insurance policy limits they recommend be purchased. High-touch brokers use technology to supplement the evaluative process, whereas some low-touch brokers rely on data and security scans as a substitute for the traditional broker-buyer relationship. Insurance companies act as intermediaries for organizations. They drive a compliance response centered on risk management services and emphasize reliance on big data, technology, and information security. In the cyber context (unlike the contexts of employment [Edelman 2016] and consumer protection [Talesh 2012]), the technologization of insurance drives the managerial and efficiency goals of insurers.

Chapter 4 explores the effects and implications of the merging of technology and insurance in the cyber context. Together, the two chapters reveal the increased linkage of technology and insurance and the implications for insurers, policyholders, and society at large.

CHAPTER FOUR

The Effects and Implications
of the Technologization
# of Insurance

This chapter highlights the effects and implications of the technologization of insurance. Although reliance on technology and data is increasingly transforming the way insurers advertise, underwrite, and price insurance, the actual impact on insurer behavior seems to have remained minimal and is largely symbolic. Insurtech interventions and innovations have been, to date, largely ineffective in enhancing organizations' cybersecurity or assisting insurers in managing uncertainty in the market. Even though they utilize big data and technology, insurers, by and large, are not requiring organizations to improve their cybersecurity health prior to offering them insurance. Surprisingly, my empirical findings also indicate that most insurers do not even offer significant premium discounts for specific cybersecurity improvements.

In contrast to the narrative that big data can produce greater efficiency and more precise pricing and risk predictions for insurers, my analysis of a big data database that I purchased reveals that big data in the cyber context is an unreliable tool often manipulated by the insurance industry and used to nudge buyers toward purchasing more insurance. Instead of providing a comprehensive and more precise picture of cyber events and risks, the data provide a biased view that works to the detriment of consumers. Although cyber insurers are turning to big data and technology as mechanisms for understanding risk, such models often are not fully integrated into the underwriting and risk management processes. Technology is mobilized as a tool for managing uncertain cyber and legal risks and regulating policyholders in a manner that is efficient but allows insurers discretion.

BIG DATA, AN UNRELIABLE TOOL

Despite increasing the amount of information that buyers and sellers have access to in the cyber context, the big data database I accessed and examined reveals that the data are limited and not always accurate or reliable. To begin with, the quality and sources from which information is compiled are limited and paint an incomplete picture of any peer group's cybersecurity posture and associated risk. This deficiency is largely due to the database's reliance on publicly available data to create sets of peer groups. Hence, there are events the database does not record. In other words, the fact that the database includes only a few cyber events in a specific peer group does not necessarily mean that this peer group is less prone to cyber events. It could mean, rather, that cyber events experienced by companies in that peer group are not public knowledge or did not make their way into the public domain by way of reporting or lawsuits, or it could mean that the database compilers simply missed some of the incidents. As one underwriter noted in an interview, "You don't really know what anything costs unless it was a publicly traded company" (former broker and underwriter, interview 12, June 25, 2019). Because cyber insurance lacks a mandated, standardized, or centralized line of reporting, no source of information is complete, and disparate sources contain different types and amounts of data. Although most states require organizations to notify customers when a breach occurs, no law requires insurance companies to share data on cyber attacks. Moreover, what information there is may be especially selective and unrepresentative because large insurance companies use their own data sets of cyber losses when pricing insurance, purposely excluding incidents of their insureds from public record databases.

The varied type and quality of the data used by insurance-related data providers is a major concern. Many insurers do not share their data with big data providers for fear of losing a competitive advantage in the market. As one insurer and big data provider I spoke with described the privacy concerns that insurers have:

> [We're] not going to give [a data provider] our data. And a lot of insureds don't want this stuff to go public. They're not publicly traded, or they don't have to answer to a regulator; they're going to close it out. They'll do their notification and unless somebody happened to write a newspaper article about it, your [big data provider] people aren't going to find it. . . . [They're] basically throwing darts. . . .
>
> Most of the stuff, most of the breach responses are done under privilege with counsel. They don't want to share with the FBI to track down the criminals, let alone share with some public actors putting together a database to talk about numbers. So they're just trying to bring in data from any point they can get. But it's still so early in the ballgame that it's really hard to get there. (interview 31, September 16, 2019)

Moreover, the database examined as part of this book is entirely backward-looking, which is to say that its compilers seek to offer benchmark recommendations on policy limits based on events in the past that do not account for changing cyber threat patterns. Benchmarking involves estimating what the potential loss could be if different scenarios happen to a prospective buyer of insurance. Many brokers and industry leaders that I interviewed critiqued this benchmarking approach by big data providers because it is backward-looking and unreliable. "And they always say [they'll] give me some benchmarking," a former broker and underwriter told me. "Well, I mean, I get so angry whenever I hear that . . . you've got this evolving threatscape in front of you, and you're going to drive the car by looking in the rearview mirror to see what the clowns behind you, who are just as blind as you, are doing? It's crazy. I would say, no, benchmarking is useless; do a ground-up analysis" (interview 12). Another insurance industry expert noted: "Data benchmarking to evaluate limits is not too reliable. [It's] [o]kay to use a little, but don't rely on it exclusively" (broker, interview 54, July 25, 2019).

Limits and deficiencies in the data used by insurance-related data providers have several negative implications. Because these databases often rely on reported losses, there may be certain types of events, as well as risk, affecting a company's cybersecurity posture unaccounted for in any policy for cyber insurance that used a database relying on an incomplete source of data. A forensic security expert also questioned the reliability of third-party databases and indicated that such data did not align with "what we're seeing in the insurance world" (forensic security consultant, interview 16). As one insurance industry expert stated: "For me, the big issue is the credibility and the source of the data" (interview 37, April 21, 2020). Hence, although all agree that big data providers are fueling the increased use of AI and predictive analytics in the cyber context, my analysis calls into question the robustness and completeness of the data and suggests that it is likely insufficiently reliable to form a rational basis for the numerous significant cyber insurance decisions being made based on such data and analysis.

BROKERS AND UNDERWRITERS USING
DATABASES TO NUDGE CLIENTS TOWARD
PURCHASING MORE INSURANCE

One could argue that any large amount of data—even if admittedly incomplete and flawed—is better than nothing and that the incompleteness is not the fault of the data providers or the result of nefarious motivations on the part of any participants in the cyber insurance ecosystem. My research, however, uncovered a more insidious problem with the use of big data in cyber insurance. Careful examination and analysis of the data broker's database reveal that the compilers do not discount outliers of excessive loss amounts when presenting or calculating key statistics. Throughout my analysis of various peer groups, the database consistently included outlier loss amounts experienced by companies in a particular peer group in presentations of data through figures and in calculations of key summary statistics. In other words, the database inflates the potential cost of losses and nudges buyers of insurance to purchase more limits.

Figure 2 shows how not discounting outliers impacts insurance policy limit recommendations for prospective buyers of insurance. After users select the industry type, revenue range, premium, limits, and retention amounts, the database presents users with a chart. This chart reveals prior loss amounts experienced by, and median limits of, companies in the selected peer group (based on industry type and revenue range).

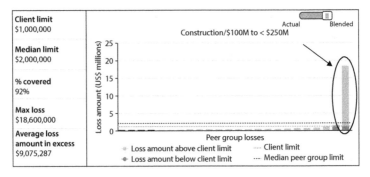

Figure 2. The chart that insurance brokers present to prospective buyers after they select a particular peer group and choose a client limit. In this case, one outlier breach significantly raises the maximum loss estimate for this peer group. Each bar represents a prior cyber event the database has recorded. The dotted horizontal line represents the client's chosen limit of $1 million. The dashed horizontal line represents the median limit of policies obtained by companies in the selected peer group ($2 million). The left panel presents a series of summary statistics that tell the user the client's selected limit, the median limit of policies held by companies in this peer group, the percentage of the losses plotted that would be covered under the client's selected limit, the maximum loss amount recorded among companies in this peer group, and the average loss amount that exceeds the client's chosen limit.

In plotting this information, however, the database does not discount either low or high loss amount outliers in the data. Especially when the data include a high outlier, a visual inspection of the plot suggests that one company may experience a much higher-than-average loss and thus would significantly raise the insurance coverage limits on the policy (and, in turn, require buyers to pay higher premiums). In Figure 2, there is one outlier, represented by the bar circled on the far right. Through a quick and cursory visual inspection, a user may be misled to believe that a high loss amount is more common than not or that the maximum loss amount is higher than it actually is.

To account for the outlier, the graph presents the average loss amount in excess and max loss in the pane on the left. In this format, the maximum loss estimate is $18,600,000, and the average loss amount in excess of the $1,000,000 proposed limit is $9,075,287. The average loss amount in excess is the difference between the limit chosen by the client in creating the simulation and the average of all losses recorded in the database that are greater than that limit. There are only two losses greater than the client's selected limit of $1,000,000 in figure 2: With a loss event estimated to be $1,550,574 and the outlier event of $18,600,000, the average loss amount in excess (i.e., the average loss amount $10,075,287 and the client's chosen limit of $1,000,000) is $9,075,287. In other words, this figure suggests the average loss amount in excess of an insurance policy limit of $1,000,000 for a particular buyer will be over $9,000,000. Thus, this chart suggests the limit of insurance of $1,000,000 is probably way too low and that the buyer should purchase more insurance.

While not discounting outliers is not necessarily incorrect methodologically, and while insurance exists, of course, to protect against unforeseen losses, the practice can be misleading, particularly if it's not fully and clearly explained. For example, because outliers are not discounted, insurance brokers using this database are able to suggest to buyers that the impact of loss may be much greater than what their selected limit would cover. However, in this case, if the outlier were discounted, the story would be different. The max loss would be about $550,574, over the client's selected limit of $1,000,000, and the average loss amount in excess would be $550,574, because only one event amount would be greater than the client's limit. Compare this to the average loss amount of $9,075,287 when an outlier is kept in the analysis. Without including the outliers, the average loss amount is about 15 times less than the average loss amount calculated with outlier events included. Therefore, the client's selected limit of $1,000,000, would seem, at first glance, more appropriate to losses experienced by the peer group (see figure 3).

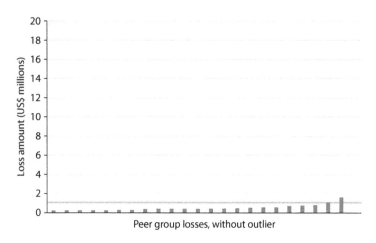

Figure 3. The losses experienced by the peer group identified in figure 2, this time without any outliers. The horizontal line is the client's selected limit of $1,000,000.

If a user were presented with this visual, as opposed to one with the outlier, the user's selected limit of $1,000,000, even at a quick glance, would look more appropriate to the losses more commonly experienced by this peer group. Not discounting outliers in the model allows brokers to nudge clients toward purchasing more insurance. This result is not a rare occurrence but, to the contrary, consistent with the majority of simulations I ran using the database.[1]

Industry experts explain that because many of the big data providers rely on publicly available data, their models tend to recommend higher limits and higher costs for data breach events: "A lot of the times," an insurer and big data provider observed, "[a data provider uses] . . . all public data. [They] are relying on disclosures by publicly traded companies or companies in regulated industries. . . . So their numbers are so high. You say, wow, that's really expensive if you have a breach. It doesn't track with what we see day to day" (interview 31).

My own evaluation of the database is consistent with the way insurers and brokers I interviewed described using big data. They employ big data to manage uncertainty and nudge buyers toward buying a high limit because the data serve as a legitimizing tool in a context where actuarial data and data specific to the client seeking insurance are spare or missing. As one broker noted, "We manage the uncertainty . . . by showing the peer data. We show them what our models generate[,] [w]hat third-party models like [big data providers] generate" (interview 8, June 20, 2019). Insurance brokers rely on the database to advocate for the purchase of higher limits, as the graph or chart can "sort of nudge the client into understanding what the recommendation is in respect to limit" (wholesale broker and underwriter, interview 23). Big data is clearly being mobilized to persuade the buyer of insurance: "Absolutely, these graphs, these reports don't do much good if . . . they're not . . . shown to the client" (wholesale broker, interview 22). One of the big data aggregators and providers commented that one way companies use third-party databases is to "[get] people over the starting line to begin with, just to make the purchase," and to convince midsize and smaller companies that "they actually need to buy the coverage." Using a database that aggregates and presents information about peer group losses can be a "persuasive way to show the kinds of events that happen to companies at a particular industry of a particular size" (data aggregator and big data provider, interview 33, part 1). Indeed, no brokers whom I interviewed indicated they present big data to prospective buyers to reduce the number of policy limits purchased. Insurance brokers explained that these databases legitimize their recommendation that prospective insureds purchase insurance at particular limits. As one broker outlined a common scenario: "Then the client will say, 'Well, prove it,' and so, he'll show the [the big data provider's data], you know. You can put in a health care company with such and such revenue, and it'll spit out a chart of, well, okay, here are five companies similarly situated to yours, and here are the limits that, you know, they have. And he'll present that, that graph or that chart to help sort of nudge the client into understanding what the recommendation is in respect to limit" (wholesale broker and underwriter, interview 23).

Of course, this reliance on big data providers' data is effective only if the data are accurate and reliable. As in my evaluation, security experts have found that the numbers in the data do not align with what they are observing in the industry. "Our numbers are much more conservative," a forensic security consultant told me, "lower than what [the data providers'] numbers come in at. It's what we're seeing in the industry now" (interview 16).

In addition to not discounting outliers, the database presents, in the same visual, analytical conclusions based on information collected from multiple, sometimes unrelated sources, potentially undermining the reliability of decisions based on such representations. For example, where actual loss amounts are not available, the database plots simulated loss amounts of cyber events together with loss amounts actually retrieved from public records (see figure 4). Because each cyber event recorded in the database has an associated actual or simulated cost, a plot with both amounts allows users to visually evaluate the number of cyber incidents a particular peer group has faced.

In addition, this visual representation may also allow users to view the financial impact of all cyber events in a particular peer group, as opposed to only those for which an actual loss amount was publicly available. However, prospective buyers of insurance are not presented with information about how the database generates simulated values and, hence, cannot

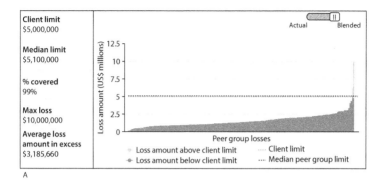

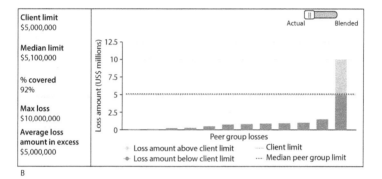

Figure 4. (*A*) Simulated and actual loss amounts blended together. Each bar represents a recorded cyber event in this peer group. Clients and brokers use this graph to ascertain how many cyber events a particular peer group has experienced, which can serve as a proxy for the frequency of cyber events. The database therefore calculates simulated loss amounts for those cyber events for which a loss amount was not publicly available. Still, sometimes many more loss amounts are simulated than are actual. (*B*) Simulation using the same peer group as in the upper panel but with only those cyber events that have actual amounts recorded.

ascertain what characteristics of a cyber event affect the loss amount. Considering this omission together with the way insurance brokers and underwriters I interviewed characterized their use of and reliance on third-party databases like the one I analyzed, it seems clear how brokers use big data to legitimize their policy recommendations.

Users can click on a particular cyber event plotted (any of the bars in figures 2–4) to reveal the number of records an event exposed, the type of records exposed and breach experienced, the name of the company that experienced the breach, and the exact simulated or actual loss amount; however, users are not given much more information about what led to the breach or any information about security or other mitigation precautions taken. Certain company-level factors that are not recorded could significantly affect a client's risk, such as the type of data storage system the client uses, the company's organizational structure, and whether the company has client-facing web interfaces. Prior research suggests that underwriters and carriers of insurance often ask in their applications about buyers' risk mitigation procedures, including whether buyers use security software (Romanosky et al. 2019), suggesting that these practices may affect a company's risk of cyber breach. As one broker put the matter:

> You could take two health systems with the same amount of revenue, the same amount of patient records, same . . . locations. What appear externally to be very similar organizations, if not identical organizations, and they could have completely different environments. So one could be on Cerner's electronic health record systems, EHR, and one could have a proprietary EHR system that was developed for them that they host in-house. And they could handle payment processing differently. One could have mobile-facing applications for patients to log in and access their PHI [protected health information]. The other one could have no such presence on the Web or anything of that nature. You can't rely on the benchmarking to say, well, you're a health care organization and you have five hundred patient records. (broker, interview 26, August 2, 2019)

Little information other than what is presented in the database plays a role in policy and price recommendations made to the prospective buyers of insurance. Except for some Fortune

500 companies that receive high-touch care by brokers (and some insurers), brokers make price recommendations to clients and advise them on the potential impact of various loss scenarios by running multiple reports or exploring various scenarios generated from these databases. However, as demonstrated in the foregoing, these reports can be misleading or, at a minimum, may not provide the client with the entire picture.

My analysis suggests that big data is transforming the underwriting process for insurers and the ways insurance brokers advise buyers of insurance. Big data is used to nudge buyers of insurance toward purchasing more insurance than the limited available data suggest they may actually need and, therefore, paying higher insurance premiums. Big data in the cyber context creates incentives for insurance companies and brokers to sell insurance and enhance profits, and databases like the one I analyzed often serve as a tool to aid that effort, not necessarily benefiting consumers.

SECURITY SCANS AND SCORING ARE NOT RELIABLE AND ACCURATE

As noted earlier, big data helps fuel AI and predictive analytics as they penetrate the cyber market. But significant problems also exist with this part of the technologization of cyber insurance. Data gathered from external scans and vulnerability scoring by information security providers may seem, at first glance, a way to assess risk and price insurance that is more rational than prior methods. On closer examination, however, the scanning, scoring, and rating process increasingly relied on by insurance underwriters to price risk may not be significantly more reliable than older methods.

Insurance industry experts whom I interviewed indicated that external scans provide only limited information: "Scanning the exterior," one told me, "doesn't tell you very much. It tells you about the web server, . . . [b]ut it doesn't really tell you what's going on inside of [a potential insured's] network" (former broker and underwriter, interview 12). Others lamented that scoring vendors' scans produce a lot of false positives, or claims that problems exist in the potential insured's cybersecurity profile when in fact their profile is fairly secure. "I see a lot of false positives," a forensic security consultant reported. "It doesn't also pick up on any of the internal side of things that we see causing claims" (interview 16).

Moreover, because information security providers are running primarily external scans, they cannot identify precisely what is causing the low cybersecurity score or rating.[2] Experts believe external scans are not very reliable because, by definition, they cannot capture the full picture of a company's cybersecurity profile: "The other thing it doesn't pick up on," the same consultant said, "is a lot of clients who outsource their most critical assets—information assets. It's not even them you need to be worried about. It's third-party. Not only third-party, there's fourth-party risk. The cloud's cloud, right? So none of those [information security providers] are looking at that" (forensic security consultant, interview 16).

Another expert noted that sometimes companies partner with information security providers that purposely leave "holes" in their security posture that can be picked up by external scans. They might do this to bait would-be cyber attackers to harmless areas of the network in order to catch them. Vendors conducting no-notice external scans and ratings will not realize what has occurred when they issue a low score. The head of a large insurer's cyber division highlights how unreliable the security ratings are:

> An external view of traffic going in and out [is] not telling the whole story. You think about other grades that you might see on a tool like that—for example, if it had a really poor grade on open ports, but the company has a managed services provider for security. Well, the reason for the poor score on open ports might be that they have some honeypots or sinkholes that they have intentionally developed, right, to capture bad actors and watch the bad, threatening traffic that is coming in. (insurance company cyber division leader, interview 19, July 22, 2019)

Apart from insurers that deal with large, high-value clients, the vast majority of insurers do not conduct a follow-up meeting with the prospective insured to discuss in greater depth the findings of a security scan. Indeed, multiple insurers and brokers repeatedly indicated in interviews that they do not disclose to the insurance buyer that they are conducting a scan or test and often do not disclose the results of the scan. For example:

> INTERVIEWER: Do you let them know that "Hey, we're going to have BitSight scan your company?"—
>
> INSURER-UNDERWRITER: No.
>
> INTERVIEWER: Oh, you don't?
>
> INSURER-UNDERWRITER: No, they're not aware at all that we're using some sort of third-party and getting some sort of rating score from a third-party vendor. (insurer and underwriter, interview 4)

In this respect, insurers miss an opportunity to engage in risk management and loss prevention. Sharing this information concerning vulnerabilities with the prospective insured could potentially improve the cyber hygiene of the organization if it prompts them to make changes based on the scans. If enough insurers adopted this practice, they might gradually nudge society to a more robust cybersecurity posture.

Although some believe the scan-and-score approach has promise, no industry expert whom I interviewed provided any data suggesting that external scans of a prospective insured's security profile are an accurate proxy for their level of risk or the amount of loss that an insured party might be reasonably expected to suffer in the wake of a successful attack. As one broker and former underwriter observed, "The external view is a proxy for their overall level of maturity. It's a theory, I wouldn't say it's proven one way or the other yet" (interview 13). In fact, some insurers do not even release the information from external security scans to the prospective buyers of insurance: "So there are a couple of different vulnerability points that they're testing. But the underwriters are telling me that they won't release the information back to the potential buyer because the data can be distorted. And it's often causing more friction with the potential buyer" (insurance broker, interview 8).

Although security scans exude legitimacy and security, the practical impact on the prospective insured's ability to improve its cybersecurity profile appears to be minimal at best and of no consequence whatsoever if they are never told of the scan or results. Moreover, insurers have incentives to sell insurance to gain market share in the growing cyber market, regardless of security scan scores.

The information security providers that provide scans and ratings do not provide continuous or ongoing scans and underwriting throughout the policy period. They are "definitely not used throughout the policy period for actual monitoring of the portfolio," as an insurer and forensic expert put it (interview 38,

April 30, 2020). Neither do they recommend how the insured can enhance its cybersecurity features. At best, then, the scans are only a snapshot in time, and they may quickly become irrelevant or even misleading because cyber threats are constantly evolving.

In addition, there appears to be insufficient incentive for the security scan providers to ensure the accuracy of their scans and analysis. An insurer and forensic expert offered an example:

> BitSight is a company that has no implications if they get it right or wrong, right? They're not going to lose money. . . . [F]irst of all, they need to sell [a] product . . . [and then] a different company, the insurance company, needs to trust what BitSight says so much that they will take huge financial bets based on what BitSight tells them. And, more often than not, this needs to not be just a reflection of what happened in the past. They have to trust BitSight with what is going to happen in the future. (interview 38)

And information security providers are unlikely to challenge, and may not even be aware of, insurers' actuarial teams rejecting their analysis:

> Let's say that you sit on the [insurance] actuary side, and you're like, "You know what, BitSight? I don't know. I hear what you're saying, but I don't trust it. I don't like it." Are you, [as] the BitSight analyst, . . . 100 percent sure that you're correct? How hard are you going to fight for the insurance company to actually use it? Are you going to jeopardize the contract? Are you going to bang on tables and say that it's an outrage that the actuarial team is dismissing or misusing or misclassifying any of it? [P]robably not, because you need to keep your customer happy. (interview 38)

On top of all the other issues uncovered in my research, it seems that insurers only rarely require prospective insureds to improve their cybersecurity posture as a prerequisite for issuing insurance, or even offer meaningful premium discounts for better cyber hygiene. When asked why they do not require changes, insurers noted that the market is so "soft" that prospective buyers can simply go to the next insurance company, which will likely issue insurance without requiring the buyer to make any changes.[3] Moreover, although many insurers I spoke with said that they rely heavily on technological tools provided by information security providers, the ways they implement these tools lacks transparency, creating a sense of arbitrary use. One expert described the lack of transparency in how security scores are incorporated into underwriting guidelines:

> And, in practice, insurance companies have been buying BitSight for three, four years. . . . I challenge you to find one underwriting guidelines document that explicitly addresses a BitSight or a Security Scorecard finding in how it applies to augmenting price. Not to mention actually declining coverage. So there is no underwriting guideline anywhere that would say, "If the BitSight score was under 500, decline." "If the BitSight score was under 700, increase price by 20 twenty percent." None of those exist. The BitSight products are used as, let's call it a second opinion portfolio overview analysis tool. (insurer and forensic expert, interview 38)

In sum, security scans and scores are not necessarily useful tools for improving the cyber hygiene of consumers.

INSURERS' TWO-TIERED TREATMENT OF POLICYHOLDERS

Managerial and business values of efficiency, cost containment, profit, and maximum managerial discretion drive insurer decision making and make the insurer mission as quasi-regulator difficult to achieve. Consumers are treated differently by insurers and brokers based on the size and wealth of the organization.

Many insurance brokers and risk managers (who buy insurance for their clients) indicated that they find the insurance application's rigid, mechanical, check-the-box format inadequate for the prospective insurance buyer to accurately communicate the company's cybersecurity posture. "We all know the problem with questionnaires," an expert asserted. "One, they ask the wrong questions. Two, the people answering them may answer them incorrectly, overtly, or maliciously—or they just don't know and so they check the box. Questionnaires are only a point in time" (forensic and information security expert, interview 14).

Particularly for small and medium-sized enterprises (SMEs; with annual revenue of less than $250 million), security scans conducted by insurance companies, or, more often, third-party information security companies that contract with insurance companies, are displacing the "old" methodology of evaluating and verifying insurance applications and conducting follow-up meetings between the insurer and the potential insured. "For a small business," a data broker told me, "they may have to answer only three or four questions on an application—online application—and they will have their policy issued within minutes. And what's going on behind the scenes is basically, they are using fairly massive data sources. . . . and usually just other sources to be able to rate the policy" (data broker, interview 33, part 2).

With this low-touch approach, efficiency and cost containment rather than safety or security shape the way insurers determine whether to engage third-party vendors to conduct security scans. Not all organizations seeking insurance are treated equally by insurers, as an underwriter observed, "and so we are using third-party data [from data brokers and information security providers] to help better distinguish good customers from bad customers and tie that directly to our rating" (interview 35). Because insurers are eager to expand into the cyber market, insurers underwrite SMEs based on the insurance application and sometimes the security scan rating from one of their information security partners. This "cash-flow underwriting" approach has created a soft market that prioritizes increasing insurance sales over regulating or nudging policyholders toward greater security.[4] Insurers rarely meet with or engage in a deep discussion of cybersecurity health with an SME. Concerns about efficiency and cost containment shape the way cyber insurers determine whether to actually meet with the prospective buyer about their cybersecurity health. "In the SME space," a broker and former insurance underwriter said, "it's more reliant on that third-party external view. You almost would never get the sixty-minute call. And the application may have some additional information. But the SMEs are really looking for an ease of transaction. The [insurance] companies that are successful are really minimizing the amount of information they are requesting. From our standpoint, we work with an insurtech that bakes in that external analysis into their underwriting" (interview 13).

Another broker described the issue strictly in terms of profit margin:

> It's 15 percent of the premium is what the broker is making. And on those deals, you're talking about maybe a thousand bucks. Probably a couple of hundred bucks. And you can't make money if you're doing a high-touch approach on that. Larger companies that are either paying a fee or you know the premiums are so much larger that the compensation to the broker is hundreds of thousands of dollars. So you can totally afford to invest in high touch [with the larger companies] and still make money." (broker and former insurance underwriter, interview 13)

Other than the security scan scores they sometimes receive, every single insurer that I interviewed indicated they rarely verify anything stated on the insurance application or meet or engage in discussions with the buyer. One insurer officer noted that "80 percent of the time we will rely on the answers on that [insurance] application" and added that only a select few larger clients warranted a deeper inquiry (insurance company cyber division leader, interview 19). Insurers are covered by the ability to engage in postclaim underwriting that essentially allows them to void the policy based on misrepresentation in the initial insurance application. As a forensic security consultant explained,

> I understand why carriers do it because they really have very little skin in the game, right? You're going to do a proper application. You're going to pay me $10,000. As long as nothing happens, it's a perfect process. Should something happen, I have the right then to come out and verify everything you told me. And, if I find anything to be untrue, I void coverage. I think that it may give the wrong perception to the buyer, saying I just have to answer these ten questions and I have insurance. (forensic security consultant, interview 16)

Perhaps unsurprisingly, large, wealthy organizations continue to have the luxury of insurance companies providing a much higher touch approach that often includes scanning and evaluating the potential insured's visible cyber risk but is supplemented by a closer evaluation of the insurance application and follow-up meetings to discuss in detail the customer's cyber risk profile and mitigation efforts. These meetings offer the opportunity for a meaningful discussion regarding the cyber hygiene of the organization, as well as for real bargaining over the terms of the insurance. For large companies, insurers sometimes even involve their internal risk engineers and technical experts and have them engage directly with the prospective buyer about their cybersecurity hygiene or at least consult with the under-writer.[5] Cyber insurers evaluate clients differently based on whether they are an SME or large organization, as one broker and former underwriter confirmed:

> Absolutely. When a carrier is putting up millions of dollars in limit, and maybe writing a very large manuscript policy, those internal resources are there to really help bridge the gap from the technical knowledge to the insurance knowledge. When you're talking about these smaller companies that we've talked about where you just fill out an application and you get a quote back really quickly, you know, the capacity that's being put up for those, even though the multi-tude—you know, there might be many, many different companies who do it. But the capacity on any one individual risk is probably limited at a million or less. And so carriers don't spend the time to go much beyond what they see from an application. (interview 10)

Managerial concerns over efficiency drive the insurance company decision-making process and approach, not a concern to fulfill a regulatory role.

Indeed, my interviews suggest that numerous well-heeled and sophisticated companies even pit one potential insurer against others in a competition to decide which the company will purchase cyber insurance from. After demonstrating to multiple potential insurers their company's cybersecurity posture, large corporations choose among bids from multiple cyber insurers pitching their services. A number of insurers whom I interviewed noted that risk managers and other buyers of insurance, particularly large companies with revenue above $250 million, expect the insurer to understand technology in order to thoroughly evaluate the risk of the buyer and how to price the risk (insurer, interview A10, June 26, 2019).[6]

Much like insurers, insurance brokers approach prospective buyers of insurance with either low-touch or high-touch approaches driven largely by the size and revenue of the organization. For large, sophisticated organizations, brokers deploy a high-touch approach that continues to rely on the insurance application and client interviews and interactions but also uses big data, predictive analytics, and security tools to enhance their evaluation of the prospective buyer of insurance.

Whereas high-touch brokers incorporate technology tools into a deeper conversation with the client about what they need, brokers engaging SMEs rely on purchasing data from big data brokers and using that information to make recommendations to clients on whether to purchase insurance and how and what their limits should be. Big data brokers that have accumulated large amounts of data particularly target smaller brokers and agents who do not have any internal resources. Many brokers whom I interviewed indicated that they often showed the charts developed by the big data aggregators to prospective buyers to explain why limits needed to be higher. Brokers are eager to share data from similar companies and leverage the fact that organizations often look to other organizations' policies and practices for guidance. "Our clients are always interested in what their peers are doing," a broker said. "They want to be able to make an informed decision. And if they need to justify what they've done, if they understand where they are in comparison with their peers, it helps them. I like the tools that the third party [data brokers] provide because it gives us objective data that's not produced exclusively by our firm" (insurance broker, interview 8).

In this respect, organizations purchasing insurance are copying one another and looking to other peer organizations for guidance on best practices (Edelman 2016). Insurance brokers use third-party data broker information on smaller companies that have less revenue because it is more efficient and cost-effective. As one underwriter observed: "You have to write a lot of SMEs to get to critical mass. And if you can find a quicker way to do that, i.e., technology, and a delivery system that allows a broker to, you know, get a quote in a matter of minutes, as opposed to him sending it to somebody like me and waiting a day or two before I turn on a quote, that's powerful. And brokers, you know, really are embracing that" (interview 11, June 25, 2019).

Whereas some brokers provide the security firm's report from the scan to the consumer, others do not tell the client the specifics of what they found in the scan. Instead, they tell the client that they can assist with the problems and presumably refer them to their security forensic consultants (wholesale broker and underwriter, interview 23). Thus, security evaluations and surveillance that are not disclosed to the prospective insurance buyer are also operationalized as an opportunity to offer companion services: "I know especially with some of the larger brokers," one broker told me, "they try to package companion services, things that they do on a consulting basis, into the placement process. That's just not what we do. And again, happy to pull third-party service providers in. We do that routinely. But certainly we're not doing anything without the client knowing what we're up [to] and why we're up to it" (interview 25, August 1, 2019).

Insurers and brokers rely on security and surveillance to analyze the risk profile of a consumer but do not always apply these tools evenly. In particular, a tension exists among brokers concerning how technology is mobilized. Brokers engaging larger organizations use a high-touch approach that uses technology to supplement the evaluative process, whereas some brokers engaging SMEs use a low-touch approach that relies on data and security scans as a substitute for the traditional broker-buyer relationship. For the most part, these increased security techniques and knowledge are not being used to push clients to become more cybersecure. The vast majority of brokers indicated that they do not require prospective buyers of insurance to make changes as a prerequisite to their agreeing to represent the buyer.

It is not necessarily unexpected or unreasonable for insurers and brokers to treat different prospective insureds differently. As cyber insurers noted in interviews, the market for cyber insurance necessitates that treatment differentiation to some degree. However, the differential treatment of insureds compromises the ability of the cyber insurance field to play a regulatory role.

Bringing chapters 3 and 4 together, as organizations legalize themselves by creating cybersecurity policies and procedures and look to insurance companies for assistance in developing a cybersecurity response, a "technologization of insurance" occurs. Although insurers filter what privacy law and cybersecurity compliance means for organizations through a managerial and risk lens, big data, information security, and emerging technologies are the mechanisms through which insurers engage in managerial responses to the unpredictable cyber insurance market. Although technology dominates the underwriting process among insurers and is mobilized by insurance brokers when engaging prospective buyers of insurance, cyber insurer usage of these tools appears largely ineffective in enhancing their insureds' cybersecurity. Big data in this sector is unreliable. The information security provider scans that insurers rely on are unreliable. Insurers use technology and security tools to scan and evaluate the cyber hygiene of a prospective insured but do not make improving their cybersecurity posture a prerequisite to obtaining coverage. Moreover, insurers are working hard to expand market share in the cyber arena and using emerging technologies more to boost policy sales and increase profit margins than to incentivize good cyber hygiene. Insurers are reluctant to reward policyholders with strong security protocols with reduced premiums. In seeking to secure as many insureds as possible, insurers weaken their ability to change or influence insured behavior. Insurers also treat different clients with high- or low-touch approaches, creating a tiered system. Thus, similar to employers (Edelman 2016) and manufacturers (Talesh 2012), insurers as regulators in the cyber context are largely symbolic: their interventions exude legitimacy to the public but provide little tangible improvement to organizations' cyber hygiene. The following chapter explores to what extent insurer loss prevention and risk management services impact policyholders' cyber hygiene.

CHAPTER FIVE

Cyber Insurance Risk Management

Ineffective, Symbolic Regulatory Interventions

The majority of the brokers that I know don't understand the threat vector. They don't understand the prebreach, the postbreach; they just know that you need insurance. So the insurance carriers are taking what I call a Prego spaghetti sauce approach. It's in there. Well, you know, we need basil. It's in there. What about—it's in there. And so, they're dumbing—they're making their products so comprehensive that even the dumbest of agents can present it.

So just think of Prego spaghetti sauce. Any ingredient you need to have a good Italian dinner—it's in there. And that's the carrier approach. Like you said, communications.

Broker and former risk manager, interview 6, June 20, 2019

Given that most organizations are undercompliant with privacy laws and underprepared for cybersecurity breaches (Talesh 2018), cyber insurers engage in risk and loss prevention on behalf of the organizations that purchase their insurance. By attempting to prevent, detect, and respond to cybersecurity breaches, insurers play a de facto regulator role. Insurers offer a series of pre- and postbreach services to purchasers of cyber insurance. Cybersecurity conferences heavily promote cyber insurance by focusing on the availability of what they refer to as "value-added" pre- and postbreach services (Talesh 2018, 438–39). Emerging technology and managed-security tools play a major role in cyber insurers' risk management approach.

My empirical research, however, finds that cyber insurers' role as quasi-regulators is largely ineffective. Consistent with new institutional theory, risk management services offered by insurers are a template for insurers to engage in managerial responses to compliance but ultimately are symbolic regulatory interventions. In addition to drawing on managerial and risk values that guide the insurance field, insurers lean heavily on using information security and emerging technologies as a pathway toward achieving greater cybersecurity. This chapter first describes the various pre- and postbreach services offered and then explains why implementation has not succeeded. Although risk management services are a mechanism through which insurers attempt to regulate and nudge organizational behavior, its impact is largely symbolic because, in fact, organizations fail to use the prebreach services. Organizations do accept and use postbreach services, but only after the breach has occurred, and therefore, their preventive impact is rendered moot.

INSURER RISK MANAGEMENT SERVICES

Prebreach services focus on preventing and detecting risks to the organization. Insurers offer new policyholders access to a set of risk prevention tools that they claim will reduce their company's likelihood of falling victim to a cyberattack.[1] Once an insured organization purchases a policy, it gains access to a portal of tools, ranging from training, written materials, incident response plans, software, free virus-scanning capability, and password management. Most important, insurers provide purchasers the opportunity to consult with forensic and information security companies that the insurers contract with. "Our real focus," one broker related to me, "has been partnering with all the major insurance companies that offer cyber risk insurance coverage of some flavor. . . . We are essentially their loss control partner, helping to assess the risks of their customers, their cyber and privacy risks" (broker and former risk manager, interview 6). Thus, in contrast to the context of directors and officers professional liability insurance (Baker and Griffith 2010), cyber insurers attempt to engage in considerable risk and loss prevention. Insurance companies either have in-house departments or contract with third-party organizations that offer an array of services aimed at preventing data breaches and violations of privacy laws from ever occurring. In this way, insurers attempt to absorb the risk prevention functions of the organization.

Risk prevention begins with a series of assessments, or what one insurer called "cyber health checks." The goals of these checks are to "give organizations a 360-degree view of their people, processes and technology, so they can reaffirm that reasonable practices are in place, harden their data security, qualify for network liability and privacy insurance, and bolster their defense posture in the event of class action lawsuits" (NetDiligence 2015). Insurers offer scans that analyze the risks of an organization's security posture. As noted earlier, the insurer or the affiliated third-party vendor performs a remotely delivered scan of the organization's perimeter network devices such as its firewall, web server, and email servers to mitigate vulnerabilities and stave off potential attacks. Insurers frame these services as unique and providing additional value (hence, "value-added").

Once the assessment is complete, insurers offer risk prevention tools. Some of the major tools include a series of training modules on password security, data privacy, and other cybersecurity issues for employees; five or so hours of consultative risk engineering services; vulnerability checks; document templates and articles on best practices; and a tabletop exercise for preparing an organization's incident response. Another risk management assessment tool focuses on cybersecurity best-practice standards in such categories as current events, security policy, security organization, asset classification and control, personnel security, physical and environmental security, computer and network management, system development and maintenance, business continuity planning, security compliance, internet liability, and privacy and regulatory compliance (NetDiligence 2015). One insurance carrier is trying to have all website activity go through the managed security provider, though that is not the norm.

Coupled with risk prevention strategies, the insurance field also offers services aimed at *detecting* data breaches before they are completed. These services include managing and tuning intrusion detection system technologies, managing host and network-based firewall technologies, managing security information and event management correlation technologies, and managing security service providers. Insurers often contract with managed security providers that offer "shunning" services. This type of service uses intel and security technology to isolate and shun communications to and from IP addresses currently being used by criminals.

Insurers offer to evaluate the people, processes, and technology involved in the client organization's cyber risk management program to ensure that the organization has a foundation on which to develop a stronger program. This approach could, in theory, allow the insurance company to absorb many of the functions of the information technology department and actively engage in loss prevention. In this vein, cyber insurers are similar to insurers offering employment practice liability insurance (Talesh 2015a) but different than directors and officers insurance (Baker and Griffith 2010). Whereas directors and officers have an incentive to have defense and indemnification liability coverage, they are less eager to have outside actors and institutions (such as insurers) interfering with their day-to-day decision making and at times risky behavior. However, with cyber insurance, in theory, the incentives are better aligned. Given the financial, legal, and reputational harm, no organization benefits from a cyberattack. Thus, cyber insurers argue, policyholders are interested in using these risk management tools to prevent and detect risks.

Although insurers alert new insureds that these services are available should they choose to use them, insureds are not required to use them. Dozens of information security providers are fighting for market share in this area, each offering products they believe help insureds reduce the chance of a data breach occurring. Indeed, the market is highly competitive, as one interviewee attested: "They are either companies with products specifically targeting the cyber insurance marketplace or ... information security providers of various sources who have products they believe would be useful in the cyber insurance space" (data aggregator and big data provider, interview 33, part 1). In theory, these risk prevention tools and security ratings could encourage insureds to work for better cyber hygiene and resiliency.

POSTBREACH SERVICES

Perhaps the most significant intervention the insurance field makes is achieved through risk management services it offers to shape the way that organizations respond in the event of an actual data breach. Traditionally, insurance covers legal defense and indemnification costs associated with a covered loss. In the cyber insurance context, insurers cover the legal, forensic, restoration, business interruption, crisis management, and credit-monitoring expenses. Cyber insurance goes beyond risk transfer in the defense and indemnification context in that it provides access to services aimed at also responding to, investigating, defending, and mitigating against the consequences of a data breach event or privacy law violation. Cyber insurers provide these risk management services, which organizations use to respond to data loss. Insurers either have departmental units that deal with various cyber related problems or contract with third-party vendors that the insured can use. Typically, the insured receives a reduced premium to use the insurer's vendors. In this respect, cyber insurance provides not just risk transfer but risk response well beyond the scope of what insurers typically handle.

Ordinarily organizations facing a cyber violation have incident response teams that try to manage and coordinate the data security event investigation, response, and reporting and the corrective action taken. Cyber insurance field actors describe the numerous voices that are part of the process. As one noted in a panel discussion: "The incident response team is made up of the incident response team leader, the privacy officer, legal and risk management services department, information security, human resources, employee relations, patient relations, outside legal counsel who is often the breach coach, crisis management and public relations person, the forensics person and the insurance company or broker. The external team members such as outside vendors, privacy breach coach, forensics, and outside counsel are part of the internal response" (insurance official, cyber risk conference, Panel 21, May 16, 2019).

Many of the members of the incident response team have direct relationships with the insurance company. Organizations that purchase this insurance often express how efficient this "one-stop shopping" can be in the event of a data breach (Talesh 2018). Through this close partnership with the insured, insurers influence the organization's compliance process. In particular, the insurance company offers a menu of services that an organization can quickly access when consumer information is stolen in a data breach. According to organizations, the most helpful aspect of cyber insurance is the postbreach risk management services:

> These services can actually be quite robust and innovative. Finally, insureds are able to tap into a built-in network of IT experts, PR firms and legal counsel experienced in cyber matters, which brings an enormous amount of value to the coverage. (Chris Andrews, cited in Hudson 2015)
>
> We use the insurance company as a resource for our decision making. (insured, conference panel 6, May 6, 2020)

Postbreach services approved by the insurer offer insureds access to law firms, forensic analysts, crisis management businesses, and credit monitoring companies.

Legal Services

Insurers provide organizations access to a suite of postbreach services, often at a discount or premium reduction, including designated panels of lawyers and law firms to assist in managing legal issues that arise when a data breach occurs. In addition to legal advice and guidance on how to deal with cybersecurity incidents, lawyers advise organizations on how to mitigate regulatory fines and liability for data breaches. Because of the variation in consumer notification laws across states, lawyers assist policyholders following a data breach in evaluating which state laws have been triggered and what steps the insured must take. In this respect, insurers are shaping the way organizations comply with privacy and cybersecurity legal challenges on the ground. Many follow lawyers' lead concerning how to respond to data breaches and often refer to them as "breach coaches." In particular, cyber insurance policy holders indicate that they like being able to contact a lawyer who has been vetted by the insurer. As one said, "Cyber insurance is a great product because of the postbreach services. My first [phone] call is to the breach coach" (insured, conference panel 6). They also like that the breach coach assures them that communications thereafter concerning the breach are privileged. Many risk managers whom I interviewed noted that the breach coach often plays a critical and primary role in developing and managing the incident response team that is formed when a data breach occurs. Moreover, these lawyers provide twenty-four-hour access to the organization's incident response lawyers through an 800 number. These lawyers and law firms are relied on in part because they are repeat players and have developed significant experience handling clients experiencing data loss.

Forensic Services

When a company's cybersecurity system is breached, an immediate concern is identifying the source and cause of the data breach, containing the breach, and ultimately restoring network processes that may have been damaged as a result of the breach. Addressing these problems often requires an information security cyber expert. Cyber insurers or their third-party vendors offer organizations the services of forensic experts. One forensic investigator I interviewed highlighted how insurers provide access to key forensic services: "firms really want us to come in and clean things up when a breach occurs and our relationship with the insurer makes it easier for the firm to access our services" (forensic investigator, interview 47, September 30, 2015). Cyber insurers not only provide the insured access to these vendors but also cover the costs to investigate the cause of the data breach, restore the network processes to normal, and retain information security forensics experts. In addition to legal expertise, the insurance company is also the primary source for forensic expertise.

Crisis Management and Public Relations

Another threat organizations face when a breach occurs is damage to its reputation. Prior studies note that more than a third of customers of companies that suffer a data breach no longer do business with those companies because of the breach (Beazley n.d.). Cyber insurers address this risk by providing access at a reduced cost to preapproved public relations and crisis management firms. These firms provide notification, advertising, and related communications assistance to help protect and restore the insured's reputation after a breach event. These crisis management and public relations firms develop and provide advertising or related communications to protect and restore the insured's reputation following a breach event. Risk managers indicated that they value this service.

Credit Monitoring and Restoration

Finally, the other major response that many organizations have to make when a data breach occurs is dealing with consumers whose financial information is stolen. In such situations, millions of people are at risk of credit and identity theft by hackers. Financial institutions, retail stores, and credit card companies that experience breaches of consumer information often have to set up credit-monitoring and restoration services for consumers. Typically this response also includes establishing a call center to respond to customer concerns and inquiries concerning data breach events. Cyber insurance provides access to companies experienced in credit monitoring and restoration that organizations can use for a reduced fee. Cyber insurance also covers the costs of credit and fraud monitoring and costs associated with setting up call centers to respond to customer concerns and inquiries as a result of data loss.

In sum, these risk management services reflect insurers' managerialized response to data privacy concerns. Taken collectively, the pre- and postbreach services can, in theory, help organizations prevent, detect, and respond to cybersecurity incidences. But do they work? Are policyholders using these services?

LARGELY INEFFECTIVE AND SYMBOLIC QUASI-REGULATORS

Cyber insurers tout their ability to regulate and shape the behavior of their insureds by preventing, detecting, and responding to cybersecurity risks.[2] The vast majority of insurers and brokers whom I interviewed indicated they believe insurers "drive some behavioral changes," act as a "motivator to get better coverage," and play a regulatory role in the cybersecurity context. To that end, insurers aggressively market and offer a wide variety of pre- and postbreach services to their insureds.

However, interviews with insurers and risk managers who purchase cyber insurance also reveal that insureds *rarely* use the prebreach services offered. Many of the interviewees lamented the low uptake rate by SMEs, and more than one risk manager stated categorically that fewer than 10 percent of organizations that purchase cyber insurance actually use the vast array of prebreach services insurers offer that would potentially reduce the insured's risk. As one former broker and underwriter observed, "The uptake was less than 10 percent in terms of the services that were being offered. But it's a great marketing tool because we're better than the other guys. Look how much free stuff you're getting from us" (interview 12). Consistent with new institutional theories on isomorphism, most insurers have developed their own prebreach tools or contract with companies that offer such services as a way of maintaining legitimacy in the market. But the impact of these services is largely symbolic. "These are marketing—these are all kind of attempts to differentiate oneself by marketing. Because the uptake isn't really there. Like all these insurers, they're spending a lot of money on these services. And then the clients just don't use them" (former broker and underwriter, interview 12).

Although insurers view offering these tools as part of establishing themselves as legitimate players in the cyber market, the rest of the cyber insurance field views these prebreach services mostly as marketing tools:

> But much of the pre-breach stuff out there is just a bunch of bullshit. The cybersecurity industry has customers on this merry-go-round of, we're going to build a reactive technology and then it's going to get out-technologized. We're going to build another one. Just keep buying, just keep buying, just keep buying. And so, there is some fatigue on customers. You have all these well-funded companies that the marketing—if you look at the marketing brochures across all these different solutions, they all kind of sound the same. (forensic and information security expert, interview 14)

One former insurance broker and underwriter noted that insurers are racing against one another to develop as many pre-breach services as they can without focusing on whether buyers actually use these services or whether they work: "If you look at AIG, AIG's offering over eight new [prebreach] services. And there's no rhyme or reason to any of them. They just keep bolting things on to try and look better than Beazley. Beazley is up to about six pre- services. NAS offers like four or five. It's a land rush for prebreach services right now" (former broker and underwriter, interview 12).

Others in the cyber field sense insurers use free assessments of an organization's cyber hygiene as an opportunity to upsell the organization on these additional prebreach services: "They'll almost want to do a free assessment just to get in with the client," a forensic security consultant told me. "And then try to upsell them all these other things" (interview 16). Thus, although pre-breach services may offer organizations some ability to enhance their cyber hygiene, insurers mobilize these services in symbolic ways that exude a sense of legitimacy and security and help bolster sales without regard to actually enhancing an organization's cybersecurity. Insurers were quite open about this instrumental approach. For example: "As a marketing expense, or as a sales tool, it's essential. So, good on us—we got the deal because we offered the thing [namely, prebreach services]" (broker and former underwriter, interview 10).

WHY ORGANIZATIONS DO NOT USE INSURER-PROVIDED PREBREACH SERVICES

Notwithstanding this marketing push, organizations are not using the prebreach services insurers offer. Interviews with risk managers who buy insurance for companies revealed the variety of reasons that they do not use insurer-sponsored prebreach services. Many buyers of cyber insurance do not trust insurer-sponsored services. Some do not think the quality of the services is very good. Others think allowing insurer-sponsored information and managed-security companies to evaluate an organization may allow insurers to use the information against the insured in the event of a claim: "How do I know the insurance company isn't going to use this information that the service provider obtained against me when I have a claim? There's suspicion we're going to get screwed" (risk manager, interview 9, June 25, 2019). Many brokers and underwriters noted that the prebreach services, while multifaceted and diverse, ultimately are unreliable because they are external scans of an organization's cyber health. Multiple forensic experts indicated that the insurance premium charged is too low to include high-level managed security services, leading to low-quality prebreach services being offered. For example:

> What you find is a lot of these proactive offerings that are out there are not really all that great. Especially if they're being provided by an insurance company, they tend to be cheaper, the same for everybody, out of the box. What's the word I'm looking for? . . . Cookie-cutter. (insurer and big data provider, interview 31)

> [Prebreach services have] dismal take-up rates. It makes sense economically. Because our [prebreach service] is really built to live within the insurance premium. So it's not very much money. If you have a $20,000 premium, it's hard to go to a large cybersecurity provider and put $120,000 worth of security in a $20,000 premium. There's no room. [The security provider] is not going to spend $120,000 to protect a $20,000 premium line from the insurance company. You have to have something that lives within, the small allocation of risk management services within a $20,000 premium, a $10,000 premium. It gets worse as you go down. How much risk management can you really do if you're only collecting $1,000 from a client? (forensic and information security expert, interview 14)[3]

Other organizations decline prebreach services because they underestimate the risk of cybersecurity incidences. Despite the increase in the number and size of cybersecurity breaches, many organizations simply do not think a breach will happen to their organization. Some risk managers express skepticism concerning whether prebreach services reduce the likelihood of cybersecurity breaches and refuse to purchase without more quantifiable evidence of success. Insurance brokers also lack knowledge and expertise on how these specific security tools will help buyers of cyber insurance and thus are not able to properly tailor their advice to prospective insureds on these products. Some buyers of insurance are either confused by the resources offered or are too unmotivated or busy to fully capitalize on the prebreach services offered by insurers. In fact, a survey in 2024 of technology managers who worked for organizations revealed that 46 percent of them do not review major updates to software applications (Connatser 2024). Thus, neglect, lack of motivation, insufficient time needed to conduct such reviews, and cost shape organizational responses. Insurers repeatedly highlighted their position that policyholders do not give enough attention to the services offered. As one insurance underwriter described the thought process:

> You'll mention [the prebreach services] to them, and they'll say, "Oh great! I'm going to talk internally about that," and then they never get back to us about it. It's probably just that they have a lot of things on their plate and this doesn't necessarily fall at the top of the list. They know they have that safety net in place with the insurance, so this is just like the cherry on top. Which, they may think is just sort of a bonus, but not think is an imperative to have in place. (insurance underwriter, interview 1)

Often, large organizations either use their own prebreach security tools or directly contract with managed-security companies, thereby forgoing insurer risk management interventions. Although insurers aggressively market the value of these services at cyber conferences, their ability to nudge insureds' behavior toward greater security in the real world appears to remain low.

WHY INSURERS ARE RELUCTANT TO REQUIRE INSUREDS TO ADOPT PREBREACH SERVICES

Insurers also seem unwilling to require insureds to adopt these prebreach services as a prerequisite to issuing a policy. Because cyber insurance is such a growing and soft market, insurers whom I interviewed said they worried insureds would just seek insurance from a less stringent insurer. The soft market even causes insurers to moderate the loss prevention evaluation and the inquiries in insurance applications process out of fear that too much prying drives prospective buyers away. "It's such an incredibly soft market right now," one wholesale broker and underwriter remarked, "and there is just so much competition to write this business that when another company comes out [with insurance], it just drives the pricing down. Another company comes out and you scratch off another question [on the insurance application] that you want to ask of somebody" (interview 23). Thus, although insurers have the *potential* to improve the insured's cybersecurity posture, they appear largely unable to realize it, at least in today's cyber insurance buyer's market.

This reluctance to be rigorous extends to the insurance application itself, where insurers rarely verify or check whether SMEs' assertions on the insurance application are accurate. Instead, if and when a claim is made, they verify the accuracy of representations made when the victim applied for cyber insurance. If insurers identify inaccuracies, they deny coverage based on misrepresentation (insurance expert and attorney, interview A2, May 8, 2019).

Thanks again to the soft market—and likely to maximize the efficiency of the sales process—insurers rarely hold substantive meetings with SME cyber insurance buyers after receiving an application and conducting a security scan. In fact, one chief information security officer described how his company's premiums were *lowered* despite revising their answers to an insurance renewal that showed the company to be a higher risk:

> We had a series of like forty questions to answer, you know: "Do you have a written information security plan in place?" Yes. "Do you have an incident response plan?" Yes. "Do you have, you know, annual risk assessments completed?" Yes. So that was the prior year's answer.
>
> When I took a look at it further, you know, it became clear that the person answering those questions just didn't know, but they thought they were supposed to put yes. And we decided, well, we better be as accurate as possible this next time around. And so, we put no, and I warned, you know, our CFO, hey, this is probably going to impact the premium we're charged or the amount of coverage we can get. Somebody's going to ask us questions about it, but I'd rather we're honest on the front end so that we don't jeopardize potential coverage if we ever have a claim. And, yeah, they renewed the coverage at a lower premium, and no one ever asked us any question as to why we shifted the answers on that underwriting application. (insurance attorney and former chief information security officer, interview 20, July 25, 2019)

With respect to prebreach risk management services, risk and managerial values work hand in hand. The insurance field has adopted a managerialized conception of cybersecurity and privacy law, which elaborates information and managed security structures and policies that demonstrate compliance and rational governance. Cyber insurers sell this vision by highlighting the risks posed by not developing policies and procedures and not using insurer prebreach services. Cyber insurers also provide a safety net for organizations in the form of defense and indemnification insurance coverage. But ultimately, these services are symbolic and merely exude legitimacy to the public because organizations are not actually using these services despite their widespread marketing.

Thus, insurers have opportunities to engage in risk management and promote better cybersecurity practices among their prospective insureds and actual customers by (1) closely evaluating application responses; (2) examining the cybersecurity health of the prospective insured; (3) sharing information with the insured regarding the cyber hygiene of the organization based on the security scan evaluation; (4) requiring changes as a prerequisite to issuing insurance or charging lower premiums; and (5) making sure insureds that do purchase insurance use the insurers' prebreach services to prevent and detect risks. However, my research indicates most insurers seldom do any of these things (see also Woods and Moore 2020).

Perhaps even more troubling, my research clearly indicates that large and small-to-medium organizations seeking cyber insurance are not treated equally by insurers. "Not all customers are treated the same way," an underwriter said, "and so we are using third-party data [from big data providers and information security providers] to help better distinguish good customers from bad customers and tie that directly to our rating" (underwriter, interview 35). Because insurers are eager to expand into the cyber market, insurers underwrite SMEs based on the insurance application and sometimes an external security scan rating from one of their information security partners. Insurers rarely meet with or engage in a deep discussion of the SME's specific cybersecurity posture: "In the SME space, it's more reliant on that third-party external view. You almost would never get the sixty-minute call. And the application may have some additional information. But the SMEs are really looking for an ease of transaction. The [insurance] companies that are successful are really minimizing the amount of information they are requesting. From our standpoint, we work with an insurtech that bakes in that external analysis into their underwriting" (broker and former insurance underwriter, interview 13). Concerns about efficiency and cost containment rather than the perceived preferences of the SMEs themselves shape the way cyber insurers determine whether to actually meet with the prospective buyer about their cybersecurity health.

INSURER-PROVIDED POSTBREACH SERVICES AND DATA BREACH PREVENTION

On the positive side, the insurers and risk managers whom I interviewed indicated that insureds regularly use insurers' postbreach services. Thus, it was quite common for insureds to rely on the insurers' recommended panel of lawyers, forensics, and client management specialists. Organizations repeatedly indicated that they appreciate the expedience and efficiency of being able to access a bundle of services from the insurer. However, since these services are, by definition, performed after the breach, they do not prevent successful attacks and are unlikely to improve society's overall cybersecurity posture. The uptake of postbreach services does, however, suggest that cyber insurers actually can have a positive "regulatory" impact on insureds by changing behavior with the right incentive structure.

Although postbreach services have made more of an intervention than prebreach services, there are questions about the former
services' overall value and how much influence insurers have on
legal and forensic services. Many interviewees agreed that the
law firm hired when a breach occurs is the "quarterback" of
the response plan and can guide the organization's response,
with the benefit of attorney-client privilege. In fact, often the
breach coach directs or guides the organization on its choice of
which forensics and client restoration firms to use. But many
whom I spoke with questioned whether these interactions are
really privileged. For example, whether to pay a ransom that a
cybercriminal demands, according to many industry leaders, is
a business decision for the organization that is many steps
removed from legal advice made in anticipation of litigation.
One attorney who regularly acts as a data breach coach in cyber
claims noted the ambiguity of the privilege:

> I actually just had a discussion about that this morning. If one under-
> stands what the attorney-client relationship—or privilege, rather—
> is intended to cover, it only relates to legal advice that you give, right?
> And primarily related to litigation. For instance, on the ransomware
> cases, if you are going to be paying the ransom or not paying the ran-
> som, I think that's a business decision a lot of these people make. And
> if it's a business decision, it wouldn't be covered by the privilege.
>
> And the other part of it is, well, the work that we do is all techni-
> cal. And, as a matter of course, we will provide the facts that lead to
> an opinion as to whether or not, you know, we were negligent or not
> negligent, but it'll just provide the facts of what your environment
> looked like at the time that you were breached. That could be used
> in litigation. I don't see how a privilege is going to protect that.
> (cyber insurance consultant, interview 15)

Although insurers and lawyers "heavily market that pitch,"
namely that communications with the breach coach are

privileged, the issue is largely undecided and unaddressed by courts and remains an open question concerning whether attorney-client privilege attaches for all or parts of the lawyer's actions as the breach coach (interview 15). Scholars question whether attorney advice in this capacity actually falls within the attorney client privilege (Schwarcz, Wolff, and Woods 2022).

There are also concerns about whether the entwined relationship between insurers and law firms is in the best interest of the insured. Law firms crave opportunities to be on insurer-sponsored panels of lawyers that insureds choose from. To that end, large law firms (such as Mullen Coughlin, Lewis Brisbois, and BakerHostetler, to name a few) have cornered a significant portion of the cyber breach market. These law firms use professional and social opportunities to gain the trust and business of insurers. In addition to a series of interviews, law firms "wine and dine and mix with the insurers" whenever they have an opportunity, help write articles for insurers, help insurers publish documents that they can send to their insureds, provide free training sessions for insurer internal adjusters, and donate and contribute as major sponsors at national cyber insurer conferences (insurance attorney and former chief information security officer, interview 20).

The relationship between the law firms and insurers is tangled at many levels. Once an insurer selects a particular firm to be one of the insurer-approved law firms insureds may choose from, it has tremendous access to repeat business. Insurers also disincentivize insureds from using law firms not sponsored by the insurer. In fact, insurers go so far as to instruct policyholders that if they choose to use a law firm not preapproved by the insurer, the insurer will either not pay for those legal expenses or limit their coverage of attorney fees by the standard coverage of the policy. Some insurance industry officials expressed frustration with being essentially forced to use insurer-sponsored law firms, many of which are located in a state other than where the cybersecurity incident occurred, leading to a disjointed postbreach response. As one attorney described this situation:

> [It's] less seamless. You know, if you have to use a firm, if you're a manufacturing company in Milwaukee, and you have a data breach, and my law firm has helped you with all of your policies and preparedness, but once you have the breach, if you have to use a firm out of Philadelphia because they're the one the insurer's going to approve, then it's a disjointed process and you spend a lot of time trying to teach the Philadelphia firm about how this occurred and what mechanisms you had in place to try to prevent that, what your policies say. (insurance attorney and former chief information security officer, interview 20)

These findings are consistent with what Arce, Woods, and Bohme's (2024) recent study suggests, that "policyholders opt for a panel and accept the insurer's recommended service provider even when more efficient providers are listed on the panel" (7). Insurer-provided hotlines route questions regarding legal issues directly to insurer-sponsored law firms. My interviews with insurance industry officials revealed that, despite these challenges, other law firms continually seek to break into this market and become one of the insurer-sponsored law firms. Law firms on these panels charge a discounted legal fee often made possible by generating a high volume of business.

In addition to concerns over attorney-client privilege and the cozy relationship between selected law firms and insurers, there are also questions about the quality of legal advice provided under these arrangements. The major law firms in this area often push the work on these cases to associate attorneys, who cost far less than what a partner would charge. This is the result of a prenegotiated rate between the insurer and the law firm. On one hand, this arrangement potentially lowers the price. On the other hand, it leads to less experienced lawyers working on these cases and a sense that the insured's best interests are not always the primary concern. As one attorney observed:

> There are a handful of national firms that show up on every panel for insurers, and we've been on the other side of cases with them where we've got a client whose contractor suffered a breach. The contractor has a panel for one of these national panel firms. And we end up on a call talking with them, representing our client.
>
> And we've interacted with these national panel firms quite a bit, and you're always on the phone with a different associate. You might have a series of ten calls—call one has this associate, call two has a different associate, call three another. You rarely get a partner, you know, on that phone call. And it's a frustrating experience because they're just, you know, churning associates through these files. And the underlying insured is not really getting very good representation. (insurance attorney and former chief information security officer, interview 20)

Law firms that use mill-style approaches to process large quantities of cases at discounted rates with younger attorneys staffing them often offer only generic legal advice with little effort directed to guiding the policyholder on how to make long-term systemic changes to their cybersecurity posture:

> One of the disservices that the insurance company does is hire those that are very good at a cookie cutter approach to handling a breach. They've got their list of different state breach notification laws. They've got their associates that are willing to jump in quick. They have their form letters. They have their [forensics and client management] vendors that they rely on, that they have good relationships with, that may or may not be very good, but it doesn't matter because they have good relationships with them.

Yet, if something happens, they don't take into consideration the ramifications to, let's say for example, the privacy procedures that are already in place. They don't give recommendations to how to improve. Because, again, they're not primarily privacy attorneys; they're primarily breach coaches addressing breaches. So the problem is that oftentimes when you have these incidents, you want the two rolled up together because, in real time, as you're addressing certain things, you can help mold the policy by explaining how things should be different. That is a big service to the client that doesn't necessarily get done if the task of the attorney is basically just to be the breach coach and not to provide any high-level assistance. (insurance attorney, interview 18, July 17, 2019)

To be clear, the insurance industry people whom I interviewed were not suggesting that the major law firms handling these cases are not competent law firms; rather, they were saying that the current system is not narrowly tailored in a way to put the insured's interests ahead of having an efficient process for managing a high volume of cases at discounted rates. Although postbreach services in general received a more favorable view than prebreach services, there are concerns about the structure of the relationship and quality of the service.

In sum, while cyber insurers are theoretically positioned to fill the gap as a regulator of organizational behavior by offering pre- and postbreach risk management services with cyber insurance, they have not done so thus far. Consistent with my institutional theory of insurance regarding organizational responses to law, although risk management and loss prevention services are marketed aggressively and exude legitimacy to the public, they are more symbols of compliance than actual compliance, particularly regarding prebreach services.

CHAPTER SIX

How Cyber Insurers and Managed Security Companies Influence the Meaning of Privacy Law and Cybersecurity Compliance

Despite significant evidence suggesting cyber insurers do not work well as regulators, insurtech companies have influenced the content and meaning of privacy law and cybersecurity compliance. Here we see the bottom-up new institutional theory of insurance come full circle: it was not the federal government that passed a law instructing insurance companies to create cyber insurance and accompanying risk management services. Rather, it was insurers, in response to cybersecurity threats and ambiguous privacy laws, that created and institutionalized a series of risk management practices that they claim help improve an organization's cyber hygiene. This chapter reveals that, although the federal government envisioned a public-private partnership to address cybersecurity threats that included the assistance of insurance companies, it provided no framework and little guidance as to how insurers should meaningfully assist organizations facing cybersecurity threats. Consequently, insurance institutions were provided the discretion and space to shape the content and meaning of cybersecurity compliance.

Insurer and information security company constructions of privacy law compliance and cybersecurity focus largely on appearing legitimate to the public and avoiding being sued as opposed to creating structures likely to keep organizations cybersecure. Similar to employers in the civil rights context (Edelman 2016) and manufacturers in the consumer protection context (Talesh 2012), cyber insurers are actively constructing the content and meaning of privacy law and cybersecurity compliance because so much deference is given to insurers as regulators. Despite the ineffectiveness of cyber insurers as regulators, public legal institutions such as legislators and regulators continue to defer to cyber insurance as a legitimate form of regulation in the cybersecurity and privacy law context without evidence that such interventions actually improve organizations' cybersecurity.

I begin by exploring to what extent cyber insurance policies address law and compliance obligations and responsibilities in the policy itself. Next, I explain how cyber insurers and affiliated entities have shaped what privacy laws mean when interpreting and implementing cyber policies against policyholders. Finally, I explore how these insurer constructions come full circle and ultimately influence the manner in which public legal institutions understand privacy laws and cybersecurity compliance.

CYBER INSURANCE POLICY LANGUAGE DOES NOT FOCUS ON PRIVACY LAW AND COMPLIANCE

Cyber insurers' focus on law and compliance can be evaluated in part by looking at how insurers construct their policies and what scrutiny and attention are paid to holding their insureds accountable to the prevalent privacy laws and cybersecurity standards. If cyber insurers care about whether their insureds comply with privacy laws, it presumably might be reflected in their insurance policies. The insurance contract structures the relationship and outlines the obligations of the insurer and insured. In some respects, insurers' policy language reflects what they value and choose to focus on regarding the structure of the insurer-insured relationship.

I analyzed twenty-six cyber insurance policies and evaluated whether each policy references HIPAA, HITECH, CCPA, GDPR, the Graham-Leach-Bliley Act, PCI or other, related regulations and standards. In various capacities, these laws require organizations to be consistent with privacy laws and cybersecurity protections. To the extent a particular insurance policy did so, I evaluated whether the policies interpret or define requirements, articulate specific requirements for complying with these laws, or provide incentives for compliance or penalties for noncompliance. I was surprised to find that although insurance policies often referred to law, they rarely cited specific provisions of the laws and often only vaguely referred to privacy laws. Table 2 highlights whether and how these policies referenced particular laws. The most common mention of laws or phrases relating to compliance was found in the policies' definition section.

Although some laws furthered compliance provisions by requesting annual audits, such expansions of the requirements set forth by law were rare. In fact, most insurance policies simply refer to the binding law by name, leaving the insured to determine what it must do to comply based on its interpretation of those laws. Although the insurance policies sometimes suggested a means of compliance with the statutes and regulations

TABLE 2

Insurance policy references to law

Statute or regulation	Number of policies that referenced (*n* = 26)	Type of reference
HIPAA	15	Interpretation: 5
		Compliance: 1
		Penalties: 0
HITECH	9	Interpretation: 3
		Compliance: 0
		Penalties: 0
GDPR	5	Interpretation: 0
		Compliance: 0
		Penalties: 0
GLBA	11	Interpretation: 5
		Compliance: 1
		Penalties: 0
PCI	12	Interpretation: 2
		Compliance: 3
		Penalties: 8
Legal references generally	11	Interpretation: 5
		Compliance: 2
		Penalties: 7

that would bind the insured, the suggestions were exactly that—suggestions. If the insured did not abide by the suggested mode of compliance, the insurer seemed simply to ask the insured to explain its method of ensuring compliance, thereby deferring to the insured's judgment.

The insurance policies made no mention of incentives for compliance. Although the policies mentioned the possibility of penalties and damages, such references were largely symbolic. The insurer in almost every circumstance agreed to cover all fines, penalties, costs, or damages as a result of a breach unless they resulted from criminal conduct or were not allowed to cover these costs by law. Only one policy stated that the insurer would not cover breaches or a failure to comply with the law deemed to have been done willfully or knowingly.

In sum, insurance policies make weak, veiled references to privacy law and compliance. Such policies also do not provide incentives for compliance or suggest a focus or connection to privacy law standards and regulations in ways that might cause an insured to alter their cybersecurity approach for fear that coverage will be denied. Thus, insurance policy language is not a vector for promoting or nudging more proactive cybersecurity behavior by insureds.

THE SOCIAL CONSTRUCTION OF "REASONABLE SECURITY MEASURES" IN PRIVACY LAWS

The lack of clarity in insurance policy language concerning the responsibilities of the insured to comply with privacy laws is coupled with the fragmented state and federal privacy law standards in the United States. When laws regulating organizations are ambiguous or vague, it leaves space for organizations to respond in ways that are often shaped by managerial and risk values. This ambiguity in privacy laws is especially amplified by the dearth of published court cases on what compliance means. As one privacy lawyer noted, "Courts aren't doing anything because these issues aren't getting to them [due to settlement]" (privacy lawyer and data privacy adviser, interview 24, July 31, 2019). Because of such uncertainty, insurance field actors noted, most cases settle prior to trial, thereby limiting the level of guidance such cases could provide to other organizations. In these situations, it is insurers, in partnership with managed- and information security companies, that frame what compliance means for organizations tasked with complying with such laws and regulations.

The best illustration of how cyber insurers and affiliated entities assist in constructing the meaning of compliance is the case of what "reasonable security measures" means in various statutes. Other than in health care and finance, Congress has not clarified what constitutes *reasonable* cybersecurity measures. The Federal Trade Commission (FTC) establishes appropriate standards for financial institutions to secure the confidentiality of customer records and information and protect against unauthorized access. Although the FTC does not have an explicit definition of reasonable security practices, it has implied in various cases that reasonably designed programs are those that, at a minimum, "contain administrative, technical, and physical safeguards appropriate to" the organization's size and sophistication, the "sensitivity of the personal information collected from or about consumers," "identify internal and external" security risks through an assessment process, "design and implement" safeguards to control risks, and "evaluate and adjust" the program as testing and monitoring takes place (Shackelford, Boustead, and Makridis 2022, 99). These broad-based categories force courts, which often lack technical expertise, to arbitrate complex cases and determine what is a reasonable cybersecurity practice. Shackelford and colleagues (2022) examined reasonable security measures across state and federal jurisdictions and suggest that, absent clear standards, companies underinvest and seek to avoid or evade guidance and that the FTC ultimately will not be able to enforce a standard that is constantly evolving.

In the virtual absence of a federal definition of reasonable security measures, states have filled the void by passing a series of privacy-related laws encouraging organizations to institute reasonable security measures. California has long been considered a leader in cybersecurity and data privacy legislation. In 2002, it was the first state to enact a data security breach notification law, Senate Bill (SB) 1386, requiring organizations to inform consumers of a data breach. In 2018, California passed the California Consumer Privacy Act (CCPA) (Cal. Civil Code §§ 1798.100–1798.199.100). Since January 1, 2020, this law has provided California residents more control over their personal information. California residents have the right to notice, access, opt out (or opt in), and non-discrimination. Although the CCPA grants residents a private right of action, it limits its exercise "to only those instances where the underlying business fails to maintain 'reasonable' security." (Stockburger 2021). The CCPA does *not* define reasonable. During the same period, California also enacted the California Internet of Things (IoT) Security Act (California Senate Bill 327), which set a new benchmark requiring all connected devices to have "reasonable" security features appropriate to the protection of the device and information it collects (Cal. Civil Code §§ 1897.91.04). As one analyst has noted, the California IoT Security Law requires "any manufacturer of a device that connects 'directly or indirectly' to the internet [to] equip it with 'reasonable' security features, designed to prevent unauthorized access, modification, or information disclosure" (Robertson 2018). Because of the lack of clear definition, the California attorney general's office recommended that organizations use cybersecurity best practices such as multi-factor authentication and strong encryption in addition to implementing "all the controls that apply to an organization's environment as set forth in the Center for Internet Security's Critical

Security Controls" (Stockburger 2021). Other states have followed California's lead in an effort to protect consumer privacy and device security, with many states requiring organizations to take steps to protect consumer information. However, the definition of reasonable security measures remains vague and ambiguous and leaves tremendous opportunity for organizations— and, in particular, insurers acting as de facto regulators—to define what such security measures look like on the ground.

My interviews with cyber insurance field actors confirm two things: (1) those involved in the cyber field believe "reasonable security measures" is not well defined in statutes; and (2) "reasonable security" is socially constructed by cyber insurers, managed security professionals, privacy lawyers, and other consultants operating in the cybersecurity area. Although most believed that HIPAA and the Gramm-Leach-Bliley Act offer some guidelines or information on what constitutes a reasonable security measure by an organization, most believe privacy laws are not clear, provide little guidance, and as one lawyer noted, "purposely leave it vague" because the circumstances vary from case to case (insurance attorney and former chief information security officer, Interview 20). In this situation, organizations are not avoiding or ignoring privacy laws but instead turning to cyber insurers and other consultants to construct what reasonable security measures mean on the ground. Reasonable security measures in the cyber context is what the managed security consultants and other experts say it is: "We work with our specific security consultants on what is becoming the standard of care," as one privacy lawyer and data privacy adviser said (interview 21, July 25, 2019). The attorney, who worked with the insurance industry, added, "Reasonableness is established by the standard of care. You're either within the standard of care or you fall below the standard of care, and that's established by essentially industry practice." In other words, what is considered reasonable is based on the standard of care, and the standard of care is shaped and influenced by private organizations and the cyber insurers acting as de facto risk managers and regulators.

MULTI-FACTOR AUTHENTICATION, AN ORGANIZATION-DRIVEN REASONABLE SECURITY MEASURE

Multi-factor authentication (MFA) in the health care context provides another example of how the cyber insurance field and affiliated entities are constructing the meaning of compliance and driving what is considered compliant behavior by organizations subject to laws and regulations. MFA is used primarily to provide an additional layer of defense and make it more difficult for an unauthorized person to gain access to a network or database by requiring the user to submit an authentication factor in addition to their username and password. MFA helps decrease the chance of automated attacks and identity theft, account spoofing, and phishing. The banking and finance industry has long used MFA technology. In addition to MFA, any organization that processes and stores card payment information with the use of ATMs also has to comply with payment card industry data security standards (PCI DSSs) and provide MFA to ensure their security. US law enforcement agencies that use information from the Criminal Justice Information Services Division of the FBI require MFA to access the National Crime Information Center.

Other industries urge tight security controls but do not require MFA. For example, the Sarbanes-Oxley Act of 2002 does not explicitly state that MFA is a compliance requirement but does call for strict internal controls on financial information.

The Gramm-Leach-Bliley Act does not mandate MFA but does require businesses to create and follow appropriate measures to safeguard their customers' financial information. Under HIPAA, health care organizations need to put measures in place to enforce password security. Although HIPAA does not require MFA, organizations are supposed to maintain reliable password security practices.

MFA in health care organizations has come to be seen as evidence of compliant organization behavior. For example, in January 2015, Anthem Blue Cross and Blue Shield announced that the personal information of approximately 79 million former and current policyholders nationwide had been stolen in a cyberattack of the company's IT system. Law firms that affiliate with cyber insurers began emphasizing the need to move to MFA, even though MFA was not required by law at the time. Health care organizations responded by installing MFA. Eventually, these same privacy lawyers noticed that state attorney generals' (AGs') offices began to expect MFA as a reasonable security measure among health care organizations complying with HIPAA. Though not expressly stated in HIPAA, MFA is currently a baseline measure of compliance with HIPAA requirements, as one privacy lawyer explained:

> We helped a couple of other Blue Cross Blue Shield plans throughout the country with multimillion persons being impacted by [the Anthem breach]. And health care institutions, you guys better get up to snuff and get multifactor in place, or you're going to be behind the game. Now fast-forward four years later: we see regulators now saying—state AGs offices, departments of insurance, and the office of civil rights—now are focused on MFA. Did you consider it on your risk assessment? Did you do something about it? Do you have it there? You know, this kind of thing. So it's what I tell my clients now, is it has become the standard of care. (privacy lawyer and data privacy adviser, interview 21)

In this instance, compliance and reasonable security measures are shaped not by formal legal mandates but by organizations and affiliated entities advising organizations, such as insurers, managed security companies, and law firms. This is particularly important in the HIPAA context since few cases ultimately go to trial and those that do are looking to the parties to establish what constitutes reasonable behavior: "It's sort of the Wild West when it comes to having both the litigants and judges having to decide what role HIPAA is going to play in the context of litigation" (privacy lawyer and data privacy advisor, interview 24). Regardless of whether it is required by law or not, many organizations, especially large ones, encourage MFA as a best practice.

To be clear, developing compliance standards based on recommendations from insurance and managed security officials may very well be the most effective approach to solving a particular problem. However, these security measures—as articulated by cyber insurers and privacy lawyers—are often based on what other organizations are currently doing, without careful evaluation of whether any of the security measures work. One insurance attorney described the sequence: "[A] consultant draws up a report, benchmarks our environment against what the consultant purports others in the industry to be doing, identifies any major gaps, and then the parties move on, feeling that they've followed a process that was designed to identify any major gaps against what is the industry standard according to the consultant" (insurance attorney and former chief information security officer, interview 20). A cybersecurity and privacy lawyer noted that when evaluating the standard of care in the health care context, she examines "what is everybody else doing that's raising the standard of care" (privacy lawyer and data privacy adviser, interview 21), and a risk manager noted, "I've got to assume there's a lot of other companies doing it too, so it makes you really want to move forward" (risk manager and director of information technology, interview 5, June 18, 2019).

Insurance industry officials and affiliated entities are, therefore, creating the standard of care. Security measures that depend heavily on technology are seen as the legitimate institutionalized response, much as developing employer policies and procedures are seen as a legitimate response to antidiscrimination laws and are isomorphically replicated by other similarly situated organizations (Edelman 2016). Thus, although states have suggested that organizations take "reasonable security measures" to protect data privacy and security, they have largely left what that term means undefined. Cyber insurers and affiliated entities are influencing what those measures actually look like on the ground and establishing a de facto standard of care. To the extent such security practices merely exude legitimacy but really do not provide meaningful protection of consumer data, deference by public legal institutions only exacerbates the problem and does not lead to greater cybersecurity.

GOVERNMENT SAFE HARBORS AS TOOLS FOR COMPLIANCE

Some states are attempting to provide safe harbors that reward organizations by reducing liability in the event of a breach if they develop and invest in recognized cybersecurity standards and frameworks, such as the National Institute for Standards and Technology (NIST) Cybersecurity Framework.

A small group of states have enacted legislation to incentivize businesses to develop and implement data security standards. For example, the Ohio Data Protection Act (DPA) provides cyber safe harbors from liability for organizations that comply with one of five security standards (such as NIST) (Kersten 2019). To be eligible for the safe harbor in Ohio, a covered entity must "create, maintain, and comply" with a written cybersecurity program that "reasonably conforms" with one of the five preapproved security standards. The entity bears the burden of proving that its program satisfies these requirements. On one hand, Ohio's law takes a step in the right direction by requiring organizations to meet one of five well-regarded security standards. On the other hand, it is an open question as to how a regulator would monitor whether the organization is truly compliant and how much deference regulators will give to the organization's proclamations of compliance. One of the leading cybersecurity "breach coach" attorneys that works on behalf of insurers with organizations noted that how organizations establish compliance with this law remains vague: "It's interesting because you have to wonder how will a regulator be able to opine that you are permitted to take advantage of the safe harbor, without looking in detail or at least receiving some detail about the security that you have in place" (data privacy lawyer, interview 30, September 9, 2019). Somewhat relatedly, any government inquiry could open the door to enhanced regulatory investigations into the organization that is not legally required, as the breach coach explained:

> They [the state agencies] have broad enforcement powers to ask questions and they may ask questions that take them down another rabbit hole that you otherwise wouldn't have opened the door [to] if you hadn't taken the position that this safe harbor applies to you. So I think it's a step in the right direction, but I think there needs to be eyes wide open, an eyes-wide-open approach, when you are going to argue that it applies to you, because a regulator may start asking questions. And one of the things that regulators are always interested in when we do investigations and response is, well what did you look at? Do you have a forensic investigation report? We want to see it. And the report may have *F*s on that report card. (data privacy lawyer, interview 30)

Thus, although the Ohio DPA and other similar laws in other states are possibly moving in the right direction, there needs to be more transparency concerning the type of technology tools insurers are actively using and more scrutiny by state regulators of the accuracy and reliability of these tools.

CYBER INSURER COMPLIANCE RECOMMENDATIONS FOCUS ON AVOIDING LITIGATION, NOT FOSTERING A CYBERSECURE ENVIRONMENT

Cyber insurers focus on reasonable security measures in various laws, but it is typically with an eye toward avoiding a lawsuit rather than fostering a safer cybersecurity environment (Baker and Shortland 2022b). In this respect, cyber insurers follow a playbook familiar to employment practice liability insurers (Talesh 2015a). After emphasizing the uncertain legal risk that organizations face, insurers inflate the threat of a cybersecurity incident and the need for risk reduction in order to entice organizations to purchase cyber insurance. As one underwriter put it, "I think they're all in the business such as our marketing folks, including me, in scaring the shit of our companies so that they buy insurance. Which is ultimately our task. That's what we do. That's what all these seminars do, right?" (underwriter, interview 2, June 17, 2019). My interviews suggest, consistent with prior empirical research of employers and manufacturers, that insurer-sponsored training appears largely symbolic and is geared to signaling responsiveness on the part of the organization without really making the organization more cybersecure. One insurance broker summarized the ineffectiveness of cyber insurer–sponsored trainings and other pre- and postbreach services: "It's to tick the box. It's to say that you did it. So again, on an [insurance] application, you can tick the box to say, yes, we provide employee training. It's no different than human resources doing sexual harassment training and all of these other things. You've got too many employees that just aren't incentivized to care" (broker, interview 25). In response to the CCPA, insurance companies have been driving the compliance process with recommendations and trying to facilitate changes, as an insurer explained:

> Here's a nice, shiny fourteen-page brochure that lays out what you need to do. We have this in place. Here's step one. Let's get the instant response plan done. Let's get the policies and procedures done. Let's test them. Let's do a tabletop. Let's go ahead and get some scans of your system and a pen test and figure out where your strong security lies. And we can take these steps. You have a 30-day period to cure in California under the CCPA, right? If you have a breach within that 30 days, if you can come back and say, okay, we figured out what it was and remediated it. (insurer and big data provider, interview 31)

Insurers and lawyers involved with data privacy repeatedly stress that they urge organizations to make at least cursory changes to satisfy the reasonableness standard in various privacy laws and to protect themselves from regulatory fines and lawsuits. One lawyer said he thought it sufficient "just to show that you put a reasonable process in place to avoid, where you reasonably could, cyber risk, and then to have a process in place for responding to an event, and have a process in place for training and education and reporting of risks to an executive level ... [to] protect from [law]suit, or you know, regulatory investigation" (insurance attorney and former chief information security officer, interview 20). Adopting policies and procedures that reflect at least a symbolic gesture toward a compliant environment will, according to one wholesale broker and underwriter, help "elevate the security posture to what a regulator would deem as reasonable" (interview 23). Privacy law and compliance are seen as posing risk, and risk is neutralized by an emphasis and reliance on insurer risk management guidance that ultimately focuses on avoiding litigation and regulatory interventions, as opposed to fostering a cybersecure environment.

Equally important is the fact that most insurers either have managed security as part of their menu of services or contract with managed-security companies. Partnering with security firms is a mechanism through which insurers and brokers establish the legitimacy of cyber insurance to prospective buyers, regardless of whether buyers ever use these services. Insurers and brokers emphasized to me the need to offer risk management services regardless of whether anyone uses them. For example: "Brokers ask for it, like 'Hey, tell us not that you just have a policy, tell us what services come with it.' Even if the client doesn't use the services" (forensic security consultant, interview 16). Thus, compliance management as articulated by insurers is as much focused on signaling that a response has occurred and avoiding being sued as it is fostering a cybersecure environment.

STATE AND PRIVATE REGULATORS' DEFERENCE TO CYBER INSURER CONSTRUCTIONS

Previous chapters demonstrate that insurers rely on flawed data when developing cyber risk management and loss prevention policies. Even more troubling, these same flawed data—coupled with insurer constructions of what privacy law compliance means—may be shaping the content and meaning of actual laws and rules intended to regulate cyber insurers (Talesh 2015b). Insurtech companies that blend insurance and managed security are influencing the content and meaning of state, federal, and private regulatory provisions and policies. For example, private rating agencies *and* state regulators are working with the very same information that security providers and insurers use to develop their own rating, risk, and monitoring systems to regulate insurance companies. An insurer highlighted the extent to which private and state regulators rely on insurer data to develop their own regulatory policies:

> We work with carriers. We work with regulators and rating agencies like Standard & Poor's. For example, Standard & Poor's, what they've done is they use some of [our] analytics, and they've embedded them into a report that any companies and users can go buy about themselves. And it will have a variety of things and benchmarks and comparisons. . . .
>
> [W]e've worked with state regulators to come up with frameworks for how they should be evaluating cyber exposures. . . .
>
> And so, a lot of times what we've been doing is trying to couple our analytics with their processes. . . .
>
> [T]he regulators we work with are state insurance regulators or bodies like Lloyd's. So the people that are overseeing the insurance companies and the financial services companies, those are the regulators we're primarily focused on. (insurer and information security provider, interview 32)

Consistent with my new institutional theory of insurance, state and private regulators are looking to and ultimately deferring to insurance and affiliated entities on what privacy law and cybersecurity compliance means on the ground. The National Association of Insurance Commissioners, a quasi-private, quasi-public body that regulates the insurance industry in the United States, also strives to incorporate and listen to insurtech companies on compliance issues, an insurer and information security provider affirmed: "If you went to the NAIC . . . conference, they even had a mini–pitch session for insurance tech companies. So I'd say the regulators are definitely interested and integral to all the innovation you see in the insurance space in general, as well as for cyber" (interview 32).

To the extent these predictive analytic models developed by information security providers are based on inaccurate, unreliable, and incomplete data (as prior chapters suggest), state regulators and private standard-setting organizations are adopting and legitimizing a flawed model developed by insurers into their regulatory framework.

The ineffectiveness of insurers as regulators to date is compounded by the impact of information quality and reliability issues on the actual state and federal regulators themselves. For example, although AI and predictive analytics are being used by cyber insurers, one information security provider that provides the AI tools for insurers indicated that such tools are not being incorporated into the filings with state regulators. Insurers are actively incorporating AI:

> INTERVIEWER: Your sense is that the cyber insurers are actively using AI in ways of evaluating risk and pricing risk?
>
> INSURER AND INFORMATION SECURITY PROVIDER: They're working with us. And they're using our models, but they still have state regulations. So, they're filing their actuarial model. A traditional actuarial model. And according to the regulations and according to the state filings, that's how they have to price the business. But people are working with us to maybe apply some of the outputs of our model and input it into their rating model. (interview 32)

With the way these antiquated regulations are drafted, the insurance companies must include traditional actuarial methodologies in their required reports, regardless of how they actually price and underwrite cyber insurance. Thus, the information security companies are also influencing cyber insurer rating models.

Federal Government Deference to Cyber Insurers' Construction of Compliance

The federal government has also bought into the institutionalized and "rationalized myth" concerning the value of cyber insurers as regulators, without interrogating whether cyber insurers work well as regulators (Edelman Uggen, and Erlanger 1999). In fact, at multiple stages where the federal government has engaged in cybersecurity and privacy law reform, it has consistently turned to cyber insurers as potential agents of change and reform.

Josephine Wolff's (2022) history of cyber insurance notes that as far back as the early 2000s, the framework for managing cybersecurity risks relied on public-private partnerships. In February 2003, the National Strategy to Secure Cyberspace declared the private sector as the "best equipped and structured to respond to an evolving cyber threat" (US DHS 2003). The Department of Homeland Security (DHS), which issued the strategy, noted that cyber insurers offer "a means of transferring risk and providing for business continuity." In 2011, the US Department of Commerce Internet Policy Task Force (2011) averred that cyber insurance is an "effective, market-driven way of increasing cybersecurity."

From 2012 to 2016, the DHS's National Protection and Programs Directorate convened working sessions and roundtables with the insurance industry, government employees, cybersecurity experts, and other stakeholders to discuss ways to make public and private institutions more cybersecure. Using cyber insurance as a tool for encouraging organizations to improve security and loss prevention techniques, thereby reducing the number and severity of cybersecurity incidents, was clearly one of the goals of these meetings. While acknowledging that the cyber insurance market was nascent as compared to other lines of insurance, the DHS report concluded that cyber insurance is vital: "A robust cybersecurity insurance market could help reduce the number of successful cyberattacks by: (1) promoting the adoption of preventative measures in return for more coverage; and (2) encouraging the implementation of best practices by basing premiums on an insured's level of self-protection" (US DHS 2017a). Moreover, the report devoted extensive attention to improving risk management within organizations—the very kinds of services that cyber insurance companies currently offer (US DHS 2014). In March, 2015, Senator Jerry Moran in a Senate subcommittee hearing praised cyber insurance "as a market led approach to help businesses improve their cybersecurity" (*Examining the Evolving Cyber Insurance Marketplace* 2015).

In March 2020, the US Cyberspace Solarium Commission (CSC) issued its final report, which focused heavily on the role of insurance. In particular, the CSC emphasized the role that insurers can play as de facto regulators of cybersecurity issues among organizations. Despite little evidence that cyber insurers operated effectively as regulators, the CSC stated that "a robust and functioning market for insurance products can have the same positive effect on the risk management behavior of firms as do regulatory interventions" (US CSC 2020, 79). Although the CSC acknowledged insurers were not yet living up to this promise, it rationalized the lack of success as a product of not having proper standards and frameworks with which to price risk and the lack of systematized data. The CSC then proceeded—consistent with prior pronouncements by the legislative and executive branches—to emphasize the need to use cyber insurance to promote cybersecurity and to express optimism that it would work well. The CSC report devotes considerable attention to the idea that cyber insurers can incentivize organizational cybersecurity and that the federal government should assist in promoting the expansion of cybersecurity insurance products. In fact, the CSC urged the federal government to work with states and private actors to develop models for and certifications of cyber insurance products, as well as claims adjuster and underwriting training. Mindful that insurance regulation is largely a state practice, the CSC recommended Congress provide DHS funds to create a "federally funded research and development center" that would work collaboratively with insurers, state regulators, and experts in cyber risk management to develop these certifications.

The CSC's proposals continued where the DHS left off in emphasizing the need for continued public-private collaboration on modeling cyber risk. The CSC suggested that Congress establish a Bureau of Cyber Statistics within the Department of Commerce that would collect, process, analyze, and disseminate statistical data on cybersecurity incidents that federal and state governments and the private sector can rely on. The CSC even suggested "placing a cap, via standards or certifications of insurance products, on insurance payouts for incidents that involve unpatched systems" (US CSC 2020, 77). Finally, the CSC recommended that the US government protect the cyber insurance industry by developing a "government reinsurance program to cover catastrophic cyber events," modeled on a similar program created by the Terrorism Risk Insurance Act. The history of cyber insurance is filled with repeated pronouncements by federal legislative and executive officials that offer unequivocal support for the idea that cyber insurers can play a reliable regulatory function. Thus, even in 2020, the CSC deferred to cyber insurers as de facto regulators that should be harnessed and cultivated, even though little to no empirical evidence suggested that cyber insurers effectively improve organizational behavior in preventing cybersecurity incidents. Consistent with new institutional theories of insurance, federal and state policymakers appear to have adopted the logic of the insurance industry that cyber insurance provides valuable regulatory value and appear committed to looking to insurers as drivers of organizational compliance.

European Deference to Cyber Insurance Risk Management Practices

European countries appear to follow the US government's lead in giving cyber insurers considerable regulatory weight. The legitimacy of cyber insurance as a driver of cybersecurity compliance is multiplied by the fact that many European countries have also sought ways to expand the cyber insurance model. Josephine Wolff (2022) notes that, rather than follow insurance industry association recommendations for more stringent and standardized reporting requirements of the General Data Protection Regulation and NIST directive, European regulators sought guidance from US regulators and cybersecurity experts, who continuously call for expanding the role of cyber insurance as a driver of organizational compliance: "Rather than trying to tailor a cyber insurance model that suited their own regulations, European policymakers kept looking to the United States to figure out how to stabilize and grow their cyber insurance market to little avail" (199). Similar to the US government, European governments seem to approve of cyber insurers as regulatory actors, despite little evidence of success.

CONCLUSION

The new institutional theory of insurance introduced in this book explains how cyber insurers influence and shape cybersecurity compliance among businesses. In addition to weak and fragmented privacy laws, there is a dearth of court cases to provide guidance to organizations as to what cybersecurity compliance means on the ground. In response to ambiguous and fragmented privacy laws and cybersecurity regulations and organizations' undercompliance and underpreparedness for data breach events, insurance companies have partnered with managed security companies in offering pre- and postbreach services aimed at curbing cybersecurity incidents. In turn, these insurance and managed-security companies, working together, have filled in this space and constructed what compliance means on the ground.

Technological innovation has been a key part of the cyber insurance story. Although technology and big data offer some promise, the intersection of insurance and technology is problematic. Big data in this sector is limited, inaccurate, and misleading. Insurers use technology and security tools to scan and evaluate the cyber hygiene of a prospective insured but do not make improving the organization's cybersecurity posture a prerequisite to obtaining coverage. Moreover, insurers are fighting aggressively for market share. Because of a desire to secure as many insureds as possible, insurers' ability to change or influence insured behavior is weakened. Insureds that do have strong security protocols do not necessarily reap the benefits of such good behavior in the form of lower premiums. Although insurance companies offer security programs and tools that, in theory, could help an insured protect itself against being breached, most insureds do not take advantage of these prebreach services, even when offered free of charge.

Thus, my research indicates that, at least for now, cyber insurers are not significantly improving the cybersecurity posture of most insureds. And once insurance is issued, most insurers do not monitor the insured's cyber hygiene. Even though insurers tout their role as de facto regulators of organizational behavior, their impact so far appears to be marginal in terms of heightening the insured's cybersecurity readiness. Cyber insurers are not reducing a policyholder's potential exposure to cybersecurity breaches. There is not much evidence that cyber insurers' regulatory interventions work. In fact, insurance-as-regulator responses are often more focused on avoiding litigation and regulatory fines than on making organizations more cybersecure. Even more concerning is the fact that private industry and federal and state lawmakers and regulators continue to defer to the insurance industry as a viable actor assisting organizations in complying with privacy laws and protecting against cybersecurity threats. This deference bubbles up even into private, federal, and state standards, regulations, and laws that allow insurers tremendous space in which to influence and shape cybersecurity policy in society. Insurance companies and affiliated entities are influencing what privacy law and cybersecurity compliance means on the ground. The following chapter offers a series of proposals that policymakers should consider concerning how the government and private industry can address the various problems with insurers acting as regulators.

PART III

Policy Reforms
and Pathways Forward

CHAPTER SEVEN

What Can Be Done?

Policy Reforms and Pathways Forward
for Cyber Insurers and Governments

If insurance companies are symbolic regulators, what is the path forward? Can cyber insurers act as regulators in a substantive way? What role, if any, should the government take? What role and responsibility should organizations take in attempting to become more cybersecure? If co-regulation and public-private partnerships constitute the regulatory regime we live under, how do we calibrate the relationship between government, organizations, and the insurance industry in ways that meaningfully adhere to privacy laws and protect consumers' personal information? These questions are a natural outgrowth of the empirical findings presented in the previous chapters. This chapter pivots toward rethinking cybersecurity policy and the role for government, the insurance industry, and private organizations that look to become more cybersecure. My recommendations are based in part on interviews with leading insurance companies, brokers, data scientists, lawyers, risk managers, big data providers, and forensics specialists. Thus, like the others, this prescriptive chapter has benefited from my talking to experts involved in cybersecurity, privacy law, and insurance. It is also based on analysis undertaken by the government, including the National Cybersecurity Strategy issued by the White House in 2023 and the US Cyberspace Solarium Commission report issued in 2020. My recommendations seek to articulate an effective cybersecurity strategy while also accounting for the role that insurance companies can play. The suggestions offered in this chapter are not a cure-all but can be thought of as forming an approach geared to achieving more substantive compliance among organizations tasked with cybersecurity challenges. I also calibrate the regulatory balance between insurers, the government, and private organizations. The solutions, therefore, are necessarily multidimensional and involve multiple stakeholders. Insurers, governments, and private organizations all have a role to play in improving the cyber hygiene of society. This chapter lays out a way forward. I start with how insurance companies can act as more effective regulators of policyholder cyber health. Next, I recommend some structural reforms in society. I end with recommendations for how the federal government can play a more effective role as regulator, including providing a federally funded government backstop for potential catastrophic risks that insurance companies insure.

HOW CYBER INSURANCE COMPANIES CAN BECOME BETTER REGULATORS

Nothing in this book should be read as arguing that cyber insurers cannot play a meaningful role in improving their insureds' cybersecurity posture and, eventually, that of society as a whole. Big data, AI, and new technologies are revolutionizing the delivery and practice of insurance, and there is no turning back. Despite the challenges articulated in this book, insurtech can, in theory, be a part of the solution and help increase organizations' cybersecurity and insurers' ability to play a positive regulatory role in society. The lessons from the new institutional theory of insurance presented in this book provide guidance on how the insurance industry can be substantive as opposed to symbolic regulators.

At least two fundamental facts must change. First, the government should not defer to insurers or assume they are playing or can play a regulatory role without demonstrated evidence. Too often public legal institutions defer to institutionalized and normalized practices as evidence of an organization's compliance without interrogating whether such practices lead to improved compliance and fidelity to legal regulations. Organizational sociologists and political scientists have taught us this lesson over and over. In this case, insurers play a critical intermediary role between the goals of privacy laws and organizations' effectuation of cybersecurity in their environments. But insurers cannot simply tout their risk management role and governments cannot just accept their putative interventions as legitimate.

Second, insurers are more likely to play an effective role as quasi-regulators if they address some of the problems identified in this book and alter how cyber insurance and the accompanying services are delivered. To be clear, I am not arguing that an insurance-company-as-regulator model will necessarily work. Rather, if it is going to work, insurers will need to address some of the problems I identify earlier. Specifically, insurance companies should (1) engage in continuous evaluation and underwriting throughout the life of cyber insurance policies, (2) make insurance premium pricing contingent on reliable evidence of good cybersecurity practices (i.e., reward good behavior with reduced premiums), (3) when necessary, require prospective insureds to make changes to improve their cybersecurity posture as a prerequisite to issuing insurance, and (4) engage in dynamic risk management and loss control throughout the policy period to reduce insureds' risk of loss. These are some of the biggest problems identified in this multimethod study.

The potential benefits to a widespread adoption of such recommendations are not theoretical. Some insurance companies are trying to integrate some of these practices into the ways they deliver insurance. Coalition Inc., Boxx Insurance, and At-Bay are three companies that, unlike traditional insurance companies, contract with third-party vendors to provide background security analysis of prospective insureds, embed technology and security in the insurance company itself (full integration), and incorporate some of what I recommend here with modest success. Founded in the past decade by individuals with security and technology backgrounds, these fully integrated insurtech companies combine comprehensive insurance and proactive cybersecurity tools to underwrite exposure and help businesses manage and mitigate cyber risk. One insurance broker who dealt directly with Coalition described how they operate:

> They basically are a tech company with some insurance people involved. So, for Swiss Re, there is a gentleman that used to be the head of Aon's international privacy security liability practice [and who] helped form this startup. And they had venture capital to help form this startup. And they hired tech people to evaluate the risk using these external scans. Now, they feel very confident about the scans that they're doing. And they're using it to basically decide, "Yay or nay, are we going to write this risk?" and then price it based upon the controls that they see. (insurance broker, interview 8)

Insurtech companies are often financed by leading global insurers because one cannot sell insurance without being a licensed insurance company. Coalition is supported by Swiss Re Corporate

Solutions, Lloyd's of London, and Argo Group (Coalition 2020). At-Bay is supported by Munich Re (At-Bay n.d.; Wood 2020).[1] These insurtech companies primarily focus on offering insurance to small and medium-sized companies. They are, however, expanding and now offer insurance in all fifty states. Recognizing that cyber threats constantly evolve, these companies focus on using security and technology to evaluate the cyber hygiene of the company and issue a quote within three to five minutes of receiving a company's information. On receiving basic information filled out online, these companies rely on technical and domain expertise and have built proprietary and automated tools that conduct external scans of the dark web, internet, and relevant IP addresses. Once they identify the risks and assign a risk score, they use an automated machine that relies on predictive analytics and modeling to issue an insurance quote within particular parameters. If the scan does not trigger any flags or warnings, a quote is generated. If the scan does trigger a warning, the application is referred to an underwriter to make a final determination. At-Bay asserts that its model relies on asset discovery and automation:

> We're collecting information ourselves by scanning the company. We also collect threat intelligence from a bunch of resources out there. Honestly, there are two steps to it. There's the asset discovery part. The company doesn't give you a list of all of their machines and all of their IP and all of their inventory. You kind of have to discover that yourself. So the first part is discovering their assets, and the second part is understanding to what extent those assets or configurations are vulnerable to attacks. That's the first thing that we do that is very different. And then all that information flows into a machine that makes all of its decisions by itself. So we've removed the human from the underwriting decision process unless there's either a red flag or the risk is big. [T]here are parameters. (insurer and forensic expert, interview 38)

Whereas traditional insurers measure a company's risk based on its past behavior, these firms measure the company's risk based on what they can find on the web and dark web and, in doing so, analyze the company's future risk. As the same interviewee explained: "Instead of underwriting for last year's risks, can you underwrite for this year's risks? And how do you do that if those risks keep on changing? The answer is real-time underwriting and real-time risk management" (interview 38).

Continuous Underwriting and Dynamic Risk Monitoring throughout the Policy's Life Span

According to the traditional model, once the insured agrees to an insurance contract, its coverage is locked in for one year regardless of whether the risk changes. But fully integrated insurtech companies instead conduct continuous underwriting and "a more involved, active risk management and monitoring of the security of [their] insureds throughout the year" (insurer and forensic expert, interview 38). Whereas most mainstream cyber insurers offer prebreach services that policyholders use only 10 percent of the time, fully integrated insurtech companies embed prebreach monitoring security features into the insurance itself and significantly increase adoption by insureds. If they detect that a threat is imminent, they alert the company and work with its personnel to avert the threat. Such insurers offer risk transfer and risk management simultaneously.

Fully integrated insurtech companies also take the distinctive step of scanning and evaluating the cyber hygiene of the insured throughout the length of the insurance policy. This continuous underwriting and risk management sets these companies apart in the cyber context and seems to work as a more robust and effective form of regulatory nudge to the insured to improve its cyber hygiene. As the expert I spoke with described the procedure:

> The last part is, once a company is in our portfolio, we use the exact same underwriting engine that we've used to provide a quote in the beginning of the policy period. We run that engine basically once a month on every one of our policyholders.
>
> And if that engine now shoots up an alert, then we have a security team who would reach out to the insured and say basically, "Look, we already sold you a policy. We're not trying to get any more money from you. We're on the hook to pay most of it. But you're also on the hook. We're seeing this new attack come in, and we can see that you're vulnerable. Here are the details of specifically what the attack is. Here's your specific machine that's vulnerable. Our team is here at your disposal to help you fix it."
>
> And just to give you a few examples, over the last couple months, . . . [w]e ha[d] almost two dozen companies that had a Citrix installation that was vulnerable to a ransomware campaign that was exploiting that vulnerability. . . . We had a Palo Alto Networks issue that we helped solve. We helped solve RDP [remote desktop protocol] ports issues with, whatever, BlueKeep and some of the other issues that happen with RDP.
>
> [W]e're just kind of going one by one. And whenever there's a new alert or a new critical vulnerability, it flows from the research team to the model. And then the model runs on all of our portfolio [of clients] and spits out alerts. And then the security team just helps companies fix the issue. (insurer and forensic expert, interview 38)

The continuous underwriting evaluation leads to greater likelihood that insurers will request loss control interventions and policyholders will implement them, because the underwriting process is not merely a snapshot in time. Although developing a reliable rating model may be challenging for insurers who would like to build in proper reserves, one could imagine that insurers would charge a minimum premium but that policyholders would be motivated to drive toward reducing their costs and consequently improving their cyber hygiene.

Because cyber attacks are constantly evolving, a greater focus is needed on loss and risk control on the part of cyber insurance buyers (especially SMEs) throughout the life of the insurance policy. Real-time monitoring and checking for threat vectors increases the likelihood that the insured will maintain a healthy cybersecurity environment. Insurtech companies make using their risk management services a requirement under the policy and thus ensure their clients actually use the tools. As the insurtech company official noted, "Postbind prebreach [is] built into everything we do" (insurer and forensic expert, interview 38). A vulnerability test or scan that evaluates a company's cybersecurity hygiene is instructive, but there needs to be more ongoing monitoring the other 364 days of the year, given constantly changing threat vectors.

Premium Pricing Tied to the Insured's Loss Control

Unlike other insurers, some insurtech companies tie the premium to existing risk and loss control measures and reward the insured with lower premiums for heightened security:

> INTERVIEWER: Have companies said, "Sure, I will make these security changes that you suggest. And please give me the improved price." Has that experience occurred?
>
> INTERVIEWEE: Yes, it happens quite often. It happens ever more often. . . . [F]or example, the other recommendation that we ask them to do is, we ask them to add a security e-mail gateway like a Barracuda or a Mimecast or a Proofpoint. And when they do that, we give them significantly broader coverage. We have these every day. We have a few coming back and saying, "We've

added something. We've improved something. We changed our configuration. Can we please get the better terms?" And by the way, most of the time, they do it before they buy the insurance. So they get the first quote from us. They make the fixes. We improve the offer, and then they bind the insurance. (insurer and forensic expert, interview 38)

Rewarding the insured for good behavior builds on a basic concept: "The better the scan comes out, the better your premium will be" (insurance underwriter, interview 1). Despite the soft market where insurers are trying to acquire as much business as possible and are resistant to nudging insureds toward making changes to their cybersecurity posture, fully integrated insurtech companies suggest such an approach is possible.[2] In theory, this makes insureds safer, decreases the chances that the consumer data that those organizations maintain will be exposed, and allows insurers to play a more substantive, less symbolic regulatory role, ultimately to the benefit of society overall.

Others in the insurance industry whom I spoke with indicated that reducing premiums for policyholders with stronger loss control measures in place was fundamental to strengthening insurers' regulatory position, even for insurance companies that are not pure insurtech companies. As one insurance broker noted, "I think when you have a company that goes the extra mile and is doing all those extra things, they are much less likely to have a claim. And so, they should be getting less—they should be charged less. Most of these policies aren't filed, with filed rates. A lot of them are kind of written on a non-admitted basis. They have a little more flexibility in how they price things" (broker, interview A9, June 26, 2019).

The overwhelming majority of industry experts whom I interviewed also thought the insurance application process outdated and not useful for cybersecurity issues. In particular, the crude, check-the-box cyber insurance application does not prompt prospective insurance buyers to clearly and fully articulate their cybersecurity posture. Other insurers are relying on scans and security tools to evaluate the buyer's profile. Each approach comes with challenges. The checkbox application does not allow for nuance, while the pure scan approach does not allow for much dialogue with the prospective buyer. A hybrid approach would allow the insurance application to provide a drop-down menu to more fully flesh out the company's cybersecurity profile. Moreover, companies relying purely on security scans would be well served to add another layer that also accounts for the unique profile of a particular buyer of insurance. "I think," the broker told me, "moving forward, what we need to do is have a hybrid model where you have the client provide some of their own input, and then you also have an external scan of their system, so that you're covering all of your bases" (broker, interview A9). Drop-down menus and subquestions would allow the prospective buyer to describe the security controls they possess and would potentially lead to more accurate pricing.

Requiring Changes to an Insured's Cyber Hygiene

Unlike the majority of traditional insurance companies whose managers I interviewed, the fully integrated insurtech companies are not afraid to require an insured to make changes as a prerequisite to coverage. For example, remote desktop protocol (RDP) ports account for almost 25 percent of the ransomware losses insurers paid out on in 2018 and 2019. For that reason, At-Bay requires that insureds have "closed" RDP ports to reduce the chance of hacker malfeasance. An At-Bay forensic expert indicated that it currently has 0 percent of open RDP ports among its insureds, "because when you come to us and ask for insurance, if you have an open RDP port, we will say no, unless you fix it" (insurer and forensic expert, interview 38). This regulatory nudge by the insurer should result in fewer claims for the insurer, fewer breaches for the insured (often a business), and reduced harm to consumers: "Our peers experience on average about 25 percent of their losses coming from RDP ports. For us, in 2018 and 2019 it was zero percent. And our losses have been lower, and our frequency is less than half that of the industry" (interview 38). During COVID-19, as the vast majority of corporate employees worked remotely from home, insurtech companies noticed via their monitoring that a number of companies opened up unprotected RDP ports:

> I would say about half of them fixed it within 24 hours. And then probably 20 percent more, it took a week to two weeks to fix it. A few of them tried to argue why it's not an issue. With most of them we were able to figure it out. And some of them are either refusing or did not answer the phone. But that was the minority. So, yeah, we do have maybe three of them open right now, which we're frustrated by. Because it happened in the middle of the policy, we're not going to pull the policy away, but we haven't given up on helping them fix it. We do think it matters. (interview 38)

The company notified the businesses of the vulnerability and instructed them on how to fix it. When engaged in ongoing monitoring and risk management of their insureds, insurers can avert risks that others in the cyber insurance ecosystem could not.

Onboarding Prebreach Services upon Issuing Insurance

Although prebreach services do include some tools that can help make an organization more cybersecure, policyholders are not using them. As previous chapters show, cyber insurers are simply using these services as a marketing tool. Some experts whom I spoke with suggested that insurers should be more diligent in requiring policyholders to use the prebreach services as a basis for continued coverage, or should even assist in the onboarding of such services. Not much is gained by touting prebreach services if no one really uses them other than for the symbolic, marketing benefits.

To be clear, fully integrated insurtech models are not foolproof. I am not endorsing any particular insurance provider or suggesting fully integrated insurtech models are the better way of delivering cyber insurance. However, given the limited government oversight and the need to motivate insurers to regulate more effectively, the continuous underwriting and risk management approaches that fully integrated insurtech companies deploy throughout the policy period may address some of the challenges highlighted in earlier chapters and more appropriately align the incentives between insurers and insureds. Industry experts interviewed for this book indicated that insurtech's emphasis on real-time underwriting and risk management reflects the future of insurance: "They're kind of doing real-time underwriting," an underwriter and risk manager noted. "Once [a client] become[s] an insured, then they take them under their wing, and they protect them as much as they can. . . . [This is] the future of cyber insurance. . . . [I]t's going to be managed security services with insurance attached to it. I really believe that's what's going to happen" (interview 12).

If fully integrated insurtech models are successful, insurers may come to better manage and reduce uncertainty in the cyber market and improve their position as de facto regulators of the insured's cybersecurity.[3] As one industry leader put it, "Nothing we do is better than anything else that is out there already in the security industry. The one thing that we're doing which is really difficult is integrating it. Like actually injecting it into the DNA of the insurance company—not putting it as a patch on top" (insurer and forensics expert, interview 38). I view these new approaches, at minimum, as trying to address some of the deficiencies that I identify earlier. And to be even clearer, traditional insurance companies could alter their approach (and some have) and engage in continuous underwriting and risk monitoring throughout the life of the policy and reward good cyber hygiene with reduced premiums.

The larger point is that insurance companies can do more to differentiate and reward policyholders that engage in best practices. Assuming necessary protections are put in place, especially as information is migrating, many insurance experts suggested cloud-based services should be encouraged if not required for organizations. Although not foolproof, cloud storage often offers greater protection against cyberattacks than other options because such services keep infrastructure security up-to-date, patch vulnerabilities quickly, and are backed up regularly. Moreover, the monitoring for suspicious activity is continuous. As one cyber engineer stated: "Our best bet would be to use the cloud service provider as much as possible. They are going to protect our data better. So that is one thing you could do to improve the security. Otherwise, we are looking at millions of dollars to be spent building our own security. That would be a Herculean task, and probably looking at four or five cybersecurity engineers to work around the clock" (cyber engineer, interview A3, May 8, 2019).

A cloud-based approach may not be feasible for all organizations depending on their size and the scope of data and information, but certainly, large organizations should be strongly encouraged to use cloud-based storage. Organizations should also be encouraged and rewarded for "sandboxing," or isolating incoming e-mails and browser activity to confirm that they are safe before the end user can open the e-mail and respond. In other words, an employee cannot access an email from outside the company until it is quickly tested and run through a cyber filter. Although training and education are crucial (as the following section points out), services such as these help bolster cybersecurity whenever inevitable mistakes occur. "Most of the solutions are 'let's train the employees,'" a forensic security consultant said. "But that only can take you so far. . . . Like, you can lock the whole environment down. There's a really cool company out there called App River that basically lets you sandbox your email client and your browser. So you can't click on something if you're an employee, until the CIO releases it, as an example" (interview 16).

To the extent such cloud-based protection techniques can be developed in ways that do not lower worker efficiency and cause unnecessary delays, these techniques should be incentivized and potentially rewarded by insurers when evaluating whether and how to price risk.

EDUCATION AND TRAINING — FROM ELEMENTARY SCHOOL TO FOREVER

Organizations play a crucial role in society's cybersecuity health. Human error remains the biggest trigger of cybersecurity incidences. Phishing, ransomware, social engineering, and other schemes all rely on human error often due to carelessness and ignorance. As an insurance field actor mentioned, "Your weakest link is your employees" (broker and former risk manager, interview 6). Cybercriminals and attackers prey on the public's mistake-proneness, leading to cybersecurity incidents for individuals and businesses. For that reason, education and training need to be at the forefront of reforms for both organizations and the government. A complete reimagining of how we train and educate people is needed to avoid cyberinsecurity.

Mandate Cybersecurity Training and Certification
among Employers

First, governments should mandate cybersecurity education, mandate certification for particular industries, and require verification of completion. For example, the Occupational Safety and Health Administration requires that employers conduct private training for workers who face hazards on the job. Cyberattacks are one such on-the-job hazard. A federal "Institute of Cybersecurity" (or an equivalent state agency) could develop training materials, distribute training grants to nonprofit organizations, and even provide training through authorized education centers. This would institutionalize a set of baseline best practices and make employees and employers aware that they must follow them.

Relatedly, insurers in general should mandate that certain standards be maintained as a basis for issuing insurance. If federal and state governments prove unwilling to require cyber hygiene education, insurers should mandate it. Adherence to NIST standards (or an equivalent standard from the Cybersecurity and Infrastructure Security Agency), depending on the type of industry seeking insurance, would likely elevate cyber safety. Regardless of the specific best practice standards selected, there should be efforts to make sure organizations are complying with them. Enforcement, monitoring, and accountability are crucial. Currently, there is too much variation among employers, and many organizations are unable to comply with the fragmented regulatory structure. Ignoring or overlooking organizations' institutionalized lack of preparation is a policy mistake that can no longer be ignored. Just as ethics training is required for employees, there should be some minimum level of cyber education for board members, general counsel, and chief financial officers. Insurance brokers also need more education on cybersecurity so that they can have more meaningful conversations with chief information officers and risk managers buying insurance. Brokers cannot provide the right type and level of insurance if they do not understand the client's security posture and what is needed moving forward. Brokers struggle at a technical level to communicate with prospective buyers of cyber insurance. This lack of technical knowledge reduces brokers' ability to be an effective conduit between the insurer and prospective buyer of insurance. One former broker who now worked for an insurtech company noted that brokers lack the necessary expertise to be effective advisers to clients interested in cyber insurance:

> Most of the brokers now, there's only a very select few, and I like to think I know most of them, but a very select few [who] can actually have a conversation with a chief security officer. That's a different level. I thought I knew that until I left and worked for a technology company and realized how little I knew about the way network security works. So that's where brokers need to start. Forget even providing solutions. Just be able to sit down, understand what comprises a network, right? . . . The brokers are great talking to the CFO, but they just can't talk to [the chief security officer]. So, how do you find a person that can do both? (insurance broker, interview 17)

It is hard for brokers to be effective advocates if they do not understand cybersecurity issues. States should consider requiring brokers go through a certification process in order to sell cyber insurance. As one broker explained: "I think people that do what I do should have a qualification, a certification, a license for it because I have to be licensed to sell employee health benefits. I have to be licensed to sell property and casualty. I think there should be a separate license for cyber. And I think carriers should align themselves with people that are willing to understand and spread the knowledge" (broker and former risk manager, interview 6).

Although focusing on technology in the cyber insurance context makes sense to a degree given the sophistication of criminal approaches, education remains the weak link, as the broker pointed out: "Education is probably one of the aspects—of how you're educating. Every company has employees and your weakest link is your employee. And that typically happens to be the case. We emphasize to all of our insurers that obviously technology is important but equally as important is employee education. And while I think a lot of the larger companies get it or are starting to get it, a lot of the SMEs still don't educate their employees and it's a big problem" (broker and former risk manager, interview 6).

Employee education about their organization's privacy guidelines and what is expected of them should begin during the onboarding process and continue annually so that employees stay updated on best practices and emerging threats. Thirty-minute online video cybersecurity training, akin to the mandatory online sexual harassment training that many organizations use, is symbolic and not well designed to reduce risks. "Most of the folks glaze over," a broker observed. "This whole concept of owning the risk and being responsible for it goes in one ear and out the other. It's to tick the box, to say you did it—'We provide employee training'" (interview 25). Repeat victims of phishing emails and other criminal encroachments should be forced to meet with the information security and technology team to learn from their mistakes. As one former risk manager stated, "You don't want repeat offenders in your company. If they're a continuous offender, you should punish or even dismiss them. And some companies have actually started doing that. As harsh as it sounds, that's a good education plan" (broker and former risk manager, interview 6).

Use Incentives (Including Financial) to Improve Employee Cyber Hygiene

Incentives should be established to motivate individual employees and departments to practice strong cyber hygiene. If a particular department has repeated cybersecurity incidents, it should incur financial penalties. As a broker whom I interviewed indicated, a substantive compliance regime institutes and prioritizes incentives: "I think if there's financial impact, if you hit somebody in the wallet, they're going to pay attention to it. So, again, if you've got a particular division, and that division head, all of a sudden there is an incident—it comes from that specific division—there's got to be some sort of financial penalty. Absent that, I don't know of any other way to get someone's attention. I mean, every big entity does these compliance procedures" (interview 25).

Some industry officials suggested that employee bonuses should be reduced if employees are sloppy with their cybersecurity practices and it leads to losses. Conversely, if particular departments or employees demonstrate a repeated record of cybersecurity and safety, such behavior should be rewarded. In other words, organizations need to actively nudge departments and employees toward heightened cybersecurity safety and reward them. Incentivizing employees to care is crucial.

Begin Cyber Education in Elementary School

Cyber education needs to be prioritized in primary education. We teach children at the youngest ages to look both ways before crossing a street, not to talk to strangers, and not open the front door at home unless the child knows who is ringing the doorbell. Why? The answer is always safety. Yet people face greater risk of identity theft and privacy violations than of some of these more traditional safety threats. Cyber education needs to begin early on so children enter adulthood understanding the threat vectors and how to avoid problems. This is especially important since children are increasingly using technology at unprecedented rates. Many industry experts whom I spoke with thought that a long-term strategy includes education at an early age of adolescent development. One attorney explained:

> You could try and teach [cyber education] in schools. I'd love to see that happen, because the kids are so quick. Even in kindergarten they've got phones. So I would love to see it taught in schools as a form of personal and family risk training. And you get them started early to understand that. I think that would help. I don't know how capable most of our teachers are in this arena. Most of the kids in the classroom could probably show them.
>
> Their minds are malleable. You get in there and teach them about the risk, teach them to understand that giving up too much information can and always will be risky. And if you do that in the schools, then maybe you'll get employees who are better prompted to understand the risks they take for the enterprises they work for. (interview A1)

Thus, training children in cybersecurity can lay a foundation for more responsible employees since the overwhelming evidence is that human error often leads to cybersecurity incidents.

Layer Multiple Security Protocols

My interviews and other research in the cyber insurance field repeatedly led to the same conclusion: cyber fundamentals matter. In other words, if the government or the insurance industry can convince organizations to follow basic cybersecurity practices, organizations will reduce their risk and, consequently, reduce the risk of consumer information falling into cybercriminals' hands. Cyber insurance officials repeatedly emphasized that incentivizing the following practices will lead to improved cybersecurity: (1) proper configuration of network, (2) endpoint detection response, (3) strong passwords, (4) daily offline backup, (5) multi-factor authentication across assets and networks, (6) recognition of phishing attempts, (7) regular software updates, and (8) patches and proper deployment of patching data. These recommendations draw from a philosophy of layering multiple security protocols in an effort to bolster security. All interviewees routinely emphasized MFA as an essential practice for organizations of every size. To be clear, many of these recommendations are not complicated, but they require organizations to be disciplined in their security procedures. If the government or insurance industry can incentivize such discipline, organizations, consumers, and society in general will be better off.

The government seems in a position to put some of these incentives in place. In the United States, the Cybersecurity and Infrastructure Security Agency Act of 2018 created the Cybersecurity and Infrastructure Security Agency (CISA), overseen by the Department of Homeland Security. CISA publishes regularly the Binding Operational Directives (BODs) that explicitly provide actions that could be taken to improve the cybersecurity of federal civilian agencies. For example, Directive BOD-22-01 requires federal civil agencies to address new problems within two weeks of disclosure in a regularly uploaded menu of known exploited vulnerabilities. This nudge from CISA sets a timeline and standard for software and service providers to offer patches and updates for their end users. CISA limits its BOD-22-01 mandate to federal civilian agencies, but the agency does recommend that private businesses review and monitor BOD and other CISA disclosures. Perhaps insurers or the government could do more in the form of such incentives to nudge organizations to be more responsive.

In sum, if human credulity is one of the biggest problems, individuals should be educated at the earliest ages of schooling and employment in proper cyber etiquette. State and federal policymakers should aggressively encourage education. There should be training for insurance brokers so they understand the risks and can better advise their clients. Insurance companies should encourage, reward, or possibly require cyber training among their policyholders. These trainings, of course, must not be check-the-box, symbolic training. Most important, organizations need to incentivize cybersecurity with carrots and sticks, including financial incentives—for employees, departments, and the chief executive, financial officers, informational officers, and others operating at the highest levels of the organization.

THE GOVERNMENT AS SUBSTANTIVE REGULATOR

One of the big lessons that we can learn from the new institutional theory of insurance this book presents is not to defer to the institutionalized practices of organizations. The government needs to play a more prominent role in the overall governance landscape of cybersecurity, regardless of whether insurance companies choose to be active in this area.

First, the government should require the insurance industry to share anonymized data using more standardized terminology. This data sharing would increase transparency for both consumers and regulators on how data are used. It would also reduce some of the information access disparities between larger and smaller insureds and insurers. Consistent with the Cyber Solarium Commission recommendations, it makes sense for Congress to pass legislation standardizing and establishing requirements for the sharing of anonymized data by organizations. The National Association of Insurance Commissioners could play a role as well, or states could mandate a data-sharing apparatus, but the main point is that increased anonymized data sharing is needed.

Second, and concurrent with lesson one, a bureau or institute of cybersecurity should be created to administer and oversee this data repository. Insurers, brokers, risk managers, lawyers, and every other member of the cyber insurance field whom I interviewed indicated that more data and information are needed to better understand and evaluate cyber risk. Almost every interviewee said that, assuming necessary protections and safeguards are put in place, sharing anonymized data in a data repository will help the cyber insurance industry. For example: "I think if I had that magic wand, it would be to be able to have a large shared database of insured losses" (information security provider, interview 36). Others emphasized the importance of setting up a mandate that forced, perhaps through incentives, all insurers—large and small—to share data. One insurer and information security provider explained:

> If everybody's data was pooled in some way, you would be able to make leaps and bounds in the modeling in the space. But the thing is, these insurance carriers view this as their competitive advantage. So there's probably some way to get some incremental level of sharing if it's incentivized appropriately. But kind of as it stands now, you have these top ten carriers who wouldn't really have a good incentive to share in the pool. And only the people without much data would be the ones with incentive to share there. (interview 32)

Many noted that although states and the NAIC require some reporting, it is not granular enough to help insurers and others in the insurance industry model risk. "Currently the statutory reporting's done by the state. So maybe you could consolidate there. And maybe you bolster the kinds of information that are shared in those. Right now it's just, we had a breach; it was this many records" (interview 32). Persuading all insurers to buy into the value of sharing information for a greater good, as opposed to thinking only about their competitive advantage, presents some challenges. The federal government would need to ensure the data are protected and secured, not used offensively against businesses or insurers, and properly anonymized. The government should consider offering incentives for participation. As noted, more federal involvement in the form of mandating information and data sharing by insurers would help stabilize the market. A bureau or institute of cybersecurity could not only serve as a repository for collected data but also administer and issue information on best practices, statistics, and reports on data breach events. In this regard, such a mechanism would operate like the Insurance Institute for Highway Safety.

Third, as opposed to organizations trying to comply with fifty different state privacy laws and notification statutes, the federal government should create a federal privacy law to reduce the fragmented legal framework for data privacy. Coupled with this is the need to establish federal privacy standards. Currently, cybersecurity and privacy law operate in a fragmented legal environment. Various federal laws, including HIPAA, HITECH, and Graham Leach-Bliley Act, touch on privacy requirements. State regulators attempt to enforce state notification statutes as well. There is too much variation and too much guessing for organizations with regard to compliance. The multiplicity of laws and regulations is unnecessary and not working well. Congress could help organizations better understand their responsibilities if it preemptively mandated a baseline set of standards for organizations to comply with, a baseline reflecting the best practices available (such as the NIST standards) and perhaps calibrated to company size.

The US Cyberspace Solarium Commission's conclusions indicate that most organizations are woefully underprepared for data breach events and lack the most basic preventive practices (US CSC 2020). Thus, making sure organizations are taking care of the fundamentals, as noted earlier, would likely reduce some forms of human credulity and inattentiveness. Although there is great value in states tailoring regulations as they see fit, the variation in this space may well be producing less cybersecurity than confusion (and higher lawyer fees). One broker had this to say on the matter:

> The market is more keen on a federal regulation—federal standard in terms of what you need to do from a breach response standpoint. Does it qualify as a breach or not? Do you need to notify based on the nature of a breach? How do you notify? There are so many nuances. It really does vary state by state and the admin and the costs related to attracting all of those different requirements is taxing. So certainly having one standard across the country, maybe except 1 percent, I think most people would agree with that. (broker, interview A11, March 4, 2020)

Many expressed frustration with state guidelines. But the largest frustration and blame was directed toward congressional inertia and inability to intervene effectively. This lack of coordinated congressional action has led to a fragmented marketplace that forces insurers to engage in de facto regulation. "Now you're having states do that for the federal government," an insurer and underwriter observed, "because right now we all know that the federal government can't even pass bipartisan legislation if their life depended on it. So, with that in mind, I do think right now you can make the case that [insurers] are de facto regulators" (interview 4).

As noted in chapter 2, new institutional theories about compliance indicate that one of the ways to achieve substantive, as opposed to symbolic, compliance is to have less ambiguous laws. The federal government can help reduce ambiguity with regard to how to comply with laws, especially privacy laws that contain safe harbor provisions for organizations that take "reasonable security measures." Federal law, accompanied by federal standards issued by an enforcement body or agency, would provide the kind of top-down guidance that organizations need, as a data privacy lawyer explained: "The federal law's position on standards—I would love to see something that—it may address how organizations should have reasonable security standards. But then have an enforcement body issue regular guidance on what those are because reasonable security standards can change day by day, organization by organization, and it's going to be impossible to prepare a checklist that every organization will be able to check the boxes for, and that would apply to every single organization" (interview 30).

The standards or regulatory guidance should accompany any broad-based privacy law so that organizations and insurers know what is expected of them. One expert suggested that such regulations or standards take the form of a uniform security code:

I do think eventually there is going to be legislation that's going to put some teeth into some sort of standard and push a standard for those that are conducting electronic transactions. Some sort of codified or uniformed codified security code, like they do with the UCC for contracts or commercial contracts. There's going to be some sort of codification that would need to be done to provide some teeth into any sort of statutory law in place that surrounds the whole need for there to be consistent security measures." (insurer and underwriter, interview 4)

A federal law and accompanying standards would guide insurance companies in providing regulatory nudges to policyholders in the form of rewards and discounted premiums. I am not suggesting states have failed in facing the challenges of cybersecurity. Rather, I am contending that the fragmented legal framework has failed to nudge individuals and organizations in the right direction and has not provided the kind of coordinated guidance needed to get everyone on track.

Make Improved Cyber Hygiene a Public-Private
Collaborative Mission

The government should develop public-private partnerships between private industry, government, and researchers to enable two-way collaboration and cooperation in identifying, mitigating, and disrupting cyberattacks (NCFTA n.d.). CISA's Shields Up campaign offers guidance to individuals, families, organizations, and corporate leaders and CEOs on best cybersecurity practices and is a step in the right direction. As the United States cyber defense agency, CISA, through Shields Up, makes news, education, resources, and tools readily available and accessible to those interested in using them. This program is thorough but also consistent with my earlier recommendation that organizations address the fundamentals. The government should think of creative ways to make sure society is accessing and using such information.

The National Cyber-Forensics and Training Alliance (NCFTA) presents another model for preventing, detecting, and responding to cybercrime through collaboration between government and industry. As a nonprofit corporation, NCFTA allows more than 150 participants, including private industry, federal and state law enforcement, government agencies, and academia to engage one another under the protection of a nondisclosure agreement. NCFTA seeks to create a two-way collaboration in which financial institutions, federal and state law enforcement, and other entities communicate, cooperate, and disrupt and dismantle cyber threats. The NCFTA also uses in-house intelligence analysts to identify possible threats and trigger communication across industries. Some insurers are part of this collaborative public-private partnership and can assist. The NCFTA has met with representatives of dozens of countries across the world to share best practices and intelligence.

In theory, a collaborative mission—not one anchored in deference to private industry—would be useful if calibrated correctly. These kind of collaborations allow both businesses and the government to exchange information in ways that foster increased cybersecurity. Insurance companies should continue to identify best practices for their policyholders and share information to help society become and remain more cybersecure. The development of the equivalent of an AMBER alert among the government and insurers (who could communicate threat information to insureds) would be a useful tool to protect against cybersecurity threats.

Hold Software Product Manufacturers Liable for Faulty Software

One of the strongest recommendations made by the 2020 Cyberspace Solarium Commission report (US CSC 2020) and the 2023 National Cybersecurity Strategy Implementation Plan (US White House 2023) concerns expanding vendor liability. Federal law should mandate that final assemblers of firmware, software, and hardware be liable for damages caused by incidents that exploit known and unpatched vulnerabilities during the time they support the service. As the reports note, vendors too often ignore best practices "for secure development, ship products with insecure default configurations or known vulnerabilities, and integrate third-party software of unvetted or unknown provenance" (US White House 2023, 20–21). Software makers use contracts to disclaim liability and thus reduce their incentive to follow "secure-by-design" principles or "perform pre-release testing" (21). Ultimately, poor software security leads to problems with cybersecurity that are ultimately born by consumers and organizations, not the vendors that create or perpetuate these problems. Entities that do not take responsibility for, or at least take reasonable precautions against, these problems should bear some legal liability. This is one of the overwhelming concerns raised by those in the cyber insurance and cybersecurity field. For example:

> If I could change anything, I would tell you it would be revolved around the contracts, and it would be not allowing these companies to get away with not assuming risk for the product or service that they're providing. I'm not suggesting unlimited liability . . . if I was cyber czar for a day and I could make one change, the change I would make is to say, listen, these are not enforceable provisions. You cannot say in your contract that you are not liable for a revenue loss that you cause a client because you were negligent and you screwed up. (broker, interview 26)

> How our data is protected or not protected and what companies are doing or not doing, and I think in my opinion, whether it's on the insurance end or on a regulatory end, [software vendors] should be held accountable much more for protecting individuals' PII [personally identifiable information]. (insurer and former broker, interview A4)

Contract law provisions often allow the general contractor to pass the liability through to the subcontractor (and the subcontractor's insurance company) if the subcontractor is ultimately responsible for the damage during a construction event. In the cyber context, on the other hand, vendors are not sufficiently incentivized to follow best practices in making sure the products they put on the market are cybersafe. Obviously, we want organizations to make innovative software but they should be held liable and accountable when they breach their duty of care to consumers, businesses, and critical infrastructure providers. Instead of making end-users bear the costs and consequences of insecure software, responsibility should be placed on those most capable of preventing bad outcomes at the outset. This would induce producers to put safer products on the market while still preserving space for innovation.

Moreover, the larger telecommunication companies should also bear some responsibility, according to many individuals that I spoke with. As one remarked:

> My policy recommendation is somebody should be holding responsible people who actually can see what's going on. The Verizons and the AT&Ts of the world, I mean they're watching their network lit up a thousand or a million times a day by bots, and they're not doing anything about it. They just let all those people that are plugged into the network just go down. So somebody should hold them accountable. It's not going to be the FCC. And the same thing goes for the government. I mean the government is absolutely supine. It's just—I can't . . . You know, they don't do anything to kind of enforce standards. (underwriter and risk manager, interview 12)

Others pointed out that although Microsoft Office 365 (and earlier versions of Office) is used by thousands of people and Microsoft's software is the "root cause" of many problems, they avoid liability: "Their product is everywhere, and you can point to billions in dollars of losses due to the vulnerabilities of their software. So why aren't they culpable? Why is that not a product deficiency?

Microsoft makes a product that has flaws that get exploited all the time" (insurer, interview A10).

Thus, the federal government should consider passing a law that establishes liability for software and product services. At a minimum, the law should not allow manufacturers and software companies to avoid liability by contract. It should establish reasonable standards of care that companies would need to adhere to. To the extent the government could establish a standard of care for secure software development that could be verified, a safe harbor framework could be used to shield software vendors from liability. Any safe harbor that is developed, however, should draw from best practices for secure software development.

Establish a Federally Funded Financial Backstop for Catastrophic Cyber Risk

Lurking underneath a regulatory environment where (1) state and federal governments are failing to sufficiently regulate cyber risk, (2) organizations are admittedly underprepared for cyber risk, and (3) insurance companies are failing to nudge organizations toward heightened cybersecurity is the reality that the United States is at great risk of a catastrophic cyberattack directed at one of its critical infrastructures. This could cause catastrophic damage while also paralyzing the insurance industry. The SolarWinds attacks and NotPetya are among some of the more recent attacks that have had global impact. Insurance companies are attempting to deny coverage by citing policy exclusions that define such cyberattacks as acts of war (Cunningham and Talesh 2021–22). The risk to critical cyber infrastructures is real for countries across the world. The Cyber Solarium Commission directly summarized the risk and potential consequences of a catastrophic cyberattack:

The reality is that we are dangerously insecure in cyber[space]. Your entire life—your paycheck, your health care, your electricity—increasingly relies on networks of digital devices that store, process, and analyze data. These networks are vulnerable, if not already compromised. Our country has lost hundreds of billions of dollars to nation-state-sponsored intellectual property theft using cyber espionage. A major cyberattack on the nation's critical infrastructure and economic system would create chaos and lasting damage exceeding that wreaked by fires in California, floods in the Midwest, and hurricanes in the Southeast. (US CSC 2020, v)

The consensus of various reports and evaluations is that catastrophic cybercrime incidents will cost billions or even trillions of dollars and severely damage industries. The threat of a catastrophic cyberattack against a global cloud service provider that creates systemic risk across the global cyber insurance ecosystem is a major concern for those in the cyber risk field. As one risk manager stated: "It keeps Lloyd's of London up at night. They're really, you know, they almost lost their shirt in the seventies over the *Achille Lauro*. And so they do a lot of systemic risk studies these days. And they've been laser-focused on AWS [Amazon Web Services] because if it goes dark, right? Oh my God" (underwriter and risk manager, interview 12). Thus, symbolic regulation is not enough. A more substantive regulatory approach is needed that better coordinates the work of the public and private sectors.

The federal government should consider creating a financial backstop for the cyber insurance ecosystem in the event of a catastrophic cyberattack. Establishing a public-private framework is necessary to strengthen the cyber insurance industry because of the potential for catastrophic attacks. It is also necessary to improve our collective cyber hygiene and, therefore, our national and economic security. There are no commonly recognized and enforceable cybersecurity standards, particularly in the United States. As this book shows, while cyber insurers are theoretically positioned to fill this gap and meaningfully improve our collective cyber hygiene, they have not done so, and likely cannot under current conditions. The cyber insurance field currently has no financial backstop (that is, no large government guarantee of financial resources to keep insurers solvent) to prevent it from being disrupted—perhaps fatally—by a catastrophic cyberattack, or a series of them, or even a combination of cyberattacks and natural disasters. This reality is artificially distorting the cyber insurance market. In the absence of such a backstop, insurers have turned to mechanisms such as act-of-war exclusions in cyber policies that simultaneously cannot accomplish their intended purpose of preventing cyber insurance market collapse and will remain difficult or impossible to adjudicate, leading to continuing uncertainty rather than helping to stabilize the marketplace in a rational way.

There appears to be a consensus that the cyber insurance field would benefit from such government financial backstopping for truly catastrophic attacks, as well as from universally required cyberattack information reporting, so long as reasonable protections from disclosure and liability are in place for such reporting. The Cyber Solarium Commission's recommendations in 2020 were consistent with the idea that a backstop is needed. More recently, the Department of the Treasury reached a "tentative conclusion" that a potential federal insurance backstop focused on catastrophic cyber risk should be explored in 2024 (Hemenway 2023). My interviews in the insurance industry reflect a similar perspective about the need for a government backstop. "I think the risk is so ubiquitous that I don't think government can fix it," an insurance attorney told me. "I think what we can do is we can create backstops like we do for natural disasters. So, if you're completely wiped out in a natural disaster, government will come in and make some loans and do some other things. I think if we treat this kind of risk, particularly financial risk and the fact that somebody's 401(k) is cleaned out and the company that sponsored the 401(k) can't stand behind it, I think there probably ought to be something" (attorney, interview A1).

In 2021, Bryan Cunningham and I (2021–22) proposed draft legislation we titled the "Catastrophic Cybersecurity Resilience Act" that lays out a concrete proposal for how a federally funded financial backstop might work. A federal backstop for insurers could potentially be invoked after an actual catastrophic cyberattack. If calibrated carefully, such a backstop could help protect the solvency of the cyber insurance field, reduce market uncertainties that the insurance field repeatedly complains about concerning cyber risk, and assist insurers in better fulfilling their promise and claim of improving cyber hygiene among insureds and, ultimately, society.

To be eligible for the program, Cunningham and I suggest, insurers must do a few things. First, the government should mandate that all purchasers of the insurer's cyber products maintain a baseline level of cyber hygiene, as determined jointly by the secretary of the treasury, CISA, and the national cyber director (NCD). Second, all insureds should be required to timely report cyber incidents and share other information—on condition that the shared information is protected and with the understanding that the government will make the gathered information public to the greatest extent consistent with disclosure limitations and national security concerns. Third, insurers should abide by, and be precluded from challenging through litigation, newly created public "certifications of attribution" for cyberattacks, to be issued by the secretary of the treasury, in consultation with

CISA and the NCD. These determinations would be supported by the national Cyber Threat Intelligence Integration Center (wisely proposed by the CSC but not yet created). Lastly, insurers should be required to agree not to enforce act-of-war exclusions in cyberattack coverage decisions or litigation.[4] To reduce "silent cyber" risks, the backstop funds from the federal government would apply only to losses covered by standalone cyber policies or other policies explicitly including cyber coverage.

Obviously, this proposal certainly could (and likely should) be tweaked as the government moves toward formalizing legislation, but the approach would yield benefits. In particular, the government could help nudge the cyber insurance field toward its purported goal of improving overall cyber hygiene without overly aggressive, top-down regulation. The Cunningham and Talesh (2021–22) legislative approach attempts to couple government insurance backstopping for catastrophic cyberattacks with a set of requirements to qualify for such backstopping. To be clear, no insurer would be required to impose on their insureds any of the mandates provided for in this legislation. Moreover, no insured would be required to buy coverage with the requirements provided by the law. But, given all the concerns raised by the state of cyber*insecurity* in the market and how the cyber insurance industry has failed as a de facto regulator, there is a good chance that the cyber insurance industry would adopt these federal best-practice measures if the cyber insurance market stabilized, access to cyberattack information increased, there was a significant reduction or even elimination of act-of-war exclusion litigation and other "silent cyber" risks, and protection from liability for cyberattack information sharing.

As Cunningham and I noted (2021–22), such an arrangement contemplates that the treasury secretary would have the authority, in consultation with CISA and the NCD, to require that proof of losses from cyber risk coverage exceed, or be reasonably expected to exceed, $10 billion in order to certify the incident as a catastrophic attack and trigger federal backstopping. The $10 billion threshold is admittedly arbitrary and should be adjusted based on consultations between government and industry experts and on more reliable data from the cyber insurance field. Whatever number is settled on should be consistent with expected damages from cyberattacks and the level of loss payouts reasonably likely to destroy cyber insurers. Much as with the Terrorism Risk Insurance Act, certifications under the law would be final and not reviewable.

Cyber insurers need to be positioned in a way to act as meaningful quasi-regulators over their insured. Allowing them to do so on their own has not worked. The offer of federal backstopping funds would incentivize them to impose on their insureds reasonable cyber incident requirements. My prior research with Cunningham and recent congressional testimony by business leaders suggest that such requirements not only are long overdue and might for the first time have the support of key industry players, but could also over time create data sets and analysis to enable the cyber insurance market to better understand, price, and manage cyber risk, with the goal of improving our overall cyber hygiene and national and economic security (Cunningham and Talesh 2021–22). The insurer acceptance of cyberattack attribution certification for catastrophic cyberattack insurance program participation and the agreement not to assert act-of-war exclusions in such cases are crucial. Essentially, the federal law should declare war exclusions invalid and unenforceable.

To be clear, proposals like the one Cunningham and I have proposed and this book endorses require discussion, adjustment, and refinement. But this proposal builds on the lessons of catastrophic cybersecurity breaches in the past few years and on the earlier research on insurance companies as symbolic regulators. It is also responsive to the Cyber Insurance Risk Framework guidance provided by the New York Department of Financial Service (NYDFS), specifically the provision directing insurers to "employ [specific] practices . . . to sustainably and effectively manage their cyber insurance risk" (Lacewell 2021). The NYDFS's key recommendations include calling for guidance on how to "manage and eliminate exposure to silent cyber insurance risk," "educate insureds and insurance providers," and "require notice" of cyber incidents to government officials (Brown, Cunningham, and Raman 2021). Cunningham and my proposal would allow government financial backstopping only for standalone cyber policies or policies otherwise explicitly providing cyber coverage; require reasonable cybersecurity measures, including training, in order to be eligible for the proposed program; and create a national mechanism for prompt cyber incident reporting. This approach, or an approach in a similar vein, would help reduce "systemic risk," as the NYDFS recognizes the increasing concerns about such risk, which have "[g]rown in part because institutions increasingly rely on third party vendors and those vendors are highly concentrated in key areas like cloud services and managed service providers. . . . Examples of such events could include a self-propagating malware, such as NotPetya, or a supply chain attack, such as the SolarWinds trojan, that infects many institutions at the same time, or a cyber event that disables a major cloud services provider" (Lacewell 2021).

The global cyber insurance community recognizes that catastrophic losses, potentially of a magnitude to threaten the stability, or even existence, of cyber insurance, are possible. One of the main reasons such a catastrophe appears increasingly plausible is the poor state of cyber hygiene among a significant percentage of insured businesses. Cyber insurers have yet to fulfill early expectations that they would use their relationships with, and ability to incentivize, their insureds toward greatly improved cybersecurity practices and procedures.

A US government–funded financial backstop may stabilize the cyber insurance field and improve overall cyber hygiene. In the event of a catastrophic cyberattack, cyber insurance carriers would remain solvent, and this is a clear carrot. But to incentivize insurers, in return for such government protection, certain sticks are necessary: requiring their insureds to comply with new data and infrastructure security and cyber breach notification requirements; refraining from enforcing war exclusions in cyber insurance policies; and accepting newly mandated government certifications of attribution for cyberattacks (cf. Lubin 2021a, 2021b). Obviously, a proposal like the one described above would not be easily adopted by Congress and would require tremendous political advocacy. A parliamentary committee in the United Kingdom conducted a yearlong investigation in 2023–24 of that country's cyber insurance market, concluded that it was in "an extremely poor state," and suggested that the government consider developing a publicly funded backstop for cyber insurance. The government declined the request, worrying that actively intervening in the insurance market could impair competition (Asokan 2024). Such narrow, short-sided thinking ignores all the signals that suggest a catastrophic cyber attack will likely occur and that the cyber insurance field is ill-equipped to absorb the ramifications of such an attack.

In sum, the proposals in this chapter are not fool-proof. But they articulate an approach that I believe moves us away from symbolic regulation toward more substantive regulation aimed and improving cyber hygiene in society. If we want to substantively develop a cybersecurity apparatus that reduces the likelihood of cybersecurity incidences, we need a more holistic, comprehensive framework that leverages both government and civil society actors. Borrowing from the lessons of new institutional theory, public legal institutions should not blindly defer to organizations such as insurance companies attempting to play a regulatory role. Cyber education and training is essential, from elementary school students all the way to new employees starting a job. Those persons running organizations at the highest levels also need to understand cybersecurity and to prioritize safety and compliance. Brokers play a role, as well, and should be educated about the cyber insurance products they sell. Insurance companies need to consider learning from the lessons of why insurance companies acting as de facto regulators has not worked well. Specifically, they should consider rewarding good policyholder cyber health with reduced premiums, require insureds to make changes to their cybersecurity systems as a prerequisite to issuing insurance, and engage in real-time underwriting and loss control that allows insurers to be more adaptable to quickly changing threat vectors. Finally, the government needs to play a more active role, both in terms of passing laws and regulations that clearly lay out requirements and standards and in terms of setting forth a proper incentive structure for insurers that opt to have the government provide them with a backstop in the event of a catastrophic event.

These proposals and recommendations, therefore, reflect a focus not just on collaboration among public and private institutions but also on improving the behavior of insurance companies, organizations, and government institutions and creating long-term rewards for that improved behavior (Van Rooij and Fine 2021). The focus cannot be just on carrots and sticks and aligning incentives among insurance companies and the organizations they insure (which undoubtedly is important). We must also create intrinsic motivation among organizations, insurance companies as intermediaries, and even the government as a regulator to value and prioritize cyber hygiene and safety.

CHAPTER EIGHT

Symbolic Regulation and Insurer Influence on Private Organizations and Public Law

Cyber risks are among the biggest risks facing organizations operating in the twenty-first century. Organizations know it. Governments know it. Cybercriminals and hackers know it too. Cybercriminals are expanding globally and even being operationalized as a wartime tool. Despite these risks, organizations remain underprepared and undercompliant with privacy law and cybersecurity.

Amidst a regulatory environment where governments often encourage the private role in public governance, insurers have stepped up to offer organizations insurance and risk management services that they believe help prevent, detect, and respond to data breach events and increase an organizations' cyber resiliency. These risk management services convey legitimacy to the public and to buyers of cyber insurance but fall short of improving the cyber hygiene of organizations, rendering such interventions largely symbolic. Cyber insurers, in partnership with managed-security companies, market high-tech security tools that they claim reduce risk and institutionalize a norm that policyholders need these tools to avoid cybersecurity incidences. Over time, federal and state regulatory agencies and industry-based rating agencies defer to cyber insurer practices regarding cybersecurity policy without evidence that such interventions improve the cybersecurity of organizations.

This book reveals that these insurer responses have not worked well. The promise of cyber insurers enhancing insureds' cybersecurity, though theoretically possible, remains unfulfilled. Whereas prior research has shown how organizational policies, procedures, and structures in response to law can become symbolic (Edelman 2016), in this case, insurance companies, as quasi-regulators, are ineffective and largely symbolic. The new institutional theory of insurance posited in this book not only helps to explain the limitations of insurance companies as regulators and how insurers manage uncertainty but also provides a comprehensive theoretical statement of the interplay between insurance, organizations, and law.

Moving forward, the debate over whether insurance as regulation is a good or bad thing for society must shift to the question, *under what conditions* can insurers act as regulators in ways that achieve desired goals? When insurer regulatory interventions protect privacy rights, legal deference to those approaches is unproblematic and advances the goals of enhanced cyber hygiene, security, and resiliency in society. But when rating agencies, courts, legislators, and state regulators rely on gestures toward compliance, inferring security and safety from the mere presence of symbolic structures emanating from insurers without evaluating whether they make any measurable impact, privacy and consumer rights become merely symbolic. If state regulators, legislators, and courts adopt meanings of law and compliance that derive from the insurance field without proper evaluation of the viability of such approaches, insurers are in a position to influence what compliance means on the ground but only as symbolic regulators. Thus, the conclusion to draw from this book is not that insurers are always ineffective regulators but rather that we must understand how and why the insurer-as-regulator model has not worked well in this context.

NEW INSTITUTIONAL THEORY OF INSURANCE IN OTHER AREAS OF INSURANCE

Although I have developed and illustrated my institutional theory of insurance in the context of cyber insurance and cybersecurity, the theory is relevant to other areas of insurance both within and outside the US legal context. To better illustrate how insurance companies as intermediaries influence and shape the compliance behavior of organizations while also influencing legal and regulatory policy making among public legal institutions, I explicate the theory in a few specific contexts: the NAIC, EPLI, and property insurance. My goal here is to show how this theoretical framework helps explain how insurance companies shape private organizations' approaches to regulation and also how insurer-led constructions of law and compliance influence public legal institutions.

Explains How Insurers Use Intermediary Organizations to Influence Legislation and Regulation

Consistent with new institutional theories, this section highlights how the insurance industry uses intermediary organizations such as the National Association of Insurance Commissioners (NAIC) to influence legal rules.

Insurance regulation in the United States is largely governed by the states. State legislatures often delegate broad powers to insurance agencies or departments to enforce state insurance laws, promulgate rules and regulations, and conduct hearings to resolve disputed matters. This decentered approach allows each state flexibility concerning issues relating to fair pricing of insurance, protecting against insurance company insolvency, preventing unfair practices by insurance companies, and ensuring availability of insurance coverage. States have the discretion to approve insurance rates; conduct financial examinations of insurers, license companies, agents, and brokers; and monitor claims handling. Each state has a chief insurance regulator, with the title of commissioner, superintendent, or director of insurance, who is responsible for regulating the insurance markets in the state and enforcing its regulatory laws. Despite the decentralized state regulatory system, there has been a move toward centralization, uniformity, and cooperation in insurance regulation, a move largely driven by the NAIC.

Formed in 1871, the NAIC is a voluntary association of insurance regulators from all fifty states, the District of Columbia, and the US territories. The NAIC's stated goals are to ensure the solvency of insurers, protect policyholders, and preserve state regulation as well as the NAIC itself. In centralizing and unifying insurance regulatory policy across states, the NAIC seeks to eliminate ambiguity in the law and facilitate compliance on the part of insurers (Randall 1999).

The history of the NAIC, therefore, reflects a somewhat contradictory focus on preservation of autonomous state regulation and uniformity of regulation. The NAIC has centralized many basic regulatory functions and operates as a quasi–federal agency by advocating national standards across states. Somewhat like federal regulators in other industries, the NAIC performs centralized duties including setting forth requirements for standard forms for insurance companies' annual financial statements, coordinating financial examinations of insurance companies, rating non-US insurers for the states, providing periodic review and accreditation of state insurance departments, and drafting model laws and regulations that are often adopted by state legislatures.

The NAIC, however, operates as a quasi-public and quasi-private institution. NAIC membership is composed of state officials who are accountable to the governors that appoint them or to the general electorate. NAIC members also have regulatory powers and responsibilities in their states and also have influence in their own state's legislatures. While sometimes thought of as "a group of public officials imbued with the public trust" or "an instrumentality of the states," the NAIC officially defined itself in 1995 as a private trade organization (Randall 1999, 638). Thus, the NAIC has no power to compel the states or the industry to take action. Moreover, because the NAIC is a self-governing entity, it is neither accountable to voters nor subject to government oversight. Although the NAIC plays a central national role in insurance regulatory policy, it has little power to sanction insurers or regulators, and it is not subject to administrative rules or laws such as the Administrative Procedure Act of 1966 or the Freedom of Information Act (Talesh 2015b).

Through its involvement with the NAIC, the insurance field has been able to mediate the meaning of insurance regulation and policy in several ways. First, most of the NAIC's budget comes from assessments of the insurance industry (Paltrow 1998). One legal analyst has highlighted how the financing of the NAIC allows the insurance industry greater influence: "The industry directly funds the NAIC. Each year the NAIC assesses insurance companies a fee, based on premium volume, to file information in its centralized databases. In recent years, database fees account for approximately half of the NAIC's revenues. In contrast, state assessments account for less than five percent of revenues. As a result, members of the industry view the NAIC as part of the industry and accountable to the industry. Furthermore, much of the NAIC's work often appears to be in direct response to the industry" (Randall 1999, 639–40).

Second, the structure of the NAIC not only allows for substantial industry involvement in regulatory policy but provides an efficient and centralized mechanism for the adoption of policies and laws that the insurance field approves. It also provides a place for the insurance field to lobby against NAIC standards if committee negotiations prove unfruitful.

For example, the NAIC's establishment of accreditation standards for state insurance departments highlights how the insurance industry's institutionalized practices can influence legal regulations. After numerous insurer insolvencies in the 1980s, the NAIC developed a new accreditation program for state insurance departments with the goal of improving solvency regulation and financial examinations by individual state regulators and creating consistency among the states. Per the initial accreditation process, a group of independent individuals knowledgeable about insurance evaluated and reviewed the laws, regulations, and standards and then submitted its report to the NAIC, which then voted on the state's accreditation (Randall 1999; Talesh 2015b). Despite initial agreement among NAIC members regarding the need for market conduct regulation (requiring insurers to operate fairly and in compliance with the law), the accreditation program also did not specify standards and guidelines for market conduct regulation. Insurance industry officials and state commissioners criticized the ambiguity and lack of specificity of standards. Moreover, the NAIC had no authority to force states to participate in the accreditation process or to monitor compliance with financial regulation standards outside the accreditation and reaccreditation process. In response to criticisms from the industry and state commissioners, the NAIC proposed provisions to tighten standards, required establishment of a written policy requiring companies to cooperate and share all information with the NAIC and other state regulators, developed a scoring standard for accreditation, and threatened potential sanctions for nonaccreditation. By establishing specific standards as a condition of accreditation, the NAIC attempted to bolster state insurance regulation and fend off calls for federal intervention.

Ultimately, the NAIC reforms were not successful because the insurance industry was able to limit market conduct regulation and the scope of the NAIC's pro-solvency standards. Aided by state legislators who had ties to the insurance industry, the insurance field weakened accreditation standards and avoided enhanced market conduct regulation through the accreditation program. Similar to employers and manufacturers in the employment (Edelman 2016) and consumer protection (Talesh 2009) contexts, the insurance field successfully argued that market conduct regulation would inhibit insurers' flexibility and discretion in conducting business. To achieve its objectives, the insurance industry withheld fees and operating funds assessed by the NAIC against insurance companies, engaged in public criticism of the program, and lobbied the NAIC. Many insurers boycotted the higher fees to the NAIC and argued that the fees were used inappropriately to subsidize market conduct activities not related to solvency regulation. The insurer boycott on fee payments crippled the NAIC and forced the association to negotiate with the industry and provide significant concessions.

Despite the NAIC's stated commitment to protecting consumers, its studies of market conduct initiatives, and its public acknowledgment of the intertwined relationship between market conduct and solvency, the NAIC deferred to the insurance industry's institutionalized notions of discretion and flexibility with respect to setting rates and failed to establish market conduct accreditation standards. Consistent with new institutional theory, these institutionalized logics shaped what the insurance industry lobbied for. In turn, the insurance industry's political mobilization shaped NAIC policy concerning accreditation. As legal scholar Susan Randall has noted, "The history of the NAIC and, in particular, its continuing failure to enhance market conduct regulation or adopt market conduct accreditation standards demonstrates that the industry has utilized its power jointly to influence and even direct the NAIC's actions.... Although federal regulation may not be necessary to guarantee effective regulation of the insurance industry, the history of the NAIC suggests . . . a systematic bias in favor of the industry" (Randall 1999, 669).

In return for ending the boycott over fees, the regulators agreed to use database fees only for solvency regulation. The regulators also agreed to curb market conduct regulation, establish a liaison committee of industry representatives that meets with the regulators' executive committee on a quarterly basis, and hire a new executive vice president, a former lobbyist for a major insurance company. Moreover, the NAIC began holding annual hearings where industry officials could question commissioners on each budgetary item. Thus, institutional and political mechanisms shaped the nature of insurance regulation at key moments.

The insurance field also embeds itself in the NAIC's structure in a way that allows insurance field actors to influence legal rules. For example, the NAIC has subcommittees and working groups tasked with influencing legislation and regulation. These committees tackle a wide variety of issues, including drafting white papers and offering recommendations on the future of insurance regulation, insurance contracts, and financial instruments. Moreover, they actively engage in lawmaking by offering amendments to existing laws, such as the Standard Nonforfeiture Law for Life Insurance, making recommendations concerning health insurance, accreditation standards, and deferring taxes on assets. Rarely are NAIC policies developed without approval from the insurance industry. The industry advisory committees, resource groups, and liaisons for the NAIC provide a mechanism for the insurance field to influence the meaning of legal regulation: "At the very least," Randall (1999) notes, "the structure of the NAIC facilitates industry participation in and potential control over the content of various regulations" (669n260). The American Alliance of Insurers (AAI), an industry organization, conducted a study in 1982 that concluded that "the NAIC functioned primarily as an evaluator and reactor to the work product of the industry advisory committee [on the NAIC]" (NAAI 1982, 65). By being actively involved in the NAIC, the insurance field gains direct influence over the content and meaning of insurance laws because the NAIC, as an intermediary, is charged with drafting model laws and regulations. Moreover, the NAIC strongly encourages states to adopt its model standards and laws by, among other means, threatening to withdraw accreditation to states that do not adopt its recommendations. Deference by the federal government to the NAIC masks the fact that the insurance industry influences the NAIC's proposals and recommendations at critical stages.

In particular, the industry's preference for managerial control and discretion with respect to risk assessments and policies is afforded considerable deference. For example, as part of a solvency modernization initiative, the NAIC in the past few years proposed their own risk and solvency assessment (ORSA) process for US insurance companies, which emphasizes risk management and culminates in a comprehensive report of the company's risk and solvency status (Wicklund and Christopher 2012). This model was based on a European proposal set to take effect in 2014. While US state regulators hesitated to follow a European proposal, the NAIC consistently supported focusing insurers on their risk management programs. After receiving feedback from the insurance industry, the NAIC ultimately released an ORSA Guidance Manual Exposure Draft in October 2011 (Wicklund and Christopher 2012). Interestingly, the NAIC relaxed the standards after the insurance industry convinced it to allow insurers the flexibility to emphasize their own policies and procedures in their own ORSA. Although the ORSA process remained largely intact, the authority to order insurance companies to change their behavior or face penalties was removed. Thus, consistent with new institutional studies, the insurance industry's institutionalized practices drove the NAIC's regulatory recommendations during the political process. Ultimately, the NAIC and state legislatures deferred to the insurance field's constructions of law and compliance.

These examples of the insurance field's involvement with the NAIC highlight how insurance law is more bottom-up than we might think. The NAIC operates as a centralizing organization that permits the states to circumvent potential federal intervention in insurance regulation, and serves to concentrate power. In turn, the insurance industry wields considerable political influence over this centralizing and intermediary organization and impacts regulatory policy. In this instance, insurance institutions are determining the content and meaning of law.

Explains Insurer Influence on Antidiscrimination Laws

As mentioned in earlier chapters, the new institutional approach helps explain how the insurance industry influences the meaning of compliance with antidiscrimination laws. In response to civil rights laws, insurers created employment practice liability insurance (EPLI). This product spread among insurers and ultimately employers that faced uncertain legal risk and heightened litigation risk and sought to take action to avert such risks. Through conferences, training programs, and loss prevention manuals, EPLI insurers translate and interpret the meaning of compliance in ways that build discretion into legal rules and recontextualize them around a nonlegal risk logic that emphasizes averting risk and making discrimination claims more defensible. Risk and managerial values work together in the context of drafting, marketing, and selling EPLI and influence the way organizations understand law and compliance (Talesh 2015a, 2015b).

In turn, public legal institutions such as courts and legislatures appear to have adopted the logic of the insurance field as to the value of EPLI and the various risk management services and encourage and, at times, require public and private organizations to purchase EPLI. Thus, it was not courts or legislatures that initially told employers to purchase EPLI. Rather, it was the insurance field that created and institutionalized a product and ultimately convinced employers to purchase it. It was also the insurance field that motivated the legislature to require, authorize, and encourage such insurance in certain instances. The meaning of civil rights compliance has been constructed at least partly by the insurance field.

To the extent that EPLI and the value-added services induce compliant behavior by private and public institutions, requiring organizations to purchase EPLI may lead to greater adherence to civil rights goals of workplace equality. However, my empirical data suggest that there is often a disconnect between the moral language that legislators, judges, and lawyers use when discussing antidiscrimination law and the risk-oriented language used by insurers, which frames litigation as inevitable and something that must be managed.

Explains How Insurance Companies Influence
Property Insurance Regulation

New institutional theories also help explain how insurance field actors influenced the meaning of property insurance regulation in the late nineteenth and early twentieth centuries in the United States. The politics of American property insurance regulation and what insurance institutions choose to lobby for when attempting to influence legislation were derived from *competing* and *evolving* field logics operating in the insurance field. During the 1950s, the American property insurance industry shifted from a system of associations that relied on shared governance to price-competitive markets and insurance companies that directly sold insurance to insureds. This shift fundamentally transformed property insurance, bringing a mass-market, large-firm system to a sector that had been a more decentralized mix of industry associations, bureau companies, independent distributors, and local insurers.

For much of its history, the property insurance industry institutionalized and embraced three logics: (1) companies distributed insurance via networks of independent agents; (2) companies and agents governed insurance cooperatively through private associations; and (3) states subjected associations to public oversight largely through rate-regulation laws passed between 1909 and 1928. These laws were created around the concept of "regulatory cooperation," whereby cooperative rate pricing (fixing) among insurers grounded in actuarial science and statistical analysis would tie rates to costs and protect consumers from insurer insolvency (Schneiberg 2005, 96–86, 105–7). While this practice was institutionalized and ultimately legally codified, the underlying structure created problems for the insurance market. Insurance associations allowed insurers to engage in monopoly pricing and rate discrimination. Moreover, states shielded insurers from competition and delegated public powers to private rating bureaus that regulated cooperation and "increased insurers' capacities for opportunistic collective action" (106). Price competition was limited, and vertical integration between insurers and insureds was virtually nonexistent. In turn, insurance agents inflated prices, raised commissions, and passed bad risks to insurers. Associations marginalized mutual insurers that were excluded from rating bureaus. Not surprisingly, consumers, regulators, and marginalized insurers grew tired of associations abusing their monopoly. These phenomena prompted increased public scrutiny and calls for public intervention.

Both consumers and marginalized insurance companies were motivated to initiate a change. While competitive pricing schemes and direct insurance writing by insurers instead of by agents would have been a natural solution, the institutionalized logic of the insurance industry association and regulated cooperation shaped the reforms that followed. The insurance industry defended the insurance association on the grounds that insurance was different from ordinary commercial transactions in terms of sophistication. Accordingly, insurance organizations underwent "incremental changes that extended, rather than replaced, the logic of associations" (Schneiberg 2005, 111). Rather than wholesale changes, these reforms sought to address the problem of monopoly cooperatively by using associations to link insurance prices to risks and to provide consumers with ways to lower rates by working within the existing system. The National Board of

Fire Underwriters and local inspection bureaus also extended the logic of associations through collective bargaining, pricing schemes, and prevention associations. These organizations adopted policies of inspecting facilities and communicating their findings to local officials. This practice of "schedule rating," combined with promises of rate hikes and reductions contingent on inspections, was adopted to address the monopoly problem cooperatively. By shielding insurers from competition and delegating public powers to private rating bureaus, regulated cooperation increased opportunities for opportunistic collective action.

Public legal institutions ultimately deferred to the logic of associations that permeated large insurers. From 1911 to 1928, thirty-three states adopted the logic of "association via regulated cooperation" into law and enacted cooperative rate regulation (Schneiberg 2005, 112; see also Schneiberg and Bartley 2001). Even though there was renewed concern over insurer manipulation of rates in the 1920s and 1930s, legislators expanded the insurance commissioners' powers and required insurers to participate in insurer data-pooling programs. Federal and state legislatures responded with a scheme that allowed significant deference to the association model. After aggressive political mobilization by insurers, Congress in 1945 passed the McCarran-Ferguson Act, which exempted insurance from federal antitrust law. Moreover, in 1946 and 1947, the vast majority of states passed "all-industry" laws that permitted and regulated associations nationwide. Thus, the legislatures affirmed the model of scientifically regulated cooperation and afforded insurers considerable control over the manner in which rates would be established.

The property insurance case study both builds on and refines recent institutional studies. Rather than ambiguous law, what stimulated a change in insurers' organizational environment was market failures and controversies surrounding property insurance associations. Despite calls for reform, property insurers responded by emphasizing the need for discretion and flexibility in controlling rate regulation and pricing through collective pricing schemes and scheduled rating. Moreover, they emphasized that regulation through associations was the taken-for-granted, well-settled industry approach in the property insurance field. Eventually, these logics were incorporated into legislation in the form of cooperative rate regulation. In this instance, property insurance legislation in the form of rate regulation looks top-down but is actually bottom-up, derived and generated by the very group—property insurers—that such laws were designed to regulate (Talesh 2015b).

While fields maintain stability, they also evolve as new logics take form. From the 1940s to the 1970s, property insurance slowly shifted from reliance on associations to price or market competition and direct insurance writing by large insurers as opposed to agents. In particular, state regulators and the insurance field began to introduce price competition that provided individual insurers some leeway and flexibility in issuing their own rates and pressuring bureaus to reduce rates. Although the goal was not to displace associations, giving insurers flexibility on rates did marginalize associations. State regulators altered laws to help facilitate insurers' direct sales of insurance to consumers and relaxed cooperative rate fixing. In the 1950s, regulators began allowing insurers to offer limited independent pricing and direct sales to consumers. As central regulating principles, independent pricing and market competition ultimately replaced cooperative rate fixing as large insurers such as State Farm began relying on their own loss data, risk classifications, and inspection routines. With the benefits being passed on to consumers, many states embraced the insurance field's affinity for price competition by deregulating its pricing practices and allowing insurers to compete with respect to rates.[1] The NAIC even adopted the evolving logic of the insurance field by altering its position and advocating for free market competition in its 1974 report *Monitoring Competition: A Means of Regulating the Property and Liability Insurance Business*. As institutionalized logics within the insurance field evolved, property insurance regulation changed. Thus, once again, in the property context, while the legal regulations looked like they were coming from public legal institutions, the content and meaning of legal regulations were determined by insurance companies.

In sum, an institutional framework that focuses on institutional logics operating within and among professions best explains how the insurance field was able to affect property insurance regulation. In particular, the property insurance case highlights how fields have contested or competing logics that are politically mobilized by different groups who choose to form, combine, or transpose logics from other fields or build different coalitions. Power and politics are important factors that led to institutional change, but what the insurance field lobbied for was often institutionally determined by the logics operating in that field.

Overall Lessons from the NAIC, EPLI,
and Property Insurance Examples

This book offers an alternative theoretical approach for understanding the relationship between insurance companies and legal regulation. Whereas most accounts discuss the forms and functions of insurance and analyze the conditions under which insurance companies impact society, I focus on the processes through which insurance institutions construct the meaning of law and compliance. Drawing on new institutional organizational theory, I suggest that conceptions of law and compliance that evolve within the insurance field can shape judges', legislators', and regulators' understandings of compliance—and ultimately the meaning of insurance law.

Building on new institutional work, I reveal how insurance company responses to law and compliance follow a complex process shaped by institutional and political practices and by the flow of risk and managerial logics from the insurance field to the legal field. The case studies that I explore show that insurance companies are not just rational actors responding to top-down laws and regulations, but are also involved in the social construction of legal meaning. Through institutional and political processes, the insurance field's ideas about the meaning of insurance law and compliance flow into cases, legislation, and regulation, and reshape the meaning of law and compliance. In particular, the insurance field filters its understanding of law through risk principles and values that are well institutionalized among actors in that field. Whereas prior new institutional research focuses on managerial values, I show how risk-based values encourage organizations to engage in managerial responses. In such cases, risk and managerial values complement each other. The cyber example also highlights emerging technologies and big data as mechanisms through which organizations mobilize risk and managerial approaches. Thus, my analysis extends new institutional theory analysis of organizational behavior and also refines the analysis to better address organizational responses in the insurance context.

While I do not contend that the insurance industry never responds rationally to top-down mandates, existing accounts of how the insurance industry impacts society that focus on insurance companies as rational actors miss a part of the intermediary role that the insurance field plays in influencing public law. Legislation, regulation, and even court decisions aimed at regulating the insurance industry are often vague, broad, and complex. As opposed to stating clear and coercive rules, laws motivate a process through which organizations collectively seek to construct legal meaning. As the EPLI, NAIC, and property insurance examples demonstrate, these processes are inherently political as insurance institutions and their employees, consumers, and competitors compete for constructions of law that favor their interests. However, this process is also influenced by institutionalized logics that gradually evolve as insurance organizations develop policies and procedures not just for risk pooling and transfer but also compliance. Insurance institutions, therefore, are social actors that both respond to and construct meaning in their field. Conversely, legislators, judges, regulators, and lawyers operate in legal fields that overlap with the insurance field in a variety of ways. As insurance and legal actors interact, the meaning of law and compliance evolves. Thus, my framework suggests the need to understand law as shaped through the processes of institutionalization and political mobilization that take place within, and at the intersection of, the insurance and legal fields.

Although some of the examples offered in this book involve insurance field responses to law and forms of compliance that favor insurers over insureds, I do not mean to suggest that insurance industry construction of the meaning of legal regulations and compliance is always harmful to insureds or other individuals who encounter law in organizational domains. Institutionalized risk management services and insurance industry construction of legal rules sometimes reflect best practices, benefit insureds, and lead to improved compliance. Moreover, these structures may infuse insurance institutions with greater awareness of legal values and principles. However, it is also important to recognize the process through which insurance institutions influence the meaning of legal regulation. This process may foster forms of compliance that tend to be more symbolic than substantive and thus unable to adequately protect insureds, consumers, and the public at large. To the extent public legal institutions are going to defer to the insurance field, society needs to more closely interrogate the insurance field's institutionalized policies, practices, and procedures.

APPLYING NEW INSTITUTIONAL THEORY OF INSURANCE IN OTHER POLICY AREAS

The subtle processes through which organizations shape the meaning of compliance deserves further exploration because countries across the world are increasingly moving toward co-regulatory frameworks. The private sector is taking a palpably increasing role in public governance across virtually all industries. Because private organizations are not merely influencing governmental institutions but also performing many traditional government functions with government approval, organizations have greater opportunity than ever before to shape legal regulations and compliance itself. Although there are potential benefits to self-regulatory and collaborative governance arrangements, this book suggests that organizations hold great power to inhibit legal ideals in the presence of weak or ineffective structures and policies.

The financial crisis of 2007–8 highlights the need to further explore how businesses construct the meaning of compliance in ways that sometimes weaken legal regulation. Just as managerial, risk, and technology logics and values transformed civil, consumer, and privacy laws, corporate culture and institutionalized organizational practices helped shape the regulation of financial and lending institutions. Laws such as the Gramm-Leach-Bliley Act and the Sarbanes-Oxley Act rely on and defer to corporations' financial disclosure policies and internal compliance structures such as ethics codes, monitoring, and auditing and reporting systems in order to protect consumers and investors from financial fraud (Krawiec 2003; O'Brien 2007).[2] Too much deference to corporations, particularly with respect to the disclosure policies of lending institutions, internal compliance structures, and auditing and reporting systems, alongside a push for flexible, collaborative regulation, failed to properly protect investors and consumers from excessive financial risk taking. As Justin O'Brien (2007) notes, financial disclosure policies and regulation were essentially symbolic. Although these corporate and lending institution policies may symbolize compliance and ethical conduct, they did not discourage financial fraud and abuse, even though governments chose to allow organizations and related intermediaries to influence the meaning of regulation. Thus, policymakers should not overlook business ability to construct the meaning of compliance in unfavorable ways and unintentionally weaken law and undermine public policy goals under the guise of co-regulation and public-private partnerships.

LEGAL INTERMEDIARIES, REGULATION, AND SOCIAL CHANGE

The relationship between law and social change has and will continue to be an important issue for scholars and policymakers to wrestle with. While prior research has shed light on the normative, instrumental, political, and cultural processes through which law produces social change, my approach helps explain the underlying mechanisms that drive those different processes. In particular, the strategic, political, cultural, and institutional ideas and tactics through which law is influenced are often derived from and shaped by the increasing professionalization of law by nonlegal actors and the ways these nonlegal actors encounter and filter what law means via nonlegal logics. The institutional theoretical framework I introduce in this book highlights how the overlap between organizational and legal fields often leads to a mix of organizational and legal logics that influence the way organizations and other stakeholders understand and implement laws.

In addition to this core finding, my new institutional theory of insurance reveals a number of broader lessons that should guide future research on the study of intermediaries and their role in social change. First, I lay out the conditions that have led to increasing involvement by intermediaries in law's construction and meaning. Discussions of law and social change need to focus less on whether and when formal legal institutions can facilitate legal change. In particular, the location of legal rulemaking has changed. While command and control, top-down regulation still exists, there has been a pivot globally toward co-regulation, self-regulation, and the contracting out of rights to civil society actors, businesses, and other stakeholders. Moreover, there are more laws and legal regulations than ever before, and these legal mandates are also complex and ambiguous with respect to how to comply. Intermediaries now possess greater space in which to actually construct what law and compliance means in action. Thus, whether law can produce social change is contingent less on the behavior of formal legal actors connected with public legal institutions than on the actions of intermediaries. These actors are positioned to play an even greater role in determining whether law facilitates or inhibits social change. Future scholarship on law and social change should be mindful of the changed conditions for fostering social change.

Second, this book highlights the variation of intermediaries along a number of dimensions. For example, intermediaries are both legal and nonlegal actors. The obvious remains true: lawyers, law firms, and in-house counsel and actors connected to formal legal institutions such as judges, legislators, and regulators play an important role in interpreting and shaping the meaning of legal rules. But nonlegal actors such as insurance companies, risk managers, insurance brokers, and information security specialists also make a key, though less recognized, contribution to facilitating and inhibiting social change, through their daily use of the legal rules that they handle in their professional practices. The increasing complexity of legal rules and the rise of professionalized services create a space for new and more decentered actors to take on quasi-legal roles.

Third, intermediaries are confronting law not just in traditional legal settings but also in a wide variety of industries and settings, ranging from labor and employment to cybersecurity, corporate behavior, arbitration, consumer protection, welfare, and health and safety. At every turn, there are formal laws and regulations. However, there is also tremendous discretion and space for organizations and individuals to implement these laws. I anticipate intermediaries playing an ever greater role in years to come across a variety of areas. The insights from insurance companies as intermediaries, therefore, should be explored, refined, and challenged in other contexts to further explore under what conditions intermediaries facilitate and inhibit social change.

Fourth, the idea of law as an instrument of social change cannot be divorced from the logics operating among organizational actors tasked with complying with laws (Edelman and Stryker, 2005). The professional field an actor works in often influences the way they understand and construct law as an intermediary. This book reveals that multiple and sometimes contested logics allow field actors to filter and mediate law's meaning in very powerful ways. Whereas earlier research focused on how managerial values filter law's meaning, here, I present a more complex picture in which multiple and competing logics (risk, managerial, technological) shape the way organizations go about complying with laws.

The ways law is filtered through risk, managerial, and technology logics can steer legal interpretation and implementation in different directions and impact in various ways law's capacity to produce progressive social change. My framework highlights how intermediaries contribute to or inhibit social change, regardless of whether we define social change along instrumental, political, or cultural dimensions (Kostiner 2003). As I have argued previously (Talesh and Pélisse 2019), legal intermediaries contribute to concrete material changes for employees, unemployed workers, scientists, and managers, as when they help find unemployed workers new jobs, preserve wage and hour equity, or attempt to bolster cybersecurity defenses. They also contribute to or inhibit political dimensions of social change by empowering employees against managers in collective-bargaining labor negotiations or by fostering increased discourse about safety in scientific laboratories. However, intermediaries often use managerial and risk logics to weaken consumer protection legislation, or encourage employers to develop symbolic policies and procedures and, consequently, make it less likely that employers can be sued for employment violations. Cyber insurers have not been successful as intermediaries in improving the cyber hygiene of policyholders.

Going forward, I hope this institutional theory of insurance will nudge others to focus on the legal intermediary's ability to shape the content and meaning of law. Although I applaud scholars for their closer examination of regulatory intermediaries across the world (Abbott, Levi-Faur, and Snidal 2017), existing approaches still view law as largely a top-down phenomenon coming from formal legal institutions. Under this framework, rulemakers "create" law for ruletakers, and rule intermediaries implement and monitor law (Abbott, Levi-Faur, and Snidal 2017). In contrast, my framework suggests that the boundaries between rulemakers, ruletakers, and rule intermediaries are much more blurred than existing approaches suggest. Legal intermediaries play an increasingly important role not just in affecting, controlling, or monitoring relations between rulemakers and -takers but also in constructing the content and meaning of law and compliance itself. Thus, I encourage scholars interested in studying law and social change not to be bound by existing frameworks that compartmentalize the intermediary role as operating within a world where lawmaking is exclusively the province of public legal institutions. Instead, I suggest focusing greater attention on intermediaries as actors that construct and shape the meaning of law and various types of legality in different regulatory settings in ways that have positive and negative impacts in society.

FUTURE RESEARCH ON LEGAL INTERMEDIARIES

Many of the issues that I raise in this chapter are unresolved empirical questions. In fact, cybersecurity and cyber insurance are exciting areas for researchers to study, because the field is relatively new and constantly evolving. Replicating this type of study in the coming years might reveal changes in the way insurance companies act as regulators. Changes in the insurance market potentially could influence how willing insurers are to set firm conditions for issuing insurance. My research on cyber insurance has evolved in the past decade, beginning with some measured optimism about insurers' potential role as regulators (Talesh 2018), only to become more pessimistic after deepening my research inquiry and triangulating my methods for the current study. Unlike my earlier study, this book uses multiple methods and draws on multiple sources (interviews, observations, insurance policies, insurance applications, analysis of big data) and, consequently, reveals a more nuanced picture of insurance companies as regulators and the conditions under which such endeavors are likely to fail or succeed. We need fewer broad, rhetorical, normative claims about the virtues and vices of insurance companies as regulators and more fine-grain research on how they operate in action.

More broadly, we need more research that explores the relationship between insurance companies and legal regulation. While cost-benefit and efficiency analysis that presupposes insurance actors as rational actors is important, scholars need to shine a light on the organizational behavior and culture of insurance institutions and investigate the various ways institutional and political mechanisms shape the meaning of law. As opposed to explaining *why* insurance companies respond to laws, we need more theoretically informed empirical research on *how* insurance companies respond to laws. I encourage insurance scholars to focus their research on insurance industry responses to law and how insurers sometimes influence and shape the meaning of law and compliance. We need more research that critically describes and evaluates the mechanisms that will likely position insurance companies, should they or society desire, to be more substantive than symbolic regulators. At a minimum, my new institutional theory of insurance provides the first step in that it sets forth a framework for understanding *how* insurance company constructions of law influence private organizations but also public legal institutions. Others will, I hope, follow and expand on this approach.

NOTES

CHAPTER ONE. INTRODUCTION

Epigraph: United States v. South-Eastern Underwriters Association, 322 U.S. 533 (1944).

1. Some federal privacy laws preempt state privacy laws on the same topic. For example, the federal law regulating commercial e-mail and the sharing of e-mail addresses preempts most state laws regulating the same activities. However, there are many federal privacy laws that do not preempt state laws, which means that a company can find itself in the position of trying to comply with federal and state privacy laws that regulate the same types of data or types of activity in slightly different ways.

2. *Cyber hygiene* refers to the ways that individuals and organizations protect and maintain IT systems and devices and implement cybersecurity best practices. For example, an organization using the best cybersecurity practices has a strong or healthy cyber hygiene profile (Sager n.d.).

3. This study was conducted primarily between 2015 and 2021. I recognize that the cyber insurance market hardened in late 2021–22, though there are projections the market will soften some again. The fact that the cyber insurance market is relatively new and thus

not stable makes it an opportune place to continue to study this area over a longer period to chart changes.

4. As they note, Baker and Shortland's recent work (2022a, 2022b) focuses on kidnapping and ransomware and does not delve deeply into how cyber insurers engage in risk management and act as quasi-regulators.

5. In addition, prevailing research on big data and technology focuses on the impact on individuals and ignores the way data impact businesses operating across many sectors.

6. Julie Cohen (2019) notes that "the most noteworthy attribute of the personal data economy has been its secrecy, which frustrates the most basic efforts to understand how the internet search, social networking, and consumer finance industries sort and categorize individual consumers" (62).

7. Given the competitive market surrounding big data providers and the importance of anonymity, I agreed not to disclose the name of the database that I accessed. To assure anonymity, I inserted "a data provider" in square brackets instead of the actual organization name wherever interviewees reference any data provider.

CHAPTER TWO. A NEW INSTITUTIONAL THEORY OF INSURANCE

1. Of course, this is not to suggest that law and economics constitute the only framework used. There are certainly other approaches. However, it is safe to say that law and economics rationales dominate thinking on insurance.

2. Of course, shifting burdens of proof sometimes affect how much social change occurs (Stryker 2001).

3. Cohen (2019) specifically notes that "scholarship in science and technology studies has shown that new technologies do not have predetermined, neutral trajectories, but rather evolve in ways that reflect the particular, situated values and priorities of both their developers and their users" (3).

CHAPTER THREE. THE INFUENCE
OF TECHNOLOGY AND BIG DATA ON
CYBER INSURANCE

1. This analysis builds on the analysis of cyber insurance questionnaires in Romanosky et al. 2019. Although I compiled my codebook in a way similar to that Romanosky and colleagues used for theirs—that is, inductively, by evaluating and categorizing questions posed in a sample of initial applications—there were differences. My codebook was organized as a series of 115 binary yes-no questions, divided into six broad categories. The first five of these align roughly to the four themes identified by Romanosky et al. The sixth category, Internet of Things, is unique to this codebook and was not included in Romanosky's analysis.

The binary structure of the codebook also allowed me to assess variations in the level of detail applications asked for. For example, in addition to coding for whether an application asked if a company stored or had access to personally identifiable or confidential data, I also coded for whether an application asked if the company stores specific types of data, such as social security numbers, health information, or financial information. Some applications specifically asked at this level of detail about the types of data companies seeking insurance had access to or stored. Other applications asked more broadly about whether a company stored personally identifiable data. Where companies asked only the latter, I recorded the application as not asking about specific types of private and confidential data. In a similar way, I coded for whether a company asked about general or specific types of third-party vendor use; compliance with specific industry standards, rules, regulations, or laws; and specific types of uses of the Internet of Things. Organizing the codebook in this way allowed me to evaluate where variation among applications lies.

In addition, by organizing the codebook into six categories based on the practical significance to insurance providers that the particular questions in those categories provided, I was able to assess variation within and between specific categories. This assessment helped provide insight into what types of risk-related behavior are most salient to insurance providers. For example, if more applications ask about questions in a particular category than in another, that finding can indicate that, generally, cyber insurance companies generally find the information relating to that category more valuable than the other.

Finally, contra Romanosky and colleagues' analysis, this coding scheme included a coder assessment, which is a numerical evaluation of the application's thoroughness. Because this reckoning was based on the coder's evaluation of how well the application covered the relevant data storage, security, and risk mitigation practices, it also provides another grouping from which to evaluate variation between applications.

2. "The data is being used to create pricing models. . . . It is also being used to create more granular pricing underwriting models" (data aggregator and big data provider, interview 33, part 1, December 6, 2019).

3. "Currently, right now, to price the risk, you're definitely using outside data along with your own, and you provide [the insurance] on a nonadmitted policy form" (insurer and underwriter, interview 4, June 19, 2019).

4. Some of the major companies in this area include RSI, RSM, Cyber Cube, Insight Cyber Group, and Symantec. See, for example, Yates 2020.

5. The term *dark web* refers to encrypted online content that is not indexed by conventional search engines. Although the dark web assists people who want to maintain privacy and freely express their views, it has also gained a reputation as a haven for illegal activities. For more background on the dark web, see Bloomenthal 2024.

6. Vulnerability scanning is a technique used to identify potential vulnerabilities in an organization's information system and hosted applications. Such scans attempt to identify problems such as software flaws, lack of updated security patching, and improper firewall or other system configurations. See, for example, NIST 2021. As the names imply, an *external* scan may be conducted from any location with an operable internet connection against the parts of an organization's IT infrastructure facing the internet,

whereas an *internal* scan must be conducted from inside the organization's firewall. The vast majority of information security providers conduct external scans. Ibid.

CHAPTER FOUR. THE EFFECTS AND
IMPLICATIONS OF THE TECHNOLOGIZATION
OF INSURANCE

1. Although I am highlighting how brokers can choose samples and statistical techniques to suit their commercial interest, I recognize that the ways the data are operationalized is a topic worthy of future focus. For example, sample and statistical techniques may lead to different results. For a thorough analysis of this debate, see Woods and Böhme 2021.

2. Interviews revealed that many in the insurance field believe the information security providers that conduct "internal" scans are equally unreliable. One insurer and big data provider referenced a company that conducts internal scans: "I can tell you that their model is nowhere near the point where we would say it's fantastic[;] it's in the early days" (interview 31).

3. For an empirical study that found cyber insurance premiums fell in absolute terms from 2008 to 2018, consistent with the suggestion of a soft market, see Woods, Moore, and Simpson 2019.

4. As one person in the industry noted, "Right now it's a soft market. There is a lot of capacity. And we see a lot of carriers doing what we call just cash-flow underwriting. I'm just going to write it, and I'll take my chances. And, for the most part, they're making a lot of money on the cyber. I think there's like 130 carriers that do some element of cyber" (forensic and information security expert, interview 14).

5. "We have what we call risk engineers. We have two guys that are cybersecurity practitioners. And they help us review the technical elements of a submission. For instance, if we have that sixty-minute call, they would be on that call to ask questions" (broker and former insurance underwriter, interview 13). "I would say for the most part the majority of the carriers that we work with do have some sort of risk engineer or internal technical expert that

can help translate the information that they're getting from an underwriting perspective, to a, what does this mean from a risk and exposure perspective?" (broker and former underwriter, interview 10).

6. Sophisticated buyers of insurance, according to many cyber insurers, understand technology: "Th[e] conversation's gotten to a point where [if] you're way out of your depth, you can't come in here and sell me an insurance policy if you don't understand what I'm telling you about my technology infrastructure. So that's sort of changing a bit" (insurer, interview A10).

CHAPTER FIVE. CYBER INSURANCE RISK MANAGEMENT: INEFFECTIVE, SYMBOLIC REGULATORY INTERVENTIONS

1. One forensic security consultant summed up the bundle of prebreach services that insurers make available to insureds: "We help customers build breach response plans that . . . they can access . . . from their iPhone at a moment's notice and connect in with a breach coach lawyer and their forensics expert and all that. The assessment side is consulting; it's prebreach. . . . There's also a lot of proactive stuff inside that portal like calculators that show them what a future data breach is going to cost them, online security training for their staff, things like that" (interview 16).

2. The following interview excerpt highlights the industry's position on its regulatory role:

INTERVIEWER: So, what do you think of the insurance company's position as positioning itself as a de facto regulator?

INSURANCE ATTORNEY: Well, I think it's a necessity, right? . . . If the federal government can't figure out how to do it, and the states are struggling to do it. (insurance attorney, interview A2)

3. Another insurance broker noted the challenges of penetrating the market: "Carriers want to buy services to help those clients, but there's only so many dollars in the premium. If I get a $30,000

premium, it's pretty hard to put a $100,000 Fire Eye solution into it. That's why [security] companies like Fire Eye have struggled to penetrate the insurance market" (insurance broker, interview 17, July 17, 2019).

CHAPTER SEVEN. WHAT CAN BE DONE?
POLICY REFORMS AND PATHWAYS FORWARD
FOR CYBER INSURERS AND GOVERNMENTS

1. There are also differences between Coalition and At-Bay. The key differences are that At-Bay does its own underwriting and claims management, whereas Coalition has Swiss Re handle its underwriting. At-Bay hires an entire team of underwriters and handles underwriting and claims decisions internally. In general, Coalition has the authority to make decisions up to about $200 million, whereas At-Bay has authority to make decisions up to $2 billion. Thus, Coalition tends to be focused on small and medium-sized businesses, whereas At-Bay also insures larger companies (Talesh and Cunningham 2021). However, both appear eager to expand, so these limits may change by the time this book is published.

2. The market hardened in 2021–22 (after the time frame of this study, 2015–21) with the rise of ransomware. Rate increases and coverage restrictions ensued as a result. The insurance industry claims to have increased prices, tightened terms, and demanded higher levels of cyber resilience from clients before providing coverage. To the extent that insurers are demanding higher levels of cybersecurity as a prerequisite to issuing insurance (and whether they are doing so is an unanswered empirical question), insurers are contributing to improving the cyber resilience of organizations. Cyber prices stabilized in the second half of 2022 and the first half of 2023, and this leveling off led to improvement for those clients renewing their cyber coverage and for new buyers. Some carriers have noted that they have seen insureds entering the market recently with improved cybersecurity defense measures in place. Because cyber insurance is so new and the market continually

fluctuates, studies such as this one should be replicated to see how (if at all) market pressures impact the way insurance companies act as quasi-regulators (Dyson 2023).

3. As one industry leader noted, "Nothing we do is better than anything else that is out there already in the security industry. The one thing that we're doing which is really difficult is integrating it. Like actually injecting it into the DNA of the insurance company. Not putting it as a patch on top" (insurer and forensics expert, interview 38).

4. These recommendations are similar to the results of collaborative work Bryan Cunningham and I (2021–22) did in drafting our model legislative proposal.

CHAPTER EIGHT. SYMBOLIC REGULATION AND INSURER INFUENCE ON PRIVATE ORGANIZATIONS AND PUBLIC LAW

1. The New York Insurance Department illustrates the logic adopted by many states: "Those who do not wish to compete in price have conjured many possible evils of open competition. . . . During the past 50 years, there has been no evidence in California [or any] other jurisdiction that rate competition leads to destructive rate wars. Their memory haunted the Merritt Committee a half-century ago, but our own experience and the findings of the most recent Congressional study should lay the spectre to rest" (New York Insurance Department 1969). For an evaluation of the pros and cons of this form of regulation, see Lubin 2021a.

2. Gramm-Leach-Bliley Act, Pub. L. No. 106-102, 113 Stat. 1338 (1999); Sarbanes-Oxley Act, Pub. L. No. 107-204, 116 Stat. 745 (2002).

BIBLIOGRAPHY

STATUTES

Cal. Civil Code § 1798.100–1798.199.100 (West 2021)
Cal. Civil Code § 1897.91.04 (West 2021)
Civil Rights Act of 1964, Title VII, 42 U.S.C. §§ 2000e–2000e-17
Gramm-Leach-Bliley Act, Pub. L No. 106-102, 113 Stat. 1338 (1999)
Sarbanes-Oxley Act, Pub. L. No. 107-204, 116 Stat. 745 (2002)

CASES

United States v. South-Eastern Underwriters, 322 U.S. 533 (1944)

PUBLISHED SOURCES

Abbott, Kenneth, David Levi-Faur, and Duncan Snidal. 2017. "Regulatory Intermediaries in the Age of Governance." *Annals of the American Academy of Political and Social Science* 670: 1–288. https://www.jstor.org/stable/i26361533.

Abbott, Kenneth, and Duncan Snidal. 2000. "Hard and Soft Law in International Governance." *International Organization* 54 (3): 421–56. https://doi.org/10.1162/002081800551280.

Abraham, Kenneth. 2013. "Four Conceptions of Insurance." *University of Pennsylvania Law Review* 161: 653–98. https://heinonline.org/HOL /P?h=hein.journals/pnlr161&i=667.

Abraham, Kenneth, and Daniel Schwarcz. 2022. "The Limits of Regulation by Insurance." *Indiana Law Journal* 98 (1): 215–74. https://www .repository.law.indiana.edu/ilj/vol98/iss1/5.

Abzug, Rikki, and Stephen J. Mezias. 1993. "The Fragmented State and Due Process Protections in Organizations: The Case of Comparable Worth." *Organization Science* 4 (3): 433–53. https://doi.org/10.1287 /orsc.4.3.433.

Acquisti, Alessandro, Laura Brandimarte, and George Loewenstein. 2020. "Secrets and Likes: The Drive for Privacy and the Difficulty of Achieving It in the Digital Age." *Journal of Consumer Psychology* 30, no. 4: 736–58. https://doi.org/10.1002/jcpy.1191.

Acxiom Corporation. 2014. *2014 Annual Report*. https://www.annual reports.com/HostedData/AnnualReportArchive/a/NASDAQ_ACXM _2014.pdf.

———. 2018. *2018 Annual Report*. https://www.annualreports.com /HostedData/AnnualReports/PDF/NASDAQ_ACXM_2018.pdf.

Ansell, Chris, and Alison Gash. 2008. "Collaborative Governance in Theory and Practice." *Journal of Public Administration Research and Theory* 18 (4): 543–71. https://doi.org/10.1093/jopart/mum032.

Arce, Daniel, Daniel Woods, and Rainer Bohme. 2024. "Economics of Incident Response Panels in Cyber Insurance." *Computers and Security* 140 (May): 1–8. https://doi.org/10.1016/j.cose.2024.103742.

Asokan, Akshaya 2024. "UK Conservatives Say 'No' to Cyber Insurance Backstop." Gov Info Security. March 10. https://www.govinfo security.com/uk-conservatives-say-no-to-cyber-insurance-backstop -a-24569?highlight=true.

At-Bay. n.d. "Insurance for the Digital Age." Accessed January 25, 2020. https://perma.cc/37CJ-ZUQY.

Ayres, Ian, and John Braithwaite. 1992. *Responsive Regulation: Transcending the Deregulation Debate*. Oxford: Oxford University Press.

Baker, Tom. 2002. "Insurance and the Law." In *International Encyclopedia of the Social and Behavioral Sciences*, vol. 11, edited by Neil J. Smelser and Paul B. Baltes, 7587–91. Amsterdam: Elsevier.

———. 2005a. "Liability Insurance as Tort Regulation: Six Ways That Liability Insurance Shapes Tort Law in Action." *Connecticut Insurance Law Journal* 12: 1–13.

———. 2005b. "Medical Malpractice and the Insurance Underwriting Cycle." *DePaul Law Review* 54 (2): 393–438.

Baker, Tom, and Thomas O. Farrish. 2005. "Liability Insurance and the Regulation of Firearms." In *Suing the Gun Industry: A Battle at the Crossroads of Gun Control and Mass Torts*, edited by Timothy D. Lytton, 292–314. Ann Arbor: University of Michigan Press.

Baker, Tom, and Sean J. Griffith. 2010. *Ensuring Corporate Misconduct: How Liability Insurance Transforms Shareholder Litigation*. Chicago: University of Chicago Press.

Baker, Tom, and Anja Shortland. 2022a. "The Government behind Insurance Governance: Lessons for Ransomware." *Regulation and Governance*.

———. 2022b. "Insurance and Enterprise: Cyber Insurance for Ransomware." *Geneva Papers on Risk and Insurance* 48: 275–99.

Baker, Tom, and Jonathan Simon, eds. 2002. *Embracing Risk*. Chicago: University of Chicago Press.

Baron, James N., Frank R. Dobbin, and P. Deveraux Jennings. 1986. "War and Peace: The Evolution of Modern Personnel Administration in US Industry." *American Journal of Sociology* 92 (2): 350–83.

Barry, Laurence, and Arthur Carpentier. 2020. "Personalization as a Promise: Can Big Data Change the Practice of Insurance?" *Big Data & Society* 7: 1–12.

Beazley. n.d. "Data Breach." Accessed January 20, 2016. https://www .beazley.com/specialty_lines/data_breach.html.

Becker, Gary S. 1983. "A Theory of Competition among Pressure Groups for Political Influence." *Quarterly Journal of Economics* 98 (3): 371–400.

Benkler, Yochai. 2006. *The Wealth of Networks: How Social Production Transforms Markets and Freedom*. New Haven, CT: Yale University Press.

Ben-Shahar, Omri, and Kyle D. Logue. 2012. "Outsourcing Regulation: How Insurance Reduces Moral Hazard." *Michigan Law Review* 111 (2): 197–228.

Bisom-Rapp, Susan. 1996. "Scripting Reality in the Legal Workplace: Women, Lawyers, Litigation Prevention Measures, and the Limits of

Anti-discrimination Law." *Columbia Journal of Gender and Law* 6 (1): 323–86.

———. 1999. "Bulletproofing the Workplace: Symbol and Substance in Employment Discrimination Law Practice." *Florida State University Law Review* 26 (4): 959–1048.

Bloomenthal, Andrew. 2024. "What Is the Dark Web?" Investopedia. Updated April 17. https://www.investopedia.com/terms/d/dark-web.asp.

Borelle, Céline, and J. Pélisse. 2017. "'Ca sent bizarre, ici': la sécurité dans les laboratoires de nano-médecine (France-États-Unis)." *Sociologie du Travail* (online), 59 (3). https://doi.org/10.4000/sdt.934.

Boyle, James. 1996. *Shamans, Software, and Spleens: Law and the Construction of the Information Society.* Cambridge, MA: Harvard University Press.

———. 2003. "The Second Enclosure Movement and the Construction of the Public Domain." *Law and Contemporary Problems* 66 (1): 33–74.

Braithwaite, John. 1982. "Enforced Self-Regulation: A New Strategy for Corporate Crime Control." *Michigan Law Review* 80 (7): 1466–1507.

———. 2002. *Restorative Justice and Responsive Regulation.* Oxford: Oxford University Press.

———. 2008. *Regulatory Capitalism: How It Works—Ideas for Making It Work Better.* Cheltenham, UK: Edward Elgar.

Brookman, Justin. 2015. "Protecting Privacy in an Era of Weakening Regulation." *Harvard Law and Policy Review* 9: 355–74.

Brothers, Lou, Carrie Camino, Greg Layok, and Brad Ptasienski. 2017. "Survey Finds Insurers Not Fully Realizing Benefits of Analytics." PropertyCasualty360. Updated March 20. http://www.propertycasualty360.com/2017/03/20/survey-finds-insurers-not-fully-realizing-benefits.

Brown, Colleen Theresa, Thomas D. Cunningham, and Sujit Raman. 2021. "New York Department of Financial Services Issues First Guidance by a U.S. Regulator Concerning Cyber Insurance." Sidley. February 9. https://datamatters.sidley.com/new-york-department-of-financial-services-issues-first-guidance-by-a-u-s-regulator-concerning-cyber-insurance.

Business Wire. 2015. "HSB Study Shows 69 Percent of Businesses Experience Hacking Incidents in the Last Year; Cyber Poll Finds

Risk Managers Not Confident about Resources Dedicated to Combat Hacking." June 3. https://www.businesswire.com/news/home/2015 0603006200/en/HSB-Study-Shows-69-Percent-of-Businesses-Experi enced-Hacking-Incidents-in-the-Last-Year.

Cain, Ashley A., Morgan E. Edwards, and Jeremiah D. Still. 2018. "An Exploratory Study of Cyber Hygiene Behaviors and Knowledge." *Journal of Information Security and Applications* 36.

Chander, Anupam, and Madhavi Sunder. 2004. "The Romance of the Public Domain." *California Law Review* 92 (5): 1331–73.

Chon, Margaret. 2006. "Intellectual Property and the Development Divide." *Cardozo Law Review* 27: 2821–2912.

CISA (Cybersecurity and Infrastructure Security Agency), US Department of Homeland Security. 2021. "AR21-013A, Strengthening Security Configurations to Defend against Attackers Targeting Cloud Services." https://us-cert.cisa.gov/ncas/analysis-reports/ar21-013a.

Coalition. 2020. "Coalition Enters Excess Cyber Insurance Market." *PR Newswire*, July 22, 2020. https://www.prnewswire.com/news-releases /coalition-enters-excess-cyber-insurance-market-301097844.html.

Coglianese, Cary. 1997. "Assessing Consensus: The Promise and Performance of Negotiated Rulemaking." *Duke Law Journal* 46: 1255–1349.

Coglianese, Cary, and Jennifer Nash. 2001. *Regulating from the Inside: Can Environmental Management Systems Achieve Policy Goals?* Washington, DC: Resources for the Future.

Cohen, George. 1997. "Legal Malpractice Insurance and Loss Prevention: A Comparative Analysis of Economic Institutions." *Connecticut Insurance Law Journal* 4 (1): 305–51.

Cohen, Julie. 2019. *Between Truth and Power.* Oxford: Oxford University Press.

Connatser, Matthew. 2024. "Firms Skip Security Reviews of Major App Updates about Half the Time." *The Register*, July 18. https://www .theregister.com/2024/07/18/security_review_failure/.

Crawford, Kate, and Jason Schultz. 2014. "Big Data and Due Process: Toward a Framework to Redress Predictive Privacy Harms." *Boston College Law Review* 55 (1): 93–128.

Cunningham, Bryan, and Shauhin Talesh. 2021–22. "Uncle Sam RE: Improving Cyber Hygiene and Increasing Confidence in the Cyber

Insurance Ecosystem via Government Backstopping." *University of Connecticut Insurance Law Journal* 28 (1): 1–84.

Davis, Anthony E. 1996. "Professional Liability Insurers as Regulators of Law Practice." *Fordham Law Review* 65: 205–32. https://ir.lawnet.fordham.edu/flr/vol65/iss1/14.

Dobbin, Frank. 2009. *Inventing Equal Opportunity*. Princeton, NJ: Princeton University Press.

Dunn, Mary B., and Candace Jones. 2010. "Institutional Logics and Institutional Pluralism: The Contestation of Care and Science Logics in Medical Education, 1967–2005." *Administrative Science Quarterly* 55 (1): 114–49.

Dyson, Ben. 2023. "Cyber Insurance Market Poised for Growth As Hard Market Eases." S&P Global. July 20. https://www.spglobal.com/marketintelligence/en/news-insights/latest-news-headlines/cyber-insurance-market-poised-for-growth-as-hard-market-eases-76602312.

Edelman, Lauren B. 1990. "Legal Environments and Organizational Governance: The Expansion of Due Process in the American Workplace." *American Journal of Sociology* 95: 1401–40.

———. 1992. "Legal Ambiguity and Symbolic Structures: Organizational Mediation of Civil Rights Law." *American Journal of Sociology* 97: 1531–76.

———. 2007. "Overlapping Fields and Constructed Legalities: The Endogeneity of Law." In *Private Equity, Corporate Governance, and the Dynamics of Capital Market Regulation*, edited by Justin O'Brien, 55–90. London: Imperial College Press.

———. 2016. *Working Law: Courts, Corporations, and Symbolic Civil Rights*. Chicago: University of Chicago Press.

Edelman, Lauren B., Steven E. Abraham, and Howard S. Erlanger. 1992. "Professional Construction of the Legal Environment: The Inflated Threat of Wrongful Discharge Doctrine." *Law and Society Review* 26 (1): 47–84.

Edelman, Lauren B., Howard S. Erlanger, and John Lande. 1993. "Internal Dispute Resolution: The Transformation of Civil Rights in the Workplace." *Law and Society Review* 27 (3): 497–534.

Edelman, Lauren B., Sally Riggs Fuller, and Iona Mara-Drita. 2001. "Diversity Rhetoric and the Managerialization of Law." *American Journal of Sociology* 106 (6): 1589–1641.

Edelman, Lauren B., L. Krieger, S. Eliason, C. Albiston, and V. Mellema. 2011. "When Organizations Rule: Judicial Deference to Institutionalized Employment Structures." *American Journal of Sociology* 117 (3): 888–954. https://doi.org/10.1086/661984.

Edelman, Lauren B., and Stephen Petterson. 1999. "Symbols and Substance in Organizational Response to Civil Rights Law." *Research in Social Stratification and Mobility* 17: 107.

Edelman, Lauren B., and Robin Stryker. 2005. "A Sociological Approach to Law and the Economy." In *The Handbook of Economic Sociology*, edited by Neil Smelser and Richard Swedberg, 527–51. Princeton, NJ: Princeton University Press.

Edelman, Lauren B., and Mark C. Suchman. 1999. "When the 'Haves' Hold Court: Speculations on the Organizational Internalization of Law." *Law and Society Review* 33 (4): 941–91.

Edelman, Lauren B., and Shauhin Talesh. 2011. "To Comply or Not to Comply—That Isn't the Question: How Organizations Construct the Meaning of Compliance." In *Explaining Compliance*, edited by C. Parker and V. Nielsen, 103–22. Cheltenham, UK: Edward Elgar.

Edelman, Lauren B., Christopher Uggen, and Howard S. Erlanger. 1999. "The Endogeneity of Legal Regulation: Grievance Procedures as Rational Myth." *American Journal of Sociology* 105: 406–54.

Elliot, Michael W. 2017. "Big Data Analytics: Changing the Calculus of Insurance." *CIPR Newsletter* (Center for Insurance Policy and Research) 20 (November). https://perma.cc/KS6C-6KEF.

Ericson, Richard, Aaron Doyle, and Dean Barry. 2003. *Insurance as Governance*. Toronto: University of Toronto Press.

Examining the Evolving Cyber Insurance Marketplace: Hearing Before the Senate Subcommittee on Consumer Protection, Product Safety, Insurance, and Data Security. 2015. 114th Cong. 171 (March 19).

Freeman, Jody. 1997. "Collaborative Governance in the Administrative State." *UCLA Law Review* 45 (1): 1–98.

———. 2000. "The Private Role in Public Governance." *NYU Law Review* 75 (3): 543–675.

Freeman, Jody, and Martha Minow, eds. 2009. *Government by Contract: Outsourcing and American Democracy*. Cambridge, MA: Harvard University Press.

Frischmann, Brett. 2012. *Infrastructure: The Social Value of Shared Resources.* Oxford: Oxford University Press.

Gerber, Nina, Paul Gerber, and Melanie Volkamer. 2018. "Explaining the Privacy Paradox: A Systematic Review of Literature Investigating Privacy Attitude and Behavior." *Computers and Security* 77: 226–61.

Gunningham, Neil. 1995. "Environment, Self-Regulation, and the Chemical Industry: Assessing Responsible Care." *Law and Policy* 17 (1): 57–109.

Gunningham, Neil, and Darren Sinclair. 1999. "Regulatory Pluralism: Designing Policy Mixes for Environmental Protection." *Law and Policy* 21 (1): 49–76.

Hagan, Bridget. 2018. "Big Data, Big Questions—Insurers and Advanced Data Analytics." *Fintech Law Report: E-Banking, Payments, and Commerce in the Mobile World* 21 (1): NL2.

Hanson, Jon S., Robert Dinneen, and Michael Johnson. 1974. *Monitoring Competition: A Means of Regulating the Property and Liability Insurance Business.* Milwaukee, WI: NAIC.

Harvey, Sarah. 2018. "What Is the Ohio Data Protection Act?" KirkpatrickPrice blog. November 29. https://kirkpatrickprice.com/blog/industry-news/what-is-the-ohio-data-protection-act/.

Haveman, Heather A., and Hayagreeva Rao. 1997. "Structuring a Theory of Moral Sentiments: Institutional and Organizational Coevolution in the Early Thrift Industry." *American Journal of Sociology* 102 (6): 1606–51.

Heimer, Carol. 1985. *Reactive Risk and Rational Action: Managing Moral Hazard in Insurance Contracts.* Chicago: University of Chicago Press.

Hemenway, Chad. 2023. "Federal Cyber Insurance Backstop is Warranted with Focus on Catastrophic Risk." *Insurance Journal*, November 28. https://www.insurancejournal.com/news/national/2023/11/28/749640.htm.

Herr, Trey. 2021. "Cyber Insurance and Private Governance: The Enforcement Power of Markets." *Regulation and Governance* 15 (1): 98–114.

Hubbart, Elizabeth O. 1996. "When Worlds Collide: The Intersection of Insurance and Motion Pictures." *Connecticut Insurance Law Journal* 3: 267–301.

Hudson, David. 2015. "Cyber Liability Insurance Is an Increasingly Popular, Almost Necessary Choice for Law Firms." *ABA Journal*

(American Bar Association), April 1. https://www.abajournal.com /magazine/article/cyber_liability_insurance_is_increasingly_popular _almost_necessary_choice.

Huising, Ruthanne, and Susan Silbey. 2011. "Governing the Gap: Forging Safe Science through Relational Regulation." *Regulation and Governance* 5: 14–42.

Jacoby, Sanford. 1985. *Employing Bureaucracy: Managers, Unions, and the Transformation of Work in American Industry, 1900–1945.* New York: Columbia University Press.

Kades, Eric. 1997. "The Laws of Complexity and the Complexity of Laws: The Implications of Computational Complexity Theory for the Law." *Rutgers Law Review* 49: 403–84.

Kagan, Robert A., Neil Gunningham, and Dorothy Thornton. 2003. "Explaining Corporate Environmental Performance: How Does Regulation Matter?" *Law and Society Review* 37: 51–90.

Kostiner, Idit. 2003. "Evaluating Legality: Toward a Cultural Approach to the Study of Law and Social Change." *Law and Society Review* 37 (2): 323–68.

Krawiec, Kimberley D. 2003. "Cosmetic Compliance and the Failure of Negotiated Governance." *Washington University Law Quarterly* 81 (2): 487–544.

Lacewell, Linda A., Superintendent, Department of Financial Services, to All Authorized Property/Casualty Insurers. 2021. Insurance Circular Letter No. 2. February 4. New York State Department of Financial Services. https://www.dfs.ny.gov/industry_guidance/circular_letters /cl2021_02.

Lessig, Lawrence. 1999. *Code and Other Laws of Cyberspace.* New York: Basic Books.

Levi-Faur, David. 2005. "The Global Diffusion of Regulatory Capitalism." *Annals of the American Academy of Political and Social Science* 598: 12–32.

Levi-Faur, David, and S. M. Starobin. 2014. "Transnational Politics and Policy: From Two-Way to Three-Way Interactions." *Jerusalem Papers in Regulation and Governance* 62: 2–38.

Lobel, Orly. 2004. "The Renew Deal: The Fall of Regulation and the Rise of Governance in Contemporary Legal Thought." *Minnesota Law Review* 89: 342–470.

Locke, Richard M. 2013. *The Promise and Limits of Private Power: Promoting Labor Standards in a Global Economy.* Cambridge: Cambridge University Press.

Lounsbury, Michael. 2002. "Institutional Transformation and Status Mobility: The Professionalization of the Field of Finance." *Academy of Management Journal* 45 (1): 255–66.

Lubin, Asaf. 2021a. "Insuring Evolving Technology." *University of Connecticut Insurance Law Journal* 28: 130–64.

———. 2021b. "Public Policy and the Insurability of Cyber Risk." *Journal of Law and Technology at Texas* 5: 45–110.

Lytton, Timothy. 2022. "Using Insurance to Regulate Food Safety: Field Notes from the Fresh Produce Sector." *University of New Mexico Law Review* 52: 282–340.

Majone, Giandomenico. 1997. "From the Positive to the Regulatory State: Causes and Consequences of Changes in the Mode of Governance." *Journal of Public Policy* 17: 139–67.

Marshall, Anna-Maria. 2005. "Idle Rights: Employees' Rights Consciousness and the Construction of Sexual Harassment Policies." *Law and Society Review* 39 (1): 83–124.

McPherson, Chad Michael, and Michael Sauder. 2013. "Logics in Action: Managing Institutional Complexity in a Drug Court." *Administrative Science Quarterly* 58 (2): 165–96.

Mott, Gareth, Sarah Turner, Jason R. C. Nurse, Jamie MacColl, James Sullivan, Anna Cartwright, and Edward Cartwright. 2023. "Between a Rock and a Hard(ening) Place: Cyber Insurance in the Ransomware Era." *Computers and Security* 128: 103162.

Müller-Graff, Peter-Christian, and Ola Mestad, eds. 2014. *The Rising Complexity of European Law.* Berlin: Berliner Wissenschafts-Verlag.

NAAI (National Alliance of American Insurers). 1982. NAIC in Transition: A Discussion Paper on Issues Facing the National Association of Insurance Commissioners.

NAIC (National Association of Insurance Commissioners). 2020. "Insurtech." Last modified February 19, 2020. https://perma.cc/SRD3 -ZA6X.

NAIC (National Association of Insurance Commissioners) Staff. 2022. "Report on the Cyber Insurance Market." October 18. https://content

.naic.org/sites/default/files/cmte-c-cyber-supplement-report-2022-for
-data-year-2021.pdf.

NCFTA (National Cyber-forensics and Training Alliance). n.d. "One
Team, One Goal." Accessed January 27, 2021. https://perma.cc/7NXC
-8D8J.

NetDiligence. 2015. "2015 Cyber Claims Study." https://netdiligence.com
/wp-content/uploads/2016/05/NetDiligence_2015_Cyber_Claims_Study
_093015.pdf.

New York Insurance Department. 1969. The Public Interest Now in
Property and Liability Insurance: A Report to Governor Nelson A.
Rockefeller.

NIST (National Institute of Standards and Technology). 2022. *Assessing
Security and Privacy Controls in Information Systems and Organiza-
tions*. NIST Special Publication 800-53A. https://doi.org/10.6028/NIST
.SP.800-53Ar5.

NPPD (National Protection and Programs Directorate). 2014. "Insurance Industry Working Session Readout Report: Insurance for
Cyber-Related Critical Infrastructure Loss—Key Issues." Cybersecurity and Infrastructure Security Agency. July. https://www.cisa.gov
/resources-tools/resources/cybersecurity-insurance-reports.

O'Brien, Justin. 2007. "The Dynamics of Capital Markets Governance."
*Private Equity, Corporate Governance, and the Dynamics of Capital
Market Regulation*, edited by J. O'Brien. London: Imperial College
Press.

O'Malley, Pat. 1991. "Legal Networks and Domestic Security." *Studies in
Law, Policy, and Society* 11: 171–90.

Paltrow, Scot J. 1998. "The Converted: How Insurance Firms Beat Back
an Effort for Stricter Controls—State Regulators' Alliance Began
Tackling Issues; Then, the Boycott Began—A Fateful Dinner in
Chicago." *Wall Street Journal*, February 5.

Parashchak, Oleg. 2024. "Big Data in Insurance: Use Cases of Data Analytics Technology." *Beinsure*. February 25. https://beinsure.com/big
-data-in-insurance/.

Pasquale, Frank. 2015. *The Black Box Society: The Secret Algorithms That
Control Money and Information*. Cambridge, MA: Harvard University
Press.

Pélisse, Jérôme. 2011. "Se donner le droit: La force des organisations face à la loi (introduction)." *Droit et société* 77: 5–17.

———. 2014. Le travail du droit: Trois enquêtes sur la légalité ordinaire. Mémoire pour l'habilitation à diriger des recherches en Sociologie, Sciences Po Paris.

———. 2016. "Legal Intermediaries as Moral Actors." Paper presented at the Society for the Advancement of Socio-economics (SASE) meeting, Berkeley, CA, June 24.

———. 2017. "Gérer les risques par le droit en France et aux États-Unis: quelles intermédiations juridiques?" *Droit et Société* 96 (2): 321–36. https://doi.org/10.3917/drs.096.0321.

Ponemon Institute. 2015. *Fifth Annual Benchmark Study on Privacy and Security of Healthcare Data.* Traverse City, MI: Ponemon Institute.

———. 2016. *Closing Security Gaps to Protect Corporate Data: A Study of US and European Organizations.* Traverse City, MI: Ponemon Institute.

Posner, Richard A. 1974. "Theories of Economic Regulation." *Bell Journal of Economics and Management Science* 5 (2): 335–58.

Randall, Susan. 1999. "Insurance Regulation in the United States: Regulatory Federalism and the National Association of Insurance Commissioners." *Florida State University Law Review* 26: 625–99.

Rao, Hayagreeva, Philippe Monin, and Rodolphe Durand. 2003. "Institutional Change in Toque Ville: Nouvelle Cuisine as an Identity Movement in French Gastronomy." *American Journal of Sociology* 108 (4): 795–843.

Rappaport, John. 2017. "How Private Insurers Regulate Public Police." *Harvard Law Review* 130 (6): 1539–1614.

Reidenberg, Joel R. 1997–98. "Lex Informatica: The Formulation of Information Policy Rules through Technology." *Texas Law Review* 76 (3): 553–593.

Robertson, Adi. 2018. "California Just Became the First State with an Internet of Things Cybersecurity Law." *The Verge*, September 28. https://www.theverge.com/2018/9/28/17874768/california-iot-smart -device-cybersecurity-bill-sb-327-signed-law.

Romanosky, Sasha, Lillian Ablon, Andreas Kuehn, and Therese Jones. 2019. "Content Analysis of Cyber Insurance Policies: How Do Carriers

Price Cyber Risk?" *Journal of Cybersecurity* 5 (1): 1–19. https://doi
.org/10.1093/cybsec/tyz002.

Sager, Tony. n.d. "Cleaning Up a Definition of Basic Cyber Hygiene." Center for Internet Security. Accessed March 14, 2025. http://cissecurity
.org/blog/cleaning-up-a-definition-of-basic-cyber-hygine.

Schneiberg, Marc. 2005. "Combining New Institutionalisms: Explaining Institutional Change in American Property Insurance." *Sociological Forum* 2 (1): 93–137.

Schneiberg, Marc, and Tim Bartley. 2001. "Regulating American Industries: Markets, Politics, and the Institutional Determinants of Fire Insurance Regulation." *American Journal of Sociology* 107: 101–46.

———. 2008. "Organizations, Regulation, and Economic Behavior: Regulatory Dynamics." *Annual Review of Law and Social Science* 4: 31–61. https://doi.org/10.1146/annurev.lawsocsci.4.110707.172338.

Schwab, Klaus. 2017. *The Fourth Industrial Revolution.* New York: Crown Business.

Schwarcz, Daniel, Josephine Wolff, and Daniel Woods. 2022. "How Privilege Undermines Cybersecurity." *Harvard Journal of Law and Technology* 36 (2): 1–61. https://dx.doi.org/10.2139/ssrn.4175523.

Security Magazine. 2022. "Over 22 Billion Records Exposed in 2021." February 10. https://www.securitymagazine.com/articles/97046
-over-22-billion-records-exposed-in-2021.

Shackelford, Scott, Anne Boustead, and Christos Makridis. 2022. "Defining 'Reasonable' Cybersecurity: Lessons from the Public and Private Sectors." *Yale Journal of Law and Technology* 25 (1): 86–143.

Silbey, Susan. 2017. "Governing Green Laboratories: How Scientific Authority and Expertise Mediate Institutional Pressures for Organizational Change." Unpublished paper, Massachusetts Institute of Technology, Cambridge, MA.

Silbey, Susan, and T. Agrawal. 2011. "The Illusion of Accountability: Information Management and Organizational Culture." *Droit et Société* 77 (1): 69–86.

Simon, Jonathan. 1994. "In Place of the Parent: Risk Management and the Governance of Campus Life." *Social and Legal Studies* 3: 14–45.

Statistica. 2023. "Cybersecurity Worldwide." Updated September 2023. https://www.statista.com/outlook/tmo/cybersecurity/worldwide#cost.

Stigler, George J. 1971. "The Theory of Economic Regulation." *Bell Journal of Economics and Management Science* 2 (1): 3–21.

Stockburger, Peter. 2021. "Decoding 'Reasonableness' under California's IoT Law." Dentons. April 7. https://www.dentons.com/en/insights /articles/2021/april/7/decoding-reasonableness-under-californias-iot -law.

Stryker, Robin. 1994. "Rules, Resources, and Legitimacy Processes: Some Implications for Social Conflict, Order, and Change." *American Journal of Sociology* 99 (4): 847–910.

———. 2000. "Legitimacy Processes as Institutional Politics: Implications for Theory and Research in the Sociology of Organizations." *Research in the Sociology of Organizations* 17: 179–223.

———. 2001. "Disparate Impact and the Quota Debates: Law, Labor Market Sociology, and Equal Employment Policies." *Sociological Quarterly* 42: 13–46.

———. 2011. "L'intermédiation scientifique dans la mise en oeuvre des lois anti-discriminatoires américaines." In *Droit et régulations des activités économiques: Perspectives sociologiques et institutionnalistes*, edited by C. Bessy, T. Delpeuch, and J. Pélisse, 183–202. Paris: LGDJ.

Stryker, Robin, D. Docka-Filipek, and P. Wald. 2012. "Employment Discrimination Law and Industrial Psychology: Social Science as Social Authority and the Co-production of Law and Science." *Law and Social Inquiry* 37 (4): 777–914.

Sugarman, Stephen. 1989. *Doing Away with Personal Injury Law: New Compensation Mechanisms for Victims, Consumers, and Business.* New York: Quorum Books.

Swedloff, Rick. 2020. "The New Regulatory Imperative for Insurance." *Boston College Law Review* 61 (6): 2031–84.

Talesh, Shauhin. 2009. "The Privatization of Public Legal Rights: How Manufacturers Construct the Meaning of Consumer Law." *Law and Society Review* 43: 527–62.

———. 2012. "How Dispute Resolution System Design Matters: An Organizational Analysis of Dispute Resolution Structures and Consumer Lemon Laws." *Law and Society Review* 46 (3): 463–96.

————. 2014. "Institutional and Political Sources of Legislative Change: Explaining How Private Organizations Influence the Form and Content of Consumer Protection Legislation." *Law and Social Inquiry* 39 (4): 973–1005.

————. 2015a. "Legal Intermediaries: How Insurance Companies Construct the Meaning of Compliance with Antidiscrimination Laws." *Law and Policy* 37 (3): 209–39.

————. 2015b. "A New Institutional Theory of Insurance." *UC Irvine Law Review* 5: 617–50.

————. 2015c. "Rule-Intermediaries in Action: How State and Business Stakeholders Influence the Meaning of Consumer Rights in Regulatory Governance Arrangements." *Law and Policy* 37: 1–31.

————. 2018. "Data Breach, Privacy, and Cyber Insurance: How Insurance Companies Act as 'Compliance Managers' for Businesses." *Law and Social Inquiry* 43: 417–40.

————. 2021. "Public Law and Regulatory Theory." In *Handbook on Theories of Governance*, 2nd edition, edited by C. Ansell and J. Torfing. Cheltenham, UK: Edward Elgar.

Talesh, Shauhin, and Bryan Cunningham. 2021. "The Technologization of Insurance: An Empirical Analysis of Big Data and Artificial Intelligence's Impact on Cybersecurity and Privacy." *Utah Law Review* 5: 967–1027.

Talesh, Shauhin, and Jérôme Pélisse. 2019. "How Legal Intermediaries Facilitate and Inhibit Social Change." *Studies in Law, Politics, and Society* 79: 111–45.

Thomas, Rob, and Patrick McSharry. 2015. *Big Data Revolution: What Farmers, Doctors, and Insurance Agents Teach Us about Discovering Big Data Patterns*. Chichester, UK: Wiley.

Thornton, Patricia H. 2002. "The Rise of the Corporation in a Craft Industry: Conflict and Conformity in Institutional Logics." *Academy of Management Journal* 45 (1): 81–101.

Thornton, Patricia H., and William Ocasio. 1999. "Institutional Logics and the Historical Contingency of Power in Organizations: Executive Succession in the Higher Education Publishing Industry, 1958–1990." *American Journal of Sociology* 105: 801–43.

US CSC (Cyberspace Solarium Commission). 2020. "Final Report of the United States Cyberspace Solarium Commission." March. https://www.solarium.gov/report.

US Department of Commerce Internet Policy Task Force. 2011. "Cybersecurity, Innovation and the Internet Economy." June. https://www.nist.gov/system/files/documents/itl/Cybersecurity_Green-Paper_Final Version.pdf.

US DHS (Department of Homeland Security). 2003. "The National Strategy to Secure Cyberspace." February. https://georgewbush-white house.archives.gov/pcipb/.

———. 2014. "Insurance for Cyber-Related Critical Infrastructure Loss: Key Issues." Insurance Industry Working Session Readout Report. Washington, DC.

———. 2017a. "Cybersecurity." https://www.dhs.gov/topics/cybersecurity. April 23, 2017

———. 2017b. "Cybersecurity Insurance." Updated April 23. https://www.dhs.gov/cybersecurity-insurance.

US GAO (Government Accountability Office). 2021. "Cyber Insurance: Insurers and Policyholders Face Challenges in an Evolving Market." May 20. https://www.gao.gov/assets/gao-21-477.pdf.

———. 2023. "Rising Cyberthreats Increase Cyber Insurance Premiums While Reducing Availability." September 27. https://www.gao.gov/blog/rising-cyberthreats-increase-cyber-insurance-premiums-while-reducing-availability.

US White House. 2023. "National Cybersecurity Strategy Implementation Plan." https://bidenwhitehouse.archives.gov/wp-content/uploads/2023/07/National-Cybersecurity-Strategy-Implementation-Plan-WH.gov_.pdf.

Van Rooij, Benjamin, and Adam Fine. 2021. *Behavioral Code*. Boston: Beacon Press.

Verma, Anjuli. 2015. "The Law-Before: Legacies and Gaps in Penal Reform." *Law and Society Review* 49 (4): 847–82.

Vogel, Steven K. 1996. *Freer Markets, More Rules: Regulatory Reform in Advanced Industrial Countries*. Ithaca, NY: Cornell University Press.

Wicklund, David and George Christopher. 2012. "The New Rules of Risk: The NAIC Leans Toward Having Insurers Use Solvency II-Inspired ORSA Guidelines to Manage Capital." *Best's Review*, March 1.

Wolff, Josephine. 2022. *Cyberinsurance Policy: Rethinking Risk in an Age of Ransomware, Computer Fraud, Data Breaches, and Cyberattacks.* Cambridge, MA: MIT Press.

Wood, Charlie. 2020. "Munich Re-backed At-Bay Raises $34mn in Series B Round." *Reinsurance News.* February 24. https://perma.cc /C2AQ-9LKA.

Woods, Daniel W., and Rainer Böhme. 2021. "Systematization of Knowledge: Quantifying Cyber Risk." *2021 IEEE Symposium on Security and Privacy (SP)*: 211–28. https://doi.org/10.1109/SP40001.2021.00053.

Woods, Daniel W., and Tyler Moore. 2020. "Does Insurance Have a Future in Governing Cybersecurity?" *IEEE Security and Privacy* 18 (1): 21–27.

Woods, Daniel, Tyler Moore, and Andrew Simpson. 2019. "The County Fair Cyber Loss Distribution: Drawing Inferences from Insurance Prices." *Digital Threats: Research and Practice* 2 (2): 1–21.

Yates, Helen. 2020. "Cyber Solutions 4.0: Modeling Systemic Risk." *Exposure* Magazine, May 5. https://www.rms.com/exposure/cyber -solutions-40-modeling-systemic-risk.

INDEX

Page numbers in **bold** indicate tables.

ABC Inc., 76
act-of-war exclusion litigation, 192
Acxiom, 61
Administrative Procedure Act of
    1966, 202
Advisen, 70
advocacy coalitions, 34
ambiguity of legal regulations,
    36–37
American Alliance of Insurers
    (AAI), 206
Anthem Blue Cross and Blue
    Shield, 141
antidiscrimination laws, insurer
    influence on, 207–9
Aon, 162
App River, 172
Arce, 129
Argo Group, 163
artificial intelligence (AI): and big
    data providers, 73; and insur-
    ance company efficiency, 78–82

At-Bay, 162, 163, 168–69, 231n1
ATLAS.ti, 19
attorney-client privilege, 127–30

Baker, Tom, 13, 16, 46, 226n4
Barracuda, 166
Beazley, 120
benchmarking limitations, 75
Ben-Shahar, Omri, 10
big data: brokers and
    underwriters' manipulation
    of, 87–95; limitations in cyber
    insurance, 84–87; and
    predictive analytics, 79–82;
    providers, 19–21, 72–73; as
    unreliable tool, 84–87. *See also*
    technology and big data in
    delivery of insurance
Binding Operational Directives
    (BODs), 178–79
BitSight, 76, 97, 99, 100
Blue Shield, 141

Bohme, Rainer, 129
bottom-up legal influence, 27–28
bottom-up new institutional
    theory of insurance. *See*
    privacy law and cybersecurity
    compliance
Boxx Insurance, 162
"breach coaches," 114–16, 127–28,
    131, 144
Bureau of Cyber Statistics, 152

California Consumer Privacy Act
    (CCPA), 138, 146
California Internet of Things (IoT)
    Security Act, 67, 138
casualty insurance industry, 61
Catastrophic Cybersecurity
    Resilience Act, 191–97
check-the-box cyber insurance
    application, 101, 168, 179
Citrix installation, 165
Civil Rights Act of 1964, 37
civil society groups as
    intermediaries, 35–36
cloud-based protection tech-
    niques, 171–72
cloud storage, 170–71
Coalition Inc., 162, 231n1
Cohen, Julie, 48, 49, 226n3, 226n6
collective-bargaining labor
    negotiations, 220
Colonial Pipeline Ransomware
    Attack, 3
companion services as profit
    centers, 106
consumer protection, 52, 82
consumer rights, 41
content analysis: of cyber insur-
    ance applications, 22–23; of
    cyber professional literature, 21
continuous underwriting
    evaluation, 164–66
contract law provisions, 186–87

co-regulation, increasing, 33–36
credit monitoring and restoration,
    117–18
crisis management and public
    relations, 117
CrowdStrike failure, 4
Cunningham, Bryan, 191, 192–94,
    232n4
cybercrime, cost of, 4
Cyber Cube, 228n4
cyber health checks, 111
cyber hygiene, 5–6, 176, 184–85,
    225n2
cyber insurance applications: inef-
    fectiveness of, 63–67; insurtech,
    60–63
cyber insurance conferences/
    webinars, 19, 21–22
Cyberinsurance Policy (Wolff), 14
cyber insurance risk
    framework, 194
cyber insurance risk management:
    insurer-provided postbreach
    services and data breach
    prevention, 126–31; insurer risk
    management services, 110–13;
    insurers' reluctance to require
    insureds to adopt prebreach
    services, 123–26; introduction,
    109–10; largely ineffective and
    symbolic quasi-regulators,
    118–20; organizations not using
    insurer-provided prebreach
    services, 120–23; postbreach
    services, 113–18
cyber insurance's regulatory
    role, pathways for improving:
    continuous underwriting and
    dynamic risk monitoring,
    164–66; insurtech innovation,
    162–63; onboarding prebreach
    services upon issuing
    insurance, 169–72; premium

pricing tied to the insured's loss control, 166–68; recommendations for reform, 162–64; requiring changes to an insured's cyber hygiene, 168–69

cyber insurance underwriting/ underwriters: and AI, 78–82; continuous evaluation, 164–66; differential data usage by, 72; exploiting information asymmetries, 87–95; and security scans, 95–100; and technology-based risk assessment, 75–78

cyber insurers: and brokers, use of technology by, 67–71; data providers, and regulators, 147–50; as postbreach response coordinators, 113–15; rating models, 150

cyber market, growth of, 6–7

cyber resilience, 231n2

Cybersecurity and Infrastructure Security Agency (CISA), 5, 173, 178–79, 184, 191–93

cybersecurity compliance, 15, 30–32; and privacy law, 33–40. *See also* privacy law and cybersecurity compliance

cybersecurity health evaluations and scans, 75–78

Cybersecurity Institute, 180–81

Cyber Solarium Commission, 179–80, 188–90

Cyberspace Solarium Commission (CSC), US, 6, 39, 151–52, 182, 185

Cyber Threat Intelligence Integration Center, 192

Cyence, 76

dark web, 76, 79, 228n5

data: aggregated on claims and events, 71–73; benchmarking, 86; flawed propagation, 147–48; providers, 72; quality and incompleteness, 84–86; security breach notification law, 138; sharing, standardized, 179–80; and technological transformation, 8; usage, evolution of, 61–62

data breach prevention, 126–31

data-driven approaches to cyber insurance, 71–73

Data Protection Act (DPA), 143–45

deference: judicial, 51; and legitimation, 32–33; by public legal institutions, 51–52; state and private regulators', 147–53; to symbolic compliance, 150–53

Department of Homeland Security (DHS), 11–12, 150–51

detection of data breaches, 112

differential data usage by insurer size, 72

directors and officers (D&O) insurance, 46–47

drop-down menus, 168

Edelman, Lauren, 15–16, 32, 40

education and training: beginning in elementary school, 176–77; layering multiple security protocols, 177–79; mandating cybersecurity training and certification among employers, 173–76; using incentives (including financial) to improve employee cyber hygiene, 176

Electronic Communications Privacy Act, 4

empirical research gap and technology, 48–50

employee bonuses, 176

employment practice liability insurance (EPLI), 44–45, 52, 113, 200, 207–9, 215

European deference to cyber insurance risk management practices, 153

Fair Credit Reporting Act, 4
false positives of security scans, 96–97
fear-based marketing, 146
federal government deference to cyber insurers' construction of compliance, 150–53
Federal Trade Commission (FTC), 4, 137
Financial Services Modernization Act, 4
Fire Eye solution, 230–31n3
forensic services by cyber insurers, 116–17
Freedom of Information Act, 202
fully integrated insurtech models, 17, 169–70

General Data Protection Regulation (GDPR), 5, **135**, 153
governance approaches, rise of, 35–36
government as substantive regulator: Cybersecurity Institute, 180–81; federally funded financial backstop for catastrophic cyber risk, 188–97; federal privacy law and standards, 181–84; improved cyber hygiene as a public-private collaborative mission, 184–85; software product manufacturers liable for faulty software, holding, 185–88; standardized data sharing, 179–80
Gramm-Leach-Bliley Act, 39, **135**, 139, 141, 181, 217, 232n2
Griffith, Sean J., 46

Herr, Trey, 12–13
high-touch brokers, 81–82
HIPAA (Health Insurance Portability and Accountability Act), 4, 39, **135**, 139, 141–42, 181
HITECH (Health Information Technology for Economic and Clinical Health) Act, 39, **135**, 181
human credulity, 179, 182

incentive structures, lack of, 135–36
incident response management of cyber insurers, 113–15
industrial organizational psychologists, 51–52
industry scepticism towards benchmarking, 85–87
ineffective and symbolic quasi-regulators, 118–20
information capitalism, 48
information concealment by security scans, 98
information security companies, 38, 73–78, 81, 101, 111, 137, 150
Insight Cyber Group, 228n4
institutional deference, 148–50
insurance-as-regulation responses, 31–32
insurance brokers: application of data, 71–73; challenges and responses, 69; contract with security organizations, 77–78; exploiting information asymmetries, 87–95; technology approaches, 70–71; using technology to supplement evaluation, 81
insurance companies: as intermediaries, 40–41, 200–23; as symbolic regulators, 52–55
Insurance Institute for Highway Safety, 181

insurance law scholarship, 10 17,
27–28
insurance policies, 28;
reference to law, **135**
insurer intermediation, 38–40
insurer-provided postbreach
services and data breach
prevention, 113–18, 126–31
insurer risk management services,
46, 110–18
insurers' advertised regulatory
role and reality: ineffective and
symbolic quasi-regulators,
118–20; insurer-provided
postbreach services and data
breach prevention, 126–31;
insurer risk management
services, 110–13; insurers'
reluctance to require insureds
to adopt prebreach services,
123–26; organizations avoiding
prebreach services insurers
offer, 120–23; postbreach
services, 113–18
insurer size, differential data
usage by, 72
insurers' two-tiered treatment of
policyholders: based on
client size and revenue, 100–
107; profit-driven decision
making, 102–4; regulatory
failure, 101, 103, 106, 107–8
insurtech, 60–63; innovation,
162–63; models, 17, 169–70
integrated security services, 164–66
interdisciplinary expertise, 74
interest groups as
intermediaries, 34
intermediaries: civil society
groups as, 35–36; insurance
companies as, 40–41; interest
groups as, 34; nongovernmental
actors as, 35–36; nonlegal,

51 52; organizations
influencing legislation and
regulation, 200–207; rule,
36–37; state actors as, 35–36.
See also legal intermediaries
intermediation: conditions for, 30;
insurer, 38–40; legal, 31; rule,
by nonlegal actors, 38–39
Internet of Things, 227n1

judicial deference to
organizational structures, 51

law firms and insurers, 128–30
legal ambiguity, 36–37, 42
legal complexity, 37–38
legal endogeneity theory, 15–16, 32
legal environment conducive
to insurance institutions:
ambiguity of legal regulations,
36–37; complexity of legal
rules, 37–38; from government
to governance and increasing
co-regulation, 33–36; three
conditions that call for insurer
intermediation, 38–40
legal intermediaries, 217–21;
future research on, 221–23;
insurance as, 29–31; regulation
and social change, 217–21
legal intermediation, conditions
for, 31
legalization of organizations
with insurance companies as
intermediaries, 40–41
legal reasonableness standard,
146–47
legal references, vague, 134–35
legal regulations: ambiguity
of, 36–37; and insurance
institutions, 28–29
legal rules, complexity of,
37–38

legal services by cyber insurers, 115–16
legitimation and deference, 32–33
liability insurance, 27–28
limited external view of security scans, 96
limited public information and databases, 84–85
Lloyd's, 163
Logue, Kyle, 10
loss prevention, 47, 97, 111, 123, 131, 147, 166–68. *See also* cyber insurance risk management
low-touch brokers, 81–82

machine learning and information security providers, 79–80
managed security companies, 32, 121, 122–23, 147, 154, 198–99. *See also* privacy law and cybersecurity compliance
managerialization of law, 41–43
managerial logics, 41–43, 44, 214
managerial values, 16, 30, 42, 46, 52, 75, 124–25, 208, 214, 220
McCarran-Ferguson Act, 211
Merritt Committee, 232n1
Microsoft Office 365, 187
Mimecast, 166
misaligned incentives by information security providers, 98–99
Monitoring Competition: A Means of Regulating the Property and Liability Insurance Business, 213
Moore, Tyler, 13
Moran, Jerry, 151
multi-factor authentication (MFA), 138, 140–43, 178
Munich Re, 163

NAS, 120
National Association of Insurance Commissioners (NAIC), 148–49, 180–81, 200–207, 213–15
National Board of Fire Underwriters, 210–11
national cyber director (NCD), 191–93
National Cyber-Forensics and Training Alliance (NCFTA), 184–85
National Cybersecurity Strategy Implementation Plan, 185
National Institute for Standards and Technology (NIST): Cybersecurity Framework, 143; directive, 153; standards, 173
National Strategy to Secure Cyberspace, 11, 150
natural-language processing and information security providers, 79–80
Net Diligence, 70
new institutional theory of insurance: bottom-up legal influence, 27–29; conditions for intermediation, 30; dual mechanisms of influence, 30–31; insurance as legal intermediary, 29–30; insurance companies as symbolic regulators, 52–55; legitimation and deference, 32–33; stage one, 33–40; stage two, 40–41; stage three, 41–43; stage four, 43–47; stage five, 47–51; stage six, 51–52; symbolic rather than substantive regulation, 31–32, 153–55
new institutional theory of insurance in other areas of insurance: how insurance companies influence property

insurance regulation, 209–13;
insurer influence on
antidiscrimination laws, 207–9;
insurers' use of intermediary
organizations to influence
legislation and regulation, 200–
207; NAIC, EPLI, and property
insurance examples, 213–16
New York Department of Financial
Service (NYDFS), 194
New York Insurance Department,
232n1
nongovernmental actors as
intermediaries, 35–36
nonlegal actors: and the rise of
managerial logics, 41–43; and
the role of risk logics, 43–47; and
the role of technology, 47–51
nonlegal intermediaries, 51–52
non-standardized implementation
of security scores, 99–100
NotPetya malware, 3, 188, 194

O'Brien, Justin, 217
organizational behavior, 24, 28, 51,
110, 131, 152–53, 155, 214, 222
organizational responses to law,
public legal institutions'
deference to, 51–52
own risk and solvency assessment
(ORSA) process, 206–7

Pasquale, Frank, 49
payment card industry data
security standards (PCI DSSs),
135, 140
"perform pre-release testing," 186
personal data, control over, 4–5
policyholders, insurers' two-tiered
treatment of policy holders.
See insurers' two-tiered
treatment of policyholders

policy reforms and pathways
forward: education and
training, 172–79; government as
substantive regulator, 179–97;
introduction, 159–60; pathways
for improving cyber insurance's
regulatory role, 160–72
portfolio-wide risk modeling,
73–74
postbreach response
coordinators, cyber insurers as,
113–15
postbreach services: credit
monitoring and restoration,
117–18; crisis management
and public relations, 117;
cyber insurers as postbreach
response coordinators, 113–15;
forensic services, 116–17;
ineffective and symbolic
quasi-regulators, 118–20;
insurer-provided, and data
breach prevention, 126–31; legal
services, 115–16
prebreach services, 131; and
insurer risk management
services, 110–11; insurers'
reluctance to require insureds
to adopt, 123–26; as marketing
tools, 119–20; onboarding, upon
issuing insurance, 169–72;
organizations not using
insurer-provided, 120–23
predictive analytics: and big data,
79–82; models, 149
price competition, 210, 212, 213
privacy/confidentiality barriers
during cyber events, 84–85
privacy laws, 38, 39, 47, 54, 59
privacy law and cybersecurity
compliance: cyber insurers'
approach towards security and

privacy law and cybersecurity
compliance (*continued*)
compliance in practice, 145–47;
government safe harbors as
tools for compliance, 143–45;
insurers' focus on appearance
over substance, 133–36;
introduction, 132–33; multi-
factor authentication (MFA),
140–43; social construction of
"reasonable security measures"
in privacy laws, 136–40; state
and private regulators'
deference, 147–53
privacy paradox, 6
private rating agencies and state
regulators, 148–49
proactive threat detection, 165–66
professionalization of law: and the
rise of managerial logics, 41–43;
and the role of risk logics, 43–47;
and the role of technology,
47–51
Proofpoint, 166
property insurance, 61, 209–16
provisions: for artificial
intelligence, 78–82; for
organizations taking
reasonable security
measures, 183
public law, 32, 34. *See also*
symbolic regulation and
insurer influence
public legal institutions, 51–52
public-private partnerships, 12,
152, 185

quantitative analysis of big data
provider, 19–21

Randall, Susan, 205–6
real-time monitoring, 62, 166
reasonable security measures,
39, 145; organization-driven,

140–43; in privacy laws, 136–40;
provisions for organizations
taking, 183
regulatory and legal environment
conducive to insurance
institutions: ambiguity of legal
regulations, 36–37; complexity
of legal rules, 37–38; from
government to governance and
increasing co-regulation,
33–36; three conditions that
call for insurer intermediation,
38–40
"regulatory cooperation," 209–10
regulatory dynamics, shift in,
33–36
regulatory frameworks, evolution
of, 33–35
reinsurance brokers, 80
remote desktop protocol (RDP)
ports, 165, 168–69
re-regulation and neoliberalism, 35
risk: analysis, driving sales with
aggregate, 73–75; logics,
nonlegal actors and the role of,
43–47; management as
liability avoidance, 145;
management services, 21;
monitoring, continuous
underwriting and dynamic,
164–66; prevention tools, 111;
translation function, 74–75
Romanosky, Sasha, 13, 227–28n1
RSI, 228n4
RSM, 228n4
rule intermediaries, 36–37
rule intermediation by nonlegal
actors, 38–39

sales-driving function, 74–75
sales with aggregate risk analysis,
73–75
Sarbanes-Oxley Act, 140, 217
"schedule rating," 211

secrecy challenge and data, 48–50
"secure-by-design" principles, 186
security scans, 168; and cyber
    insurance underwriting,
    95–100; third-party risk
    blindness by, 97–98
Security Scorecard, 76
security scores, non-standardized
    implementation of, 99–100
selective data sharing, 84–85
Senate Bill (SB) 1386, 138
service offerings as marketing
    tools, 147
Shackelford, Scott, 137
Shields Up campaign, 184
Shortland, Anja, 13, 226n4
"shunning" services, 112
Simon, Jonathan, 16
SME cyber insurance buyers,
    124–26. *See also* insurers'
    two-tiered treatment of
    policyholders
social construction of "reasonable
    security measures" in privacy
    laws, 136–40
software product manufacturers,
    185–88
SolarWinds trojan, 188, 194
Standard & Poor's, 148
standardized data sharing,
    179–80
Standard Nonforfeiture Law for
    Life Insurance, 206
standard of care, 139–40, 143
state actors as intermediaries,
    35–36
state privacy laws, 12
subquestions, 168
Swiss Re Corporate Solutions,
    162–63
Symantec, 228n4
symbolic compliance, 145–47;
    and managerialization of law,
    42–43

symbolic quasi regulators, 118–20.
    See also cyber insurance risk
    management
symbolic regulation, 31–32
symbolic regulation and insurer
    influence: applying new
    institutional theory of
    insurance in other policy areas,
    216–17; future research on legal
    intermediaries, 221–23;
    introduction, 198–200; legal
    intermediaries, regulation, and
    social change, 217–21; new
    institutional theory of
    insurance in other areas of
    insurance, 200–216
symbolic regulators: cyber
    insurers as, 7–8; insurance
    companies as, 50–51, 52–55

Talesh, Shauhin, 40, 192, 232n4
technologization of insurance,
    60–63, 154; big data as
    unreliable tool, 84–87; brokers
    and underwriters, 87–95;
    insurers' two-tiered treatment
    of policyholders, 100–108;
    introduction, 83–84; security
    scans and scoring, 95–100
technology and big data in
    delivery of insurance: artificial
    intelligence and insurance
    company efficiency, 78–82;
    blending of insurance and
    technology fields, 60–63;
    cyber insurance applications,
    ineffectiveness of, 63–67;
    cybersecurity health
    evaluations and scans, 75–78;
    data aggregated on claims
    and events that have already
    occurred, 71–73; driving sales
    with aggregate risk analysis,
    73–75; introduction, 59–60;

technology and big data in
delivery of insurance (*continued*)
managing uncertainty with
technology and security tools,
67–71
technology and regulatory
intermediation, 47–51
telecommunication companies, 187
Terrorism Risk Insurance Act,
152, 193
third-party risk blindness by
security scans, 97–98
tiered treatment of policy holders.
See insurers' two-tiered
treatment of policyholders
training. *See* education and
training

uncertainty with technology and
security tools, managing, 67–71
underwriters. *See* cyber insurance
underwriting/underwriters
US Department of Commerce
Internet Policy Task Force, 150

visual representations of big data,
misleading, 87–95
vulnerability scanning, 228–29n6,
228n6

Wolff, Josephine, 11, 14, 150, 153
Woods, Daniel, 13, 129
*Working Law: Courts, Corporations
and Symbolic Civil Rights*
(Edelman), 15

Founded in 1893,
UNIVERSITY OF CALIFORNIA PRESS
publishes bold, progressive books and journals
on topics in the arts, humanities, social sciences,
and natural sciences—with a focus on social
justice issues—that inspire thought and action
among readers worldwide.

The UC PRESS FOUNDATION
raises funds to uphold the press's vital role
as an independent, nonprofit publisher, and
receives philanthropic support from a wide
range of individuals and institutions—and from
committed readers like you. To learn more, visit
ucpress.edu/supportus.